T0203234

Digital Color

Digital Color

Acquisition, Perception, Coding and Rendering

Edited by

Christine Fernandez-Maloigne
Frédérique Robert-Inacio
Ludovic Macaire

First published 2012 in Great Britain and the United States by ISTE Ltd and John Wiley & Sons, Inc.

ISTE Ltd
27-37 St George's Road
London SW19 4EU
UK

www.iste.co.uk

John Wiley & Sons, Inc.
111 River Street
Hoboken, NJ 07030
USA

www.wiley.com

© ISTE Ltd 2012

Library of Congress Cataloging-in-Publication Data

Digital color / edited by Christine Fernández-Maloine, Frédérique Robert-Inacio, Ludovic Macaire.
p. cm.
Includes bibliographical references and index.
ISBN 978-1-84821-346-3
1. Image converters. 2. Digital images. 3. Color vision. 4. Color photography--Digital techniques. I. Fernández-Maloine, Christine. II. Robert-Inacio, Frédérique. III. Macaire, Ludovic.
TK8316.D54 2012
006.6--dc23

2012005893

British Library Cataloguing-in-Publication Data
A CIP record for this book is available from the British Library
ISBN: 978-1-84821-346-3

Printed and bound in Great Britain by CPI Group (UK) Ltd., Croydon, Surrey CR0 4YY

Table of Contents

Chapter 6. From the Sensor to Color Images 149
Olivier LOSSON and Eric DINET

Chapter 7. Color and Image Compression 187
Abdelhakim SAADANE, Mohamed-Chaker LARABI
and Christophe CHARRIER

Chapter 8. Protection of Color Images 227
William PUECH, Alain TRÉMEAU and Philippe CARRÉ

Chapter 9. Quality Assessment Approaches 265
Mohamed-Chaker LARABI, Abdelhakim SAADANE
and Christophe CHARRIER

Foreword

The evolution of human vision occurred naturally with time. Some anthropologists suggest that the cells that are sensitive to color, cones, were developed when we were *gatherers*, in order to distinguish fruits from foliage. In fact, each of the three kinds of cones is sensitive to a wide spectrum of electromagnetic waves. The sum of these three spectra is what we call *light*. Color does not exist in nature but it is reconstituted, or learned, by our brain based on the quantities of light received on each of the three elements. Of course there are defects inherent to this chain, related to the imperfections of the eye (aging, color-blindness, etc.), or to the learning or the diversity of our cultures. In any case, naming a color is highly subjective. Moreover we denote by the same word a color that would be obtained either by adding the three cones excited by a continuous or discontinuous spectrum of a portion of light or by a pure ray. This is what specialists call *metameric* colors. They thus have different spectral compositions and we *see* them or denote them by the same color, the same word. Colors, in human vision, are also influenced by their environment which may cause optical illusions. But we are also able to name a color by the same word even if the lighting conditions change: this is *color constancy*. All this is already very difficult to understand.

It is along this path that the authors of this book on digital imaging color, like others before them, take us. It is a difficult path fraught with questions starting from image capture up to making a decision. It is a path where the authors have added the acquired knowledge and their own research, and where each element of the chain affects the other and vice versa. Of course, they rely on human vision that, as we have seen, has its defects, while scanning an image adds even more. The selection or the variability of the illuminant, the light/matter interaction from a macroscopic point of view (reflection, diffusion, diffraction, polarization, etc.), the particle size of the object, etc., make the spectrum received by the sensor already complex and influenced by all these physical phenomena. The different technologies of the digital sensor are also added to the complexity of obtaining an objective digital image.

Reader, all this is largely explained in this book which will guide you through this science of colorimetry associated with physiology – that is to say to our body functions, which is in this case our human visual system (HVS). Other explanations will guide you in choosing different models, often standardized by the CIE (International Commission on Illumination) through to the *color appearance model* used to approach the HVS. Every word of this model clearly demonstrates the difficulty of understanding the concept of colorimetry. It is a genuine aid that is proposed to base the choices of the sensor and the model on what we want, i.e. based on our application. Algorithms and hints are included to assist you and resolve issues, while the explanations at every turn of a page increase your understanding.

So if the image is digital why not create a resemblance to reality. A whole chapter is reserved for rendering and image synthesis. You will therefore find how to perform computationally some of the issues of the first section of this preface. Representation models of light sources up to spectrum rendering passing through the simulation of light propagation (ray tracing, etc.) make us travel in this world of virtual reality. Encryption, watermarking to protect authors will have almost no secret for you. If you want to know how to set the quality of an image and contrast it with the fidelity of an image, then approaches in this thriving field will bring you, if not solutions, at least the tools for you to build a good workshop. In contrast to the sensor, there is the visualization. So, how can we measure – for the sensor as well – how to calibrate it? Nothing is simple in this field since subjectivity is ultimately the teacher. At the end of the bench there is the user, the observer, and it is here that everything escapes us. We open the time to the reader and his memory. A second book[1] by the same authors is also to be published that is complementary to this one, but with a more algorithmic and applicative vision.

I would like to extend thanks to Christine Fernandez-Maloigne (University of Poitiers), Frédérique Robert-Inacio (ISEN-Toulon) and Ludovic Macaire (University of Lille) for having successfully led this team of authors, each an expert in their field. In addition thank you to all of the authors for devoting your time and dispensing your knowledge to share with us this major work, which is obviously useful for our community and also beyond. This book is intended for all those who wish to develop a chain of acquisition, processing and analysis of color digital images. To you, reader, I wish you good reading and am sure you will find the answers to your problems in this field.

Pierre BONTON
University Blaise Pascal, Clermont-Ferrand II, France
LASMEA Laboratory, CNRS JUR 6602
March 2012

---

1 C. FERNANDEZ-MALOIGNE, F. ROBERT-INACIO, L. MACAIRE, Digital Color Imaging, ISTE, London, John Wiley & sons, New York, 2012.

Chapter 1

Colorimetry and Physiology – The LMS Specification

To test and improve the quality of color images, we need to know how the human visual system operates. Colorimetry is a method that quantitatively assesses the changes that the engineer makes to an image. Recent advances in this field are due to a better understanding of visual mechanisms.

This chapter first describes the physiological mechanisms that are transferred from the retina in the eye to the human brain, which produce the physiological perception of color. Then it presents two approaches to colorimetry: first, as recommended by the International Commission on Illumination (CIE), and second, deriving directly from the physiology of the visual system that results in the ability to specify stimuli and color differences. Finally, the chapter outlines the difficulties in defining the appearance of color and the advantages in modeling the human visual system.

Chapter written by Françoise VIÉNOT and Jean LE ROHELLEC.

1.1. Physiological basis

Light detected by the eye excites the photoreceptors that are photosensitive cells. It produces biochemical changes and yields a signal, which is relayed by different classes of post-synaptic retinal neurons. The post-synaptic retinal neurons are organized in a layer in radial and transversal directions. The information is conveyed along the radial direction of the receptors toward the bipolar cells and then toward the ganglion cells whose axons form the optic nerve.

Horizontal cells and amacrine cells form a transversal network, whose action modulates direct signals. Then, the signal travels in the form of trains of action potentials through the optic nerve toward the visual cortex, where a visual image is formed.

1.1.1. *The photoreceptors*

1.1.1.1. *Spectral sensitivity of cones, the monovariant response of a photoreceptor*

Each photon absorbed by a cone triggers a cascade of chemical reactions producing a signal at the output of the cone, regardless of the wavelength associated with that photon. As a result, the amplitude of the response of the cone to light depends only on the number of absorbed photons, and not on the wavelength associated with the photons. While light consist of wavelengths in the visible spectrum with wide energy distributions, the response of a single cone is monovariant, it varies only in amplitude. If the photon has energy close to that required for the isomerization of the photosensitive pigment included in the cone, this is absorbed by the cone. The probability of absorption is determined by the spectral sensitivity of the cone.

The *in vitro* measurements of the spectral sensitivity of the cones [DAR 83] showed the existence of three families of retinal cones with maxima at 419, 531 and 558 nm. This would correspond to *in vivo* measurements in a healthy eye, taking into account the filtering effect of the ocular media, which is about 440 nm for S cones sensitive to short wavelengths, 540 nm for M cones, sensitive to middle wavelengths,

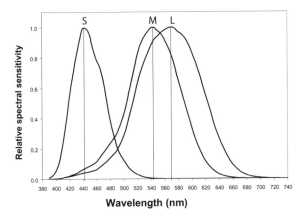

Figure 1.1. *Spectral sensitivity of the three families of cones*

and 565 nm for L cones, sensitive to longer wavelengths. The spectral sensitivity curves are widely spread over the visible spectrum, with the M and L cones being close to each other. It should be noted that there is no retinal cone whose maximum sensitivity lies in the part of the spectrum that appears red to the eye (beyond about 620 nm), indicating that the retinal cones are not simple color receptors. Red, like other colors, is reconstructed by the visual system. The M and L cones give to the eye its maximum light sensitivity of around 555 nm.

1.1.1.2. *The retinal mosaic*

Through optical or electronic microscopy, it is observed that the retina consists of two types of morphologically distinct photoreceptors: rods and cones. Rods are responsible for the vision at low illumination, and cones at higher illumination. The numerical density of cones is maximum in the fovea, that is to say in the central area of the retina, where images of the objects that we see are formed, and drops significantly toward the surrounding area. It is also possible to observe the cones *in vivo*, or at the back of the eye, using adaptive optics that neutralize the aberrations. We can also identify their corresponding families L, M or S [ROO 99, HOF 05]. Among the ten retinas that were examined, it was verified that the S cones were relatively few and that the numerical proportion of L and M cones was on average 2L for 1M, with surprising variations from person to person ranging from 1L for 2M to 16L for 1M, for normal color vision.

1.1.2. *Retinal organization*

The extraction of the color signal is achieved by comparing the signals from a family of cones with those from another family of cones. This comparison is carried out by post-synaptic retinal neurons.

1.1.2.1. *Concept of receptive field of the neuron*

Each neuron of the visual system, wherever it is located in the hierarchy of the processing, corresponds to a given area of space seen by the subject. It also corresponds to all the requested photoreceptors, within which the bio-electrical behavior of the neuron is changed. This area is called the receptive field of the neuron.

The receptive fields are small in the fovea, and larger as we move away from it. Each neuron is only a small, circular part of the visual field and the encoding of the signal responsible for each neuron depends on its immediate environment.

A retinal neuron does not perform an absolute coding of the light contained in its receptive field, but a coding related to the light status in the near vicinity. Only a differential signal (contrast) generates a signal in the neuron, which is transmitted to the next neurones in the hierarchy of visual information processing. The contrast may relate both to a difference in light or to a difference in spectral content of light.

1.1.2.2. *Two parallel pathways from the retina to the cortex*

The chemical contact between photoreceptors, bipolar cells, and horizontal cells is carried out at the terminal portion of the cone and is called "synapse". The synapse type determines a fundamental functional dichotomy of the coding of the light signal. Some bipolar cells have synapses that maintain the polarity of the signal coming from the cone, others reverse it. The ON-bipolar cells indicate an increment of light at the center of the receptive field (relative to the surrounding fields). They initiate a neural pathway called the ON pathway. The OFF-bipolar cells indicate a decrease in light at the center of the receptive field (relative to the surrounding fields). They initiate a neural pathway called the OFF pathway. These ON and OFF pathways run in parallel across each unit area of the visual space by encoding all the variations of light and remain independent up to the cortex.

1.1.2.3. *At the origin of konio, parvo and magnocellular pathways*

Different types of bipolar cells are at the origin of three separate neurophysiological pathways from the retina to the cortex: the koniocellular pathway dedicated to spectral differentiation; the parvocellular pathway dedicated to spectral differentiation and light differentiation; and the magnocellular pathway dedicated to light differentiation.

Midget bipolar (MB) cells are the most numerous. They receive signals from cones L and M. They are distinguished by the type of synapse, one belonging to the ON pathway, others to the OFF pathway (see next section).

For ease of nomenclature, a neuron whose receptive field center is ON (responding to an increase in light), will be encoded by "+", and a neuron whose receptive field center is OFF (responding to a decrease in light) will be encoded "−". The letter following the sign denotes the majority cone type in the center, either L or M (S cones will be discussed in the next section). Implicitly, the area of the receptive field receives signals from the other family of cones, either M or L, on an antagonist mode. For example, a neuron denoted +L will transmit a signal if the center is brighter than the surrounding area and/or if the spectral composition in the center favors large wavelengths. Thus, the midget bipolar cells are of four main types +L, −L, +M and −M. These neurons are the essential elements of the parvocellular pathway and the main initiators of the spectrum of colors and the range of forms and details.

Specific bipolar cells of S cones are the essential elements of the koniocellular pathway. They perform an encoding of the spectral antagonism by contrasting the signals of short wavelengths (S) to those of larger wavelengths (L and M), but are not involved in the encoding of variations in brightness.

Diffused bipolar cells are not selective of the spectral origin. Some are ON, while others are OFF. These neurons are the essential elements of the magnocellular pathway, which initiates the perception of the motion, flicker and variations in brightness.

1.1.2.4. *Functional characteristic of the parvocellular pathway (P)*

Mostly, neurons in the parvocellular pathway are sensitive to both spectral variations and light variations, thus combining two perceptually distinct variables: variation in brightness (shape precursor) and variation in chromaticity (color precursor). On the same area of the image, these neurons have two functional organizations of receptive fields: a receptive field sensitive to light variations only and a receptive field sensitive to spectral variations. For example, a neuron +L, indicates an increment of light in the center of its receptive field AND/OR, for an equiluminance stimulation, the neuron indicates that the center is covered with a light of longer wavelength than the one illuminating the surrounding area.

1.1.2.5. *Three neural pathways at the end of the retina*

Given the broad band of spectral sensitivity of cones, cone antagonism allows us, in addition to a saving of messengers, to decorrelate the signals from the cones and to minimize redundancies within and among the three pathways: magno, parvo, and koniocellular [LEE 99, ZAI 97, SHE 08].

Each cone can simultaneously interact with many types of bipolar cells. This is as if the signal of a cone was specifically transcribed according to the specialization of the neuron that it contacts, thus creating multiple filters of a single piece of information generated by the interaction of the light with the photoreceptor.

In each channel, the ganglion cells collect the signals that come from the bipolar cells modulated by the amacrine cells. These are transmitted to the neurons in the lateral geniculate nucleus of the thalamus without significant functional change and with convergence rates that vary depending on the distance to the fovea. These signals are then projected on the primary visual cortex, where they are combined (summed and/or differentiated). As one goes up the hierarchy of processing, the size of receptive fields increases, taking into account larger areas of the visual field.

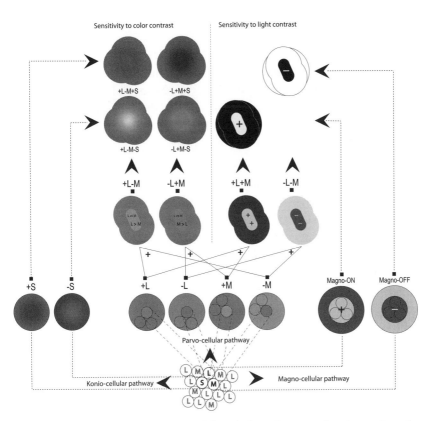

Figure 1.2. *Schematic representation of three independent neural pathways from the retina to the cortex, from the cones. First level: synaptic level of 3 types of cones, L, M and S (here, minimal version of 3 cones). Second level: the receptive fields of the neurons in the parvocellular pathway combine the signals from L and M cones. Cone antagonism appears as a center-surround organization encoding both light contrast (+ and −) and spectral contrast (L and M) giving rise to four types of units (+L, −L, +M, −M). The receptive fields of neurons in the koniocellular pathway combine the signals of S cones with the signals of the cones that are sensitive to larger wavelengths (L and M) under the form of co-extensive receptive fields that encode the chromatic contrast (S vs LM). The receptive fields of neurons in the magnocellular pathway combine the signals from L and M cones, the center-surround organization encode the light contrast (+ and −). Third level: additive combination of receptive fields of units in the parvocellular pathway, resulting in selective units at the thin chromatic contrast and selective units at the thin light contrast. The encoding of the color contrast is enhanced and refined by the summation of parvo units with the koniocellular units. The encoding of the light contrast is enhanced and refined by the summation of parvo units with magnocellular units (for a color version of this figure, see www.iste.co.uk/fernandez/digicolor.zip)*

1.1.3. *Physiological modeling of visual attributes related to color*

The De Valois and De Valois model [VAL 93] allows us to account for segregation of color and light information mixed in the early stages in the visual pathways. This model distinguishes several successive levels of development of the nerve signal leading to the perception of color.

1.1.3.1. *Conesynoptic and antagonism level*

This model is based on the existence of three types of cones: L, M and S. The S cones are arranged in a regular grid and are less numerous (for example, by proportion: 10 L for 5 M for 1 S).

Cone antagonism is differential encoding between the center and the surrounding area of the receptive field. Each cone features a large number of synaptic sites at its terminal portion. A minimal version of the model suggests that each cone establishes contact with at least eight bipolar cells, four with ON neurons (+L, +M, +S and +LMS) and four with OFF neurons (L, M, −S and −LMS).

1.1.3.2. *Third level: perceptual antagonism*

Cone antagonism of the second level provides relative, local information of a dichotomous nature (for example, areas of more light or; fewer large wavelengths). The third level reflects the separation of information regarding spectral content and that regarding light content. The signals reaching the cortex are summed taking into account the retinotopic organization (the initial vicinity on the retina is preserved). The summation of the signals of the second level sometimes enhances the contrast of light and sometimes the color contrast. When the units of different spectral origins have the same sign, for example: (+L) + (+M), the light contrast is enhanced. When they are of opposite sign, for example (+L) + (M), their joint action enhances the color contrast signal, forming a receptive field with two color antagonism between the center and the surrounding area, indicating thin variations of the color contrast.

Considering the retinotopic recovery in the cortex, the signals from the S cones are conveyed through the koniocellular pathway. The signals from the magnocellular pathway interact with the signals from parvocellular pathway, and then they refine the color signal and the light signal.

In the visual cortex, four types of information are available. Two relate to the spectral nature of the light and two to its relative intensity between the center and the surrounding area of the receptive field regardless of its spectral nature:

1) the spectral contrast, local, between the large and the shortest wavelengths (L vs M);

2) the spectral contrast, local, between the short wavelengths on the one hand and the largest wavelengths on the other hand (S vs L+M);

3) the local contrast of luminance between the center and the surrounding area of the receptive field of small size (parvocellular);

4) the local contrast of luminance between the center and the surrounding area of the receptive field of large size (magnocellular).

There is a specific associative cortical area for the processing of "color" information: the area V4. It processes signals from area V1. In this area V4, the receptive fields are large. Thus, the color signals can be interpreted based on the surrounding color context.

The modeling of color vision still needs to be developed to take into account the weight of the signals of the cones, the linear and/or nonlinear mode of summations [VAL 00, GEG 03], the role of the light and color adaptation, [VAL 08] and the nature of color constancy.

1.2. The XYZ colorimetry: the benchmark model of CIE

In colorimetry, light is a stimulus that elicits a perception of color. Colorimetry is a set of methods and data to universally specify colors.

There are two methods to reproduce colors. The additive mixture consists of adding lightbeams. Their images are projected on the retina and their effects are added. This is the method of displaying colors on screens. The subtractive mixture consists of superimposing absorbing dyes on a medium. A part of the radiation is subtracted from the light reflected by the media and, therefore, does not reach the retina. This is the process used in printers.

Colorimetry is based on visual experiments. Experiments show that the majority of colors may be reproduced by the addition of three additive primary colors, red, green and blue, in appropriate amounts. The experiment, called "color match", also shows that colors have the properties of vectors, in particular the additive property. Therefore, we apply the laws of linear algebra to colors and additive mixtures of colors. The real additive primary colors consist of the base vectors [R], [G], and [B]. A color is defined by three scalar quantities R, G, and B, called tristimulus values (not to be confused with digital intensities encoding the color of a pixel).

Since the properties of additive mixtures of colors was replicated by different observers, it was decided to establish a reference color specification system. In 1931, the International Commission on Illumination (CIE) adopted the XYZ color system obtained through the linear transformation of the RGB color system. The primaries [X], [Y], and [Z] are virtual. They were chosen so that all colors, including monochromatic radiations, have positive X, Y and Z tristimulus values, and so that the [Y] axis, alone, carries the luminance. Let $\bar{x}(\lambda)$, $\bar{y}(\lambda)$ and $\bar{z}(\lambda)$ be the spectral tristimulus values or color matching functions. Given a radiation of spectral power distribution (or density) of energy $\Phi(\lambda)$, the tristimulus values X, Y and Z of this radiation are computed as follows:

$$X = 683 \sum \Phi(\lambda)\bar{x}(\lambda)\Delta\lambda \qquad \text{[1.1]}$$

$$Y = 683 \sum \Phi(\lambda)\bar{y}(\lambda)\Delta\lambda \qquad \text{[1.2]}$$

$$Z = 683 \sum \Phi(\lambda)\bar{z}(\lambda)\Delta\lambda \qquad \text{[1.3]}$$

In case of a display, the function $\Phi(\lambda)$ is given by the measurement of spectral radiance. With the adjustment factor 683, the tristimulus value Y corresponds to the visual luminance of the radiation.

For a reflective material of reflectance $\rho(\lambda)$, which is illuminated by a source of spectral distribution of energy $\Phi(\lambda)$, the tristimulus values are compared with a white surface of unit reflectance. The tristimulus value Y is in this case equal to the reflectance:

$$X = 100\frac{\sum \Phi(\lambda)\rho(\lambda)\bar{x}(\lambda)\Delta\lambda}{\sum \Phi(\lambda)\bar{y}(\lambda)\Delta\lambda} \tag{1.4}$$

$$Y = 100\frac{\sum \Phi(\lambda)\rho(\lambda)\bar{y}(\lambda)\Delta\lambda}{\sum \Phi(\lambda)\bar{y}(\lambda)\Delta\lambda} \tag{1.5}$$

$$Z = 100\frac{\sum \Phi(\lambda)\rho(\lambda)\bar{z}(\lambda)\Delta\lambda}{\sum \Phi(\lambda)\bar{y}(\lambda)\Delta\lambda} \tag{1.6}$$

1.3. LMS colorimetry

In colorimetry, light is a stimulus that elicits a perception of color. However, the color vision begins with the absorption of photons by the visual pigments contained in the cones of the retina. Thus, the light, as a stimulus, can be defined by the three signals L, M and S that are generated in the cones, which are the input signals in the visual system.

1.3.1. *LMS fundamentals*

1.3.1.1. *Measurement of the spectral sensitivity of cones by psychophysical techniques*

Since their spectral sensitivities overlap, it is impossible to obtain the response of a single family of cones to monochromatic radiation. Instead, a psychophysical method that takes advantage of the reduction to two families of cones among some color-blinds is used. These dichromats feature only S and L cones or S and M cones. The relative spectral sensitivity of L or M cones is measured by temporally alternating between two monochromatic radiations, one serving as a reference, and the other for testing. The pace is fast enough to exclude the S-cones' response, but slow enough to leave a slight flicker. The flicker sensation is minimal when two radiations have the same visual efficiency. By doing this for all test wavelengths, we obtain the spectral sensitivity of the cone type (either L or M) that followed the flicker.

1.3.1.2. *The photosensitive pigments and the cone fundamentals: definition and properties*

The absorption phenomena of photons by the molecules of photosensitive pigments are quantum phenomena. It was found that the absorption spectra of all the photosensitive pigments of terrestrial vertebrates, measured *in vitro*, have almost the same shape on a graph whose horizontal axis is graduated in inverse of the wavelength.

The spectral sensitivity of the cones measured at the entrance of the cornea is called fundamental or cone fundamentals. It is the sensitivity of cones integrated in the eye, including all the filters such as the crystalline lens, the macular pigment and others, which absorb a fraction of the light entering the eye before it reaches the retina. Cone fundamentals should be linked to the color-matching functions through a linear relationship.

The objective measurement of the spectral sensitivity of the cones is recent. For many years, it has been accessible only by indirect experimental methods.

From the late 19th Century, by posing a few assumptions, it was possible to predict the fundamentals from color matches performed by normal and dichromat subjects. The assumptions were the absence of a family of cones among the dichromats, the need for obtaining positive cone spectral responses, and the likelihood of the shape of the absorption spectrum of photosensitive pigments.

The most accurate and complete approach is provided by colorimetry, where each monochromatic radiation is defined by its spectral tristimulus values $\bar{x}(\lambda)$, $\bar{y}(\lambda)$, $\bar{z}(\lambda)$. It remains to be seen whether the linear relationship maps these values to the $\bar{l}(\lambda)$, $\bar{m}(\lambda)$, $\bar{s}(\lambda)$ spectral response of cone fundamentals.

1.3.1.3. *The recommendations of the CIE*

The International Commission on Illumination [COM 06] published tables giving the values of relative spectral sensitivity of the fundamentals L, M and S for a field of view of 10° of angular diameter and for a field of 2°, for an average young observer with normal color vision.

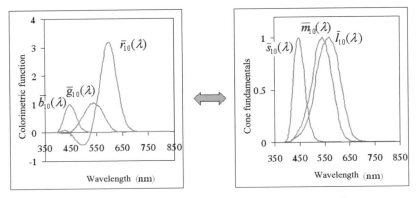

Figure 1.3. *Experimental color-matching functions $\bar{r}_{10}(\lambda)$, $\bar{g}_{10}(\lambda)$, $\bar{b}_{10}(\lambda)$ and fundamentals $\bar{l}_{10}(\lambda)$, $\bar{m}_{10}(\lambda)$, $\bar{s}_{10}(\lambda)$ linked by a linear relationship*

The recommendations incorporate the work of Stockman and Sharpe [STO 00] over several years.

For a field of view of 10° of visual angle, there is an area of diameter 10 cm seen $\bar{l}_{10}(\lambda)$, $\bar{m}_{10}(\lambda)$, $\bar{s}_{10}(\lambda)$, which is derived from color matches at 57 cm, the experiments performed on 49 observers by Stiles and Burch [STI 59]. These experimental color-matching functions $\bar{r}_{10}(\lambda)$, $\bar{g}_{10}(\lambda)$, $\bar{b}_{10}(\lambda)$ obtained with real monochromatic primaries, red (645.2 nm), green (526.3 nm), and blue (444.4 nm), exhibit high quality. The fundamentals are obtained by linear transformation:

$$\begin{pmatrix} \bar{l}_{10}(\lambda) \\ \bar{m}_{10}(\lambda) \\ \bar{s}_{10}(\lambda) \end{pmatrix} = \mathbf{A} \begin{pmatrix} \bar{r}_{10}(\lambda) \\ \bar{g}_{10}(\lambda) \\ \bar{b}_{10}(\lambda) \end{pmatrix} \qquad [1.7]$$

For a field of view of angular diameter 10°, the fundamentals exhibit a maximum of sensitivity at 568.6 nm, 541.3 nm and 447.9 nm.

The values of the color-matching function $\bar{s}_{10}(\lambda)$, tabulated by the CIE are slightly different from what would provide the linear transformation in equation [1.7], but the consequences for colorimetry are negligible. The tables are available on the Website http://www.cvrl.org/.

Unfortunately, for a field of view of angular diameter 2°, high-quality experimental data was not available. However, several physiological factors are altered with the eccentricity. It was decided to adopt a calculation scheme that enables us to predict the fundamentals consistent with known physiological and psychophysical data. The scheme consists of starting from fundamentals of a field of 10°, going up to the absorption of visual pigments included in the cones. This takes into account the absorption phenomena in several structures of the eye, the crystalline lens, the macular pigment and the photosensitive pigment density in the cones, then getting back through the opposite path in order to obtain the fundamentals $\bar{l}(\lambda)$, $\bar{m}_{10}(\lambda)$, $\bar{s}_{10}(\lambda)$ for a field of view of 2° [COM 06, SCH 07].

Figure 1.4 shows the fundamental calculation scheme validated for a field of view of 2°, and this can be generalized to any field of view of angular diameter between 1 and 10°. The CIE gives all the numerical values and equations necessary for modeling the fundamentals.

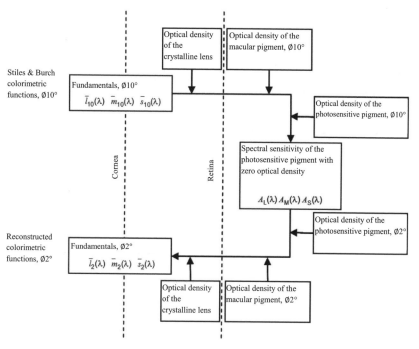

Figure 1.4. *Derivation procedure of cone fundamentals for a field of view of angular diameter 2°*

1.3.1.4. *Diversity of observers*

About 8% of the male population manifests defects of color vision in various forms and degrees. Women are practically free from that. These subjects, called color-blinds confuse certain colors that most people see clearly. The defect is caused by the absence or modification of a family of photosensitive pigments.

Individual variations are twofold in normal color vision. The numerical variations of cone populations do not significantly affect color vision and color identification, but have an effect on the visibility and the relative brightness of colors. Spectral variations of fundamentals alter color vision. As part of the normal color vision underpinned by three families of cones, there are subfamilies of photosensitive pigments whose maximum spectral sensitivity are slightly offset in wavelength by a few nanometers. Transmission variations of ocular media can also alter the fundamentals.

Recently, according to the color matches from 47 subjects examined by Stiles and Burch, it was proposed to classify the actual observers in seven categories, each accepting color matches that other categories rejected [SAR 10]. These individual variations have an impact on the assessment of colors on novel LED type displays with narrow primaries and could explain discrepancies between individuals.

1.3.2. *Application of LMS colorimetry*

Many applications directly use the LMS specification of cone excitation. The LMS specification also opens interesting perspectives for analyzing signal processing in visual pathways: color discrimination and color appearance.

1.3.2.1. *LMS specification*

The L, M, S specification of a stimulus $\phi_\lambda(\lambda)$, based on the amplitude of the excitation of three families of cones, is obtained by a calculation similar to that of tristimulus values X, Y, and Z:

$$L = k_L \sum \phi_\lambda(\lambda)\bar{l}(\lambda)\Delta\lambda$$
$$M = k_M \sum \phi_\lambda(\lambda)\bar{m}(\lambda)\Delta\lambda \qquad\qquad [1.8]$$
$$S = k_S \sum \phi_\lambda(\lambda)\bar{s}(\lambda)\Delta\lambda$$

1.3.2.2. *The luminance in LMS colorimetry*

The luminance is the sum of the activities of two families of cones L and M. The S cones do not contribute to luminance. To obtain the value Y of the luminance, the tristimulus values L and M should be computed using equations [1.8] of section 1.3.2.1, by introducing the factors $k_L = 1.98$ and $k_M = 1$.

1.3.2.3. *Real color domain*

All the colors of the real surfaces are included in a closed volume of the space, limited by the position of the optimal colors. In fact, it is physically impossible to achieve surfaces whose spectral reflection factor exceeds 100%. Once this limit is reached, the only way to increase the luminance factor Y of the surface is to broaden the reflection spectral band, which inevitably reduces the purity of color. In other words, a surface cannot be simultaneously very clear and highly saturated. The calculation shows that the *optimal colors* correspond to a set of reflectances with a square spectral profile and that they are represented by a convex surface in the color space.

Within the field of real colors, the values of the excitations of L and M cones are correlated (Figure 1.5). As it has been shown experimentally that the excitation of S cones do not contribute to the development of the luminance, the constant luminance planes are arranged parallel to the axis S. Any plane of equation L + M = constant is calculated with the factors $k_L = 1.98$ and $k_M = 1$ and is parallel to the axis S and carries the colors of constant luminance.

1.3.2.4. *The metamerism*

As a physical quantity, light is defined by the distribution of monochromatic radiations within it. As a color stimulus, light is defined only by three numbers, related to the three signals generated in the cones. The visual system is unable to analyze the spectrum of light. This explains the metamerism or phenomenon of visual origin, through which two beams of light may appear while their spectra are different. The two lightbeams appear identical because the same amount of photons is absorbed by the cones in both cases. This phenomenon is widely exploited by visualization technologies. For example, the apparent color

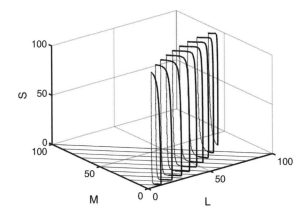

Figure 1.5. *Optimal colors in isoluminant planes of the LMS color space. The tristimulus values L, M, S, were normalized as described in the discussion*

of the clouds whose spectrum is naturally continuous is replicated by an additive mixture of primaries with discrete spectra.

With displays, yellow is obtained through an additive mixture of red and green. In the Rayleigh match [RAY 81], a metamer of the yellow radiation of 589 nm is obtained through an additive mixture of radiations of 670 nm and 546 nm. This is possible because the number of photons absorbed by the cones L, M or S is identical for the two metamers.

Let us pose the problem: What are the values of radiant flux $\Phi(\lambda)$ that provide a solution? We propose to solve the problem by using LMS colorimetry. The values $\bar{l}(\lambda)$, $\bar{m}(\lambda)$, $\bar{s}(\lambda)$ will be rounded off to facilitate the demonstration.

Let us write the color equations:

For the L cones:

$$\bar{l}(670) \times \Phi(670) + \bar{l}(546) \times \Phi(546)\bar{l}(589) \times \Phi(589) \qquad [1.9]$$

For the M cones:

$$\bar{m}(670) \times \Phi(670) + \bar{m}(546) \times \Phi(546)\bar{m}(589) \times \Phi(589) \qquad [1.10]$$

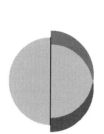

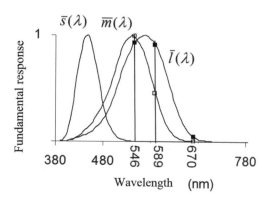

Figure 1.6. *Rayleigh match*

Let us introduce numerical values recorded on the sensitivity curves in Figure 1.6, and if a relative solution is sufficient, let us pose $\Phi(589) = 1$. It follows that:

$$\bar{l}(546) = 0.9 \quad \bar{l}(589) = 0.9 \quad \bar{l}(670) = 0.05$$
$$\bar{m}(546) = 1 \quad \bar{m}(589) = 0.5 \quad \bar{m}(670) = 0 \qquad [1.11]$$
$$\bar{s}(546) = 0 \quad \bar{s}(589) = 0 \quad \bar{s}(670) = 0$$

We have to solve the system of equations:

$$\begin{pmatrix} 0.05 & 0.9 \\ 0 & 1 \end{pmatrix} \begin{pmatrix} \Phi(670) \\ \Phi(546) \end{pmatrix} = \begin{pmatrix} 0.9 \\ 0.5 \end{pmatrix} \qquad [1.12]$$

The solution gives the proportion of radiant flux at 670 nm and 546 nm that have to be added to get the yellow color of the radiation of 589 nm:

$$\Phi(670) = 9$$
$$\Phi(546) = 0.5 \qquad [1.13]$$

1.3.2.5. *Simulation of the vision of colorblind people*

Using LMS specification, it was possible to simulate what a dichromat who has no photosensitive pigment L (protanope case), M (deuteranope

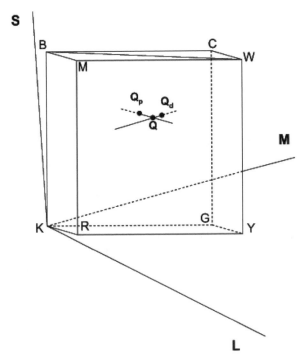

Figure 1.7. *Representation of colors confused by two types of dichromats in the LMS color space. The confusion lines are parallel to the axes L, M or S. The stimulus Q_p is confused with Q by the protanope. The stimulus Q_d is confused with Q by the deuteranope*

case) or S (tritanope case) [BRE 97] sees. For a dichromat, all stimuli located in the LMS space along a line parallel to the axis representing the family of absent cones are confused. This is known as the confusion line (Figure 1.7). The color space for the dichromat is obtained by projecting parallel to that axis all the colors of the LMS space on the surface that carries apparently identical colors for him and for a normal subject.

1.3.2.6. *The silent substitution*

Due to their spectral overlap, it is impossible to stimulate a family of cones separately, even with a monochromatic radiation. One way to stimulate a single family of cones is to alternate in time two colors that are located on a parallel to the axis representing the excitation of this family of cones. Thus, the stimulation of the other two families of cones does not vary. They remain "silent".

This technique can be extended to the stimulation of rods and melanopsin expressing ganglion cells.

1.3.2.7. Generalization of the LMS model

The LMS color model is based on a carefully established physiological basis. There is a linear relationship among the tristimulus values R, G, B, the tristimulus values X, Y, Z, and the signals L, M, S (Figure 1.8). LMS colorimetry, in future, could replace XYZ colorimetry each time the effect of a lightbeam on the visual system has to be monitored and analyzed. Pending recommendation of the CIE, we can adopt the transition matrix defined by Smith and Pokorny to transpose the tristimulus values of the XYZ space to the LMS space [SMI 75]. Factors k_L and k_M are included in the transformation such that the sum of the tristimulus values (L + M) gives the luminance Y directly. Rigorously, the transposition is applied to the tristimulus values corrected by Vos in 1978 [VOS 78]:

$$\begin{pmatrix} L \\ M \\ S \end{pmatrix} = \begin{pmatrix} 0.15514 & 0.54312 & -0.03286 \\ -0.15514 & 0.45684 & 0.03286 \\ 0 & 0 & 0.01608 \end{pmatrix} \begin{pmatrix} X \\ Y \\ Z \end{pmatrix} \quad [1.14]$$

1.3.3. Color discrimination

1.3.3.1. The isoluminant chromaticity diagram from MacLeod-Boynton

The chromaticity diagram represents the chromaticity of the colors without referring to their luminance. The chromaticity diagram x, y of the XYZ colorimetric system is an example. The chromaticity diagram l, s proposed by MacLeod and Boynton [MAC 79] is isoluminant. It lies in a constant luminance plane. The tristimulus values L and M are calculated with the factors $k_L = 1.98$ and $k_M = 1$. Therefore, the horizontal axis l carries in abscissa the contribution to the luminance of the excitation of

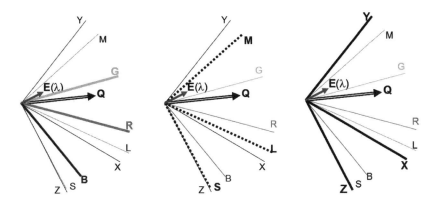

Figure 1.8. *Representation of the Q color and a monochromatic radiation E(λ) in the RGB, LMS, and XYZ color spaces. The figure is replicated in three copies to accentuate the three axes of each space, respectively. Within each space, the axes are independent and non-orthonormal. The representation in the plane of the figure makes it difficult to account for the 3D structure of each space*

L cones and the vertical axis carries the variation of the excitation of the S cones alone, relative to luminance. So, by posing:

$$l = \frac{L}{L+M} \quad and \quad s = \frac{S}{L+M} \qquad [1.15]$$

Any line of the L, M, or S space is projected along a line in the l, s chromaticity diagram. Specifically, the confusion lines of protanopes and deuteranopes are projected as straight beams that come from (1.0) and (0.0) respectively, and those of tritanopes as straight lines parallel to the s axis.

1.3.3.2. *The orientation and size of the MacAdam ellipses*

In the x, y chromaticity diagram, variations of size and orientation of MacAdam ellipses indicate the abilities of chromatic discrimination [MAC 42]. They reflect the activity of the two chromatic pathways [GRA 49]. The major ellipse axes that follow a beam of straight lines, which come from the lower left of the spectral locus, represent a variation of the excitation of S cones. The small axes are extended in directions

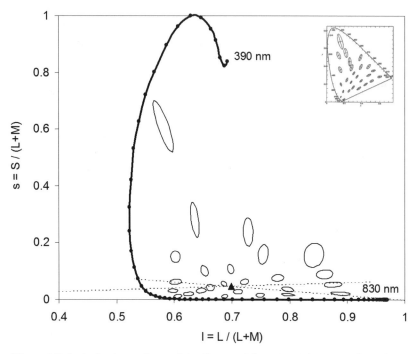

Figure 1.9. *l,s isoluminant chromaticity diagram. The unity of the tristimulus value S is such that the s coordinate does not exceed the unity. White equi-energy, (black Δ). Protan and deutan confusion lines (—-). MacAdam ellipses, arbitrary scale*

representing the variations of excitation of L and M cones (Figure 1.9, inset). We can expect to obtain a uniform representation of small color differences by exploiting the retinal processes of post-synaptic encoding. Thus, in the chromaticity diagram from MacLeod and Boynton, the chromatic discrimination thresholds are organized in circles when they are obtained on a background of the same chromaticity and in regularly arranged ellipses when they are obtained on a gray background [KRA 92] (Figure 1.9).

1.4. Colors in their context

Colorimetry specifies a lightbeam or a color stimulus presented in isolation. Once the context of the presentation (illumination or surround) changes or becomes complex as within an image, the appearance of the stimulus is changed. Therefore, the definition of the appearance of color is opposed to the specification of a single color.

1.4.1. *CIECAM02*

A color in isolation has several appearance attributes: *hue, chroma* or *colorfulness, lightness* or *brightness*. The hues form the color wheel within which four elementary hues have a special status and are opposed in pairs: red and green; blue and yellow. The CIECAM02 colorful appearance model described in Chapter 3 includes a color adaptation module, a light adaptation module, and a module for calculating the appearance attributes.

This is an empirical, operational model resulting from numerous visual observations. By introducing the nonlinearity of the signals that come from the cones, the CIECAM02 model applies to a range of light levels greater than those encountered in an office or on a screen. It predicts the appearance of an isolated color in various lighting conditions, weak or strong, artificial or natural. However, it does not reflect the complexity of the operation of the visual system. Thus, the specificity of S cone signals known in the earlier version of the Hunt model [HUN 95] is not taken into account. The phenomena of simultaneous contrast (described in Chapter 3) is not taken into account either.

1.4.2. *Chromatic adaptation*

When the lighting of a scene changes, either in luminance or in chromaticity, the appearance of color objects changes a little, as if the gain of the receptor mechanisms were adjusting to the ambient light. The chromatic adaptation mechanisms proposed in CIECAM02 have spectral sensitivity curves, which are fairly close to the fundamentals, and differ by a slightly sharpened bandwidth. Sensitivity peaks more distant from each other with slight negative sections. These signs indicate a slight antagonism activity in the chromatic adaptation, which occurs not only in cones, but also, to a lesser extent, at the level of retinal neurons in the parvo and koniocellular pathways.

1.4.3. *Partitioning of the perceptual space by the elementary hues*

The partitioning in the LMS space of the reddish colors and the greenish colors is neither flat nor continuous in the vicinity of the achromatic site. The same goes for the blue/yellow and white/black boundaries, which exclude a linear modeling of elementary hues from the cone signals. Furthermore, these boundaries are deformed when the test to be assessed appears on a colored background, which induces a chromatic adaptation. The model proposed by Chichilninsky and Wandell [CHI 99] requires a separation of the signals in increments and decrements. It includes a first step where the signals of the cones are distinguished according to their sign L+, L−, M+, M−, S+, S−, each undergoing a specific gain reflecting chromatic adaptation. In the second step where the signals of the cones are recombined linearly, the increments and decrements are again separated in pre-antagonist signals RG+, RG−, BY+, BY−, WB+, and WB−, before being recombined into antagonist signals.

1.4.3.1. *The simultaneous contrast*

The simultaneous contrast phenomenon (described in Chapter 3), according to which a surface changes its color depending on the background against which it is presented, has been widely studied. The law is stated as follows: Through their juxtaposition, two colors lose more or less of the color that is common to them ([CHE 39] Chapter IX). Therefore, a green-yellow turns green on a yellow background, and turns yellow on a green background. As opposed to the simplest assumptions, the colors induced by a background are not exactly complementary to the background, which points out the intervention of perceptual mechanisms beyond the receptors.

In the images, the contrast situations are very complex and the involved mechanisms are poorly known. Thus, in contrast to the perception of a natural scene in 3D [WEB 02], the color of a target is biased in the sense of simultaneous contrast in the digital image. The color contrasts could be treated independently, or even upstream of the color itself, which would explain our speed to decrypt the complexity of an image. To model the phenomena of color contrasts, it is necessary to introduce signal rectification processes after retinal processing (Shapiro, 2008) [SHA 08].

1.4.3.2. *Association effect and assimilation*

As opposed to the contrast, when the color of a surface tends to take the color of its surround, we talk of assimilation [KNO]. The phenomenon, easily observable with an environment of relatively high spatial frequency, results from association mechanisms whose explanation is still speculative. The white illusion in color, widely popularized, is dramatic [VIE 03].

1.5. Conclusion

This chapter gathers the physiological basis, colorimetric data and observations, which represent different approaches to color vision, and which reflect, each in their own way, the unique answer of the human visual system. Colorimetry provides a necessary yet insufficient answer on how to process an image. A color cannot be processed in isolation. The context, the surround, the conditions of adaptation and the expectation of the observer are the major parameters that significantly alter the appearance of the color. The quality of image processing comes from its compliance with the processes actually performed by the human visual system. Digital imaging can contribute to our understanding of the complexity of the HVS.

1.6. Bibliography

[BRE 97] BRETTEL H., VIÉNOT F., MOLLON J.D., "Computerized simulation of color appearance for dichromats", *Journal of the Optical Society of America A*, vol. 14, no. 10, p. 2647-2655, OSA, 1997.

[CHE 39] CHEVREUL M., *De la Loi du Contraste Simultané des Couleurs*, Pitois-Levrault, Paris, 1839.

[CHI 99] CHICHILNISKY E.J., WANDELL B.A., "Trichromatic opponent color classification", *Vision Research*, vol. 39, p. 3444-58, 1999.

[COM 06] COMMISSION INTERNATIONALE DE L'ÉCLAIRAGE, "Fundamental chromaticity diagram with physiological axes - part 1", *CIE*, vol. 170-1-2006, 2006.

[DAR 83] DARTNALL H.J., BOWMAKER J.K., MOLLON J.D., "Human visual pigments: microspectrophotometric results from the eyes of seven persons", *Proc. R. Soc. Lond. B. Biol. Sci.*, vol. 220, no. 1218, p. 115-30, 1983.

[GEG 03] GEGENFURTNER K.R., KIPER D.C., "Color vision", *Annual Review of Neuroscience*, vol. 26, no. 1, p. 181-206, 2003.

[GRA 49] GRAND Y.L., "Les seuils différentiels de couleurs dans la théorie de Young", *Revue d'optique*, vol. 28, p. 261-278, 1949.

[HOF 05] HOFER H., SINGER B., WILLIAMS D., "Different sensations from cones with the same photopigment", *J. Vis.*, vol. 5, no. 5, p. 444-54, 2005.

[HUN 95] HUNT R., *The Reproduction of Colour in Photography, Printing & Television: 5th ed.*, Fountain Press, Kingston-upon-Thames, UK, 1995.

[KNO] KNOBLAUCH K., SHEVELL S.K., CHALUPA L.M., WERNER J.S. (eds.), *The Visual Neurosciences*, p. 892-907, MIT Press, Cambridge, USA.

[KRA 92] KRAUSKOPF J., GEGENFURTNER K.R., "Color discrimination and adaptation", *Vision Research*, vol. 32, p. 2165-2175, 1992.

[LEE 99] LEE B., "Receptor inputs to primate ganglion cells", GEGENFURTNER K., SHARPE L. (eds.), *Color Vision: From Genes to Perception*, p. 203-217, Cambridge University Press, New York, 1999.

[MAC 42] MACADAM D., "Visual sensitivities to color differences in daylight", *J. Opt. Soc. Am.*, vol. 32, no. 5, p. 247-273, OSA, 1942.

[MAC 79] MACLEOD D.I.A., BOYNTON R.M., "Chromaticity diagram showing cone excitation by stimuli of equal luminance", *J. Opt. Soc. Am.*, vol. 69, no. 8, p. 1183-1186, OSA, 1979.

[RAY 81] RAYLEIGH L., "Experiments on colour", *Nature*, vol. 25, p. 64-66, 1881.

[ROO 99] ROORDA A., WILLIAMS D., "The arrangement of the three cone classes in the living human eye", *Nature*, vol. 397(6719), p. 473-475, 1999.

[SAR 10] SARKAR A., BLONDÉ L., CALLET P.L., AUTRUSSEAU F., MORVAN P., STAUDER J., "Toward reducing observer metamerism issue in industrial applications: colorimetric observer categories and observer classification", *18th Color Imaging Conference, Color Science and Engineering Systems, Technologies, and Applications, CIC18*, San Antonio, Texas, USA, 2010.

[SCH 07] SCHANDA J., *Colorimetry, Understanding the CIE system*, Wiley and Sons, Hoboken, New Jersey, USA, 2007.

[SHA 08] SHAPIRO A.G., "Separating color from color contrast", *Journal of Vision*, vol. 8, no. 1, p. 1-18, 2008.

[SHE 08] SHEVELL S., KINGDOM F., "Color in complex scenes", *Annual Review of Psychology*, vol. 59, no. 1, p. 143-166, 2008.

[SMI 75] SMITH V., POKORNY J., "Spectral sensitivity of the foveal cone photopigments between 400 and 500 nm", *Vision Research*, vol. 15, no. 2, p. 161-171, 1975.

[STI 59] STILES W., BURCH J., "NPL colour-matching investigation: final report (1958)", *Optica Acta*, vol. 6, p. 1-26, 1959.

[STO 00] STOCKMAN A., SHARPE L.T., "The spectral sensitivities of the middle-and long-wavelength-sensitive cones derived from measurements in observers of known genotype", *Vision Research*, vol. 40, no. 13, p. 1711-1737, 2000.

[VAL 08] VALBERG A., SEIM T., "Neural mechanisms of chromatic and achromatic vision", *Color Research Appl.*, vol. 33, p. 433-443, 2008.

[VAL 93] VALOIS R.D., VALOIS K.D., "A multi-stage color model", *Vision Research*, vol. 33, no. 8, p. 1053-1065, 1993.

[VAL 00] VALOIS R.D., COTTARIS N., ELFAR S., MAHON L., WILSON J., "Some transformations of color information from lateral geniculate nucleus to striate cortex", *Proc. of the National Academy of Sciences of the USA*, vol. 97, no. 9, p. 4997-5002, 2000.

[VIE 03] VIENOT F., ROHELLEC J.L., "Jeux de couleurs", *Pour la Science, Dossier hors-série*, p. 20-27, 2003.

[VOS 78] VOS J., "Colorimetric and photometric properties of a 2° fundamental observer", *Color Research and Application*, vol. 3, p. 125-128, 1978.

[WEB 02] WEBSTER M.A., MALKOC G., BILSON A.C., WEBSTER S.M., "Color contrast and contextual influences on color appearance.", *Journal of Vision*, vol. 2, no. 6, p. 505-519, 2002.

[ZAI 97] ZAIDI Q., "Decorrelation of L and M cone signals", *J. Opt. Soc. Am.*, vol. A14, p. 3430-3431, 1997.

Chapter 2

Color Constancy

2.1. Introduction

In Chapter 1, we saw that the retina and especially the cones play an important role in color perception. However, the human visual system, which consists of other parts such as the optic nerve or visual cortex, is far more complex. In particular, it is able to identify the color of objects irrespective of lighting conditions. An object that passes from the sun into shadow seems to maintain the same color. This ability is called *color constancy* [ZEK 93]. The mechanisms of color constancy also exist in other life forms, such as goldfish or bees [TOV 96]. From the viewpoint of physics, it is possible to show that the wavelength re-emitted by the objects cannot correspond to the color perceived by the observer in some cases. The brain is therefore able to interpret the color of a given object as a constant even if the illumination changes. In computer vision, it is very important to be able to define this type of descriptor. The mechanisms used by the human visual system are not yet fully known; however, many algorithms dedicated to the problems of color constancy have been developed. Several algorithms work properly under

Chapter written by Jean-Christophe Burie, Majed Chambah and Sylvie Treuillet.

certain conditions of illumination. A color object recognition algorithm can yield very good results under natural light but show poor performance under artificial light. The purpose of this chapter is to present color constancy models and correction algorithms commonly used in this type of literature.

2.2. Theoretical preliminaries and problems

2.2.1. Concept of illuminant

Light is an essential factor in the mechanism of color perception. It is therefore important to give a precise definition. Light is an electromagnetic radiation. To characterize a light source, we represent its spectral distribution of energy, which is the amount of energy emitted over a range of wavelengths. For example, the curve (D65) of Figure 2.1 shows the spectrum of the daylight over the range of wavelengths between 380 and 780 nm corresponding to the visible spectrum. We define four types of source:

– the continuous spectrum sources whose electromagnetic radiation extends continuously over all wavelengths (e.g. Figure 2.1);

– the discontinuous spectrum sources where the spectrum features many holes in which no light energy is emitted;

– the mixed spectrum sources, which correspond to the superposition of a continuous spectrum and a discontinuous spectrum;

– the line spectrum sources, which are sources that only emit in a few wavelengths (e.g. lasers).

Since the spectral distribution may vary from one source to another, the color of these sources is different. A light source can also be quantified by its color temperature (expressed in Kelvin typically between 2,000 and 10,000 K). This temperature is the one at which a theoretical black body should be heated[1] so that it produces an emission spectrum similar to the color seen in the visible range. For instance, a candle flame has a temperature of 1,850 K and is orange in color, while the midday sun has

---

1 By theoretical definition, a black body is one that fully absorbs the radiation it receives.

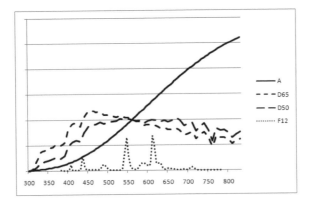

Figure 2.1. *Examples of the CIE standard illuminants*

a temperature of 5,800 K and is blue in color. In colorimetry, the spectral distribution of radiation is used to measure the color of a light source. This distribution is called *illuminant*. The International Commission on Illumination (CIE) has defined standard illuminants (Figure 2.1) that serve as a reference in industrial applications:

– illuminant A: incandescent sources whose color temperature is 2,856 K;

– illuminant B: direct daylight (4,874 K);

– illuminant C: average daylight (not including the ultraviolet zone) with a color temperature of 6,770 K;

– illuminant D: illuminant family including D50 (for *Daylight 50*), which specifies the characteristics of daylight of a temperature close to 5,000 K, D65 (6,504 K) and D75 (7,500 K);

– illuminant E: theoretical source whose energy is constant for all wavelengths;

– illuminants F: family of 12 illuminants from F1 to F12 corresponding to the light emitted by fluorescent lamps.

These reference illuminants [CIE 07] are defined in the form of tables of values of spectral density of energy and can have no corresponding existing light source.

NOTE.– The introduction of low-energy lamps replaced incandescent lamps. However, these new lamps feature color temperatures ranging from 2,700 K to 6,400 K depending on the model. The concept of the illuminant is still valid.

2.2.2. Concept of objects' reflectance

During their journey from a source to the eye (or the sensor of a camera), light rays undergo alterations that can be described by a set of successive reflections on the surface of objects constituting the scene. Light, in terms of wavelengths that compose it, is thus modified at each reflection. To explain this principle, we define a reflection model that connects the light rays arriving on an object to those leaving the object. In scientific papers, there are many models that will be recalled in detail in Chapter 4. These include the Lambert models [LAM 60], the bi-directional spectral reflectance function [NIC 65], Torrance and Sparrow [TOR 67], Wolf [WOL 67], the dichromatic model [TOM 91], etc. These models are widely used in computer vision and image synthesis (see Chapter 4). Schematically, all these models define the spectral reflectance function of a surface as a linear combination of several functions, each describing a specific element of the reflection phenomenon. Thus defined, these models have the disadvantage of being complex and time consuming in calculation. Therefore, most of them limit the phenomenon of reflection to two components: *specular* and *diffuse* reflection. The specular reflection phenomenon occurs when the incident light is returned primarily in a particular direction. In this case, the proportion of reflected light not only varies with the direction of observation, but also with the nature of the object (metal, plastic, etc.). It is this specular reflection that is the cause of reflection or the shiny characteristic of objects. When a surface returns the same proportion of incident light in all directions, this is called diffuse reflection. This component of the reflection phenomenon is often called the Lambertian component and is common to all reflectance models. Let us consider a surface that obeys the Lambertian model. We call the reflectance $R(\lambda)$ of an object, the fraction of light reflected by the surface. The light distribution $I(\lambda)$ that reaches the eye is the product of the distribution of the illuminant $E(\lambda)$ and the reflectance of a surface $R(\lambda)$:

$$I(\lambda) = R(\lambda).E(\lambda) \hspace{4cm} [2.1]$$

This shows that the color perception of an object depends not only on the properties of the material of the object, that is to say, its reflectance $R(\lambda)$, but also on the illuminant that illuminates the scene.

2.2.3. Problem of color constancy

The human visual system is equipped with mechanisms to define color descriptors that remain invariant to changes in illumination. The term "invariant" should however be used with caution because, if the human visual system can distinguish between millions of different colors, it cannot remember all these differences. Thus, if two colors are not shown simultaneously, our ability to distinguish between them significantly decreases. However, the human visual system is able, in most cases, to identify the dominant hue of an object irrespective of the illuminant. What about a device such as a digital camera or a video camera? These devices do not have this ability and the numerical values of colors can be significantly altered by a change in perspective or a change in illumination. This ability is nevertheless essential in many applications.

The values generated by these devices do not exhibit the reflectance properties of objects in the scene. The measured value for the channel k of the pixel located at (x,y), denoted $\rho_k(x, y)$, is the product of the incident illumination $E(\lambda)$, the reflectance of the surface $S(x, y, \lambda)$ and the spectral sensitivity of channel k of the camera $C_k(\lambda)$, as a function of the wavelength λ integrated over the visible spectrum ω:

$$\rho_k(x, y) = \int_{\omega} E(\lambda)S(x, y, \lambda)C_k(\lambda)d\lambda \hspace{3cm} [2.2]$$

We therefore have two unknowns: the reflectance and the type of illuminant. In color image processing, the color constancy usually consists of two steps: the illuminant estimation step and the correction step. To estimate the properties of the illuminant of the scene, an assumption is made on the distribution of pixel color of the image. Then, the color correction of the scene is performed by selecting the canonical illuminant (a canonical illuminant is the illuminant for which the sensors were calibrated) closest to the estimated illuminant. Solving the problem of color constancy therefore requires the definition of exploitable model(s) in image processing.

2.3. Color constancy models

2.3.1. *Model of the human visual system*

Information processing by the human visual system starts with the eye. Light passes through the lens before reaching the retina. The latter consists of two types of cells: rods and cones. It is the retina that will allow us to perceive the color of objects by sending information via the optic nerve to the visual cortex. Within the visual cortex, the areas dedicated to color perception have been identified [ZEK 93]. However, the human visual system is complex. Although many studies have provided a better understanding of its operation, the mechanisms implemented to perceive colors and achieve color constancy are not yet fully known. The study of color constancy has resulted in many models. According to McCann [MCC 04], there are two types of models based on very distinct mechanisms. The first is based on *chromatic adaptation*. This type of model assumes that the retinal sensitivity varies in response to illumination changes. The algorithms based on this model require the measurement of reflectance and illumination at each pixel to determine the appearance of objects. The second type is based on *spatial comparisons*. This type of model is insensitive to changes in illumination because it computes luminance ratios of different pixels of the image. The von Kries and Land models, described as follows, belong respectively to these two types. However, there are other theories that assume that color constancy is partly due to an adaptation of cones (called von Kries constancy) [CAR 00]. The rest of the adaptation is due to a spatial analysis of the scene, *a priori* knowledge of the color of some surfaces (skin color for instance) and a color comparison against stored colors.

2.3.2. *Von Kries diagonal model*

Von Kries proposed an adaptation model in 1902 that is still the basis of several algorithms of color constancy [CAR 00] and also color appearance models (see Chapter 3).

His adaptation rule states that the functions of spectral sensitivity of the eye are invariant and independent, and that the adaptation of the visual system to different illuminants is performed by adjusting three gain coefficients associated with three color channels (L, M, S) according to equation [2.3]:

$$\begin{bmatrix} L' \\ M' \\ S' \end{bmatrix} = \begin{bmatrix} k_L & 0 & 0 \\ 0 & k_M & 0 \\ 0 & 0 & k_S \end{bmatrix} \cdot \begin{bmatrix} L \\ M \\ S \end{bmatrix} \qquad [2.3]$$

where L', M' and S' are the stimuli after adaptation. The coefficients k_L, k_M and k_S are adjusted so that the stimuli of a reference white surface $(L_w, M_w$ and $S_w)$ are constant and equal to 1:

$$k_L = \tfrac{1}{L_w} \qquad k_M = \tfrac{1}{M_w} \qquad k_S = \tfrac{1}{S_w} \qquad [2.4]$$

This rule assumes that the illuminant is uniform. The correction thus removes the color of the illuminant and produces an image equivalent to that which would have been taken under white light. This adaptation model therefore requires knowledge of the appearance of a reference white surface to adapt the visual stimuli in a scene. The color of a reference white area can also be interpreted as the color of the illuminant; this method is known as a "white patch". Based on this model, several color constancy algorithms estimate the stimuli corresponding to a white surface in a scene, and then use the adjustment rule by von Kries to correct the image (section 2.4.2.2).

Worthey and Brill [WOR 86] studied the limits of the adjustment rule of von Kries by considering three theoretical retinas and testing the rule on each of these retinas. The first retina HR-1 consists of three narrowband receptors, of wavelengths λ_R, λ_G and λ_B. The von Kries rule works perfectly with this type of retina since the receivers are narrow and do not overlap. The second type of retina, HR-2, consists of a single broadband receiver. This type of retina illustrates the metamerism problem (see Chapter 1), since the same value of stimulus corresponds to different spectral reflectances.

The third type of retina, HR-3, has three broadband receivers but without overlapping, similar to those used in the acquisition devices.

Since the receivers are broadband, the metamerism problem invariably arises, but it is possible to avoid this problem by using three light sources with narrow bands of wavelengths corresponding to those of the three sensors. As the reflectances are sampled only at these wavelengths, broadband sensors do not generate "metameric" colors.

2.3.3. *Land theory*

Edwin H. Land has played a very important role in the field of color constancy. He is the proponent of one of the best known theories: the Retinex model [LAN 86]. The term "Retinex" is a combination of "retina" and "cortex", because E.H. Land was unsure whether the process was conducted at the retina or the cortex. The aim of his theory is to simulate and explain how the human visual system perceives colors. To understand how it works, Land conducted a series of experiments. During the first, conducted in an achromatic context [LAN 71], Land and McCann found that the contours of two adjacent regions of an image play a fundamental role in determining the reflectance of an object, information that they considered essential for color constancy. A second experiment was to present to different observers a board consisting of a juxtaposition of a hundred uniform colored rectangles randomly arranged (called the Mondrian experiment because of the similarity of the board with Piet Mondrian paintings [LAN 50]). Three spotlights illuminate the board with long (red), medium (green) and short (blue) wavelengths, respectively. A rectangle on the board is selected first. Its radiance is measured in each of the three wavelength bands to determine the information reaching the eye. The intensities of the three spotlights are then adjusted so that the radiance returned by a second rectangle is identical to the first rectangle.

Land noted that observers correctly identified the intrinsic color of the rectangles without being influenced by the illuminant color, although the two rectangles had exactly the same photometrically measured values. He obtained the same result when the illuminant was not uniform. Land also realized that the identification of a color depended on the area of the board that was observed. For instance, if a blue rectangle alone were visible, an observer would not be able to specify the intrinsic color of the rectangle when the spotlights were adjusted to measure a green radiation. However, if other rectangles were visible to the observer, then he would be able to specify the blue rectangle. Land concluded that the wavelength alone cannot fully explain the perception of color. As a result of these experiments, Land identified, on the one hand, the luminance (that is, the reflectivity) as the color fundamental stimulus, and on the other hand, the importance of boundaries, which allow the eye to estimate the clarity by seeking the singularities in the ratio of the flow of energy that comes from closely spaced points. It is from these observations that Land proposed his Retinex theory. According to him, the retina has three types of receptors (cones) that respond to long, medium and short wavelengths of the visible spectrum (L, M and S). Each set of receptors, acting independently, measures the energy received in different parts of the visible spectrum. For adjacent receptors of the same type, the human visual system then calculates the ratio of received energies. This operation detects the boundaries but also eliminates the effects of the illuminant. By combining information that comes from the three types of receptors, this process of color constancy allows the human visual system to perceive the color of objects.

There are two major differences compared to the von Kries model. The first is that the Retinex theory also applies to scenes illuminated by a non-uniform illuminant. The second is that the von Kries model is a correction estimated from local information while in the case of Retinex, a spatial comparison is performed. It is from these experiments that Land proposed his model of the human visual system: the Retinex algorithm (see section 2.4.2).

2.4. Color correction algorithms

The aim of color constancy algorithms is to recover the intrinsic properties of surface reflectance $S(x, y, \lambda)$ independently of the incident illumination $E(\lambda)$. The problem would have been easily solved with the availability of spectral data. Since only three sensors are typically used by acquisition devices (scanner and digital camera), it is not possible to recover the reflectance properties of surfaces as a function of the wavelength (unless to acquire multispectral images [BER 98]).

Therefore, only the tristimulus values are available. Some methods [FUN 93, SMI 99, LUC 00] propose to reconstruct the reflectance spectrum of surfaces to perform spectral processing (such as an illuminant change), but these reconstruction methods are complex, pose a number of assumptions and demonstrate a lack of precision. However, if the incident illumination $E(\lambda)$ can be estimated, it is then possible to determine the sensor response $\rho_k(x, y)$ by using a camera canonical model. It has been shown by Finlayson [FIN 93] that by posing a set of conservative assumptions, equation [2.2] can be reduced to a simpler system of equations based on a diagonal transformation:

$$R = \rho_r(x, y) = \alpha S_r(x, y)$$

$$G = \rho_g(x, y) = \beta S_g(x, y) \qquad [2.5]$$

$$B = \rho_b(x, y) = \gamma S_b(x, y)$$

To recover the surface reflectance information, the values of α, β and γ should be determined. The estimation of these parameters is to compute a color value invariant to illumination. An overview of the various existing methods of color constancy is given as follows. We essentially present basic approaches such as the algorithm of the gray world and the white patch or the Retinex algorithm of Land. More recent methods are also detailed such as the probabilistic approaches, the methods based on gamut conversion or neural network, and the perceptual approach.

2.4.1. *Gray world*

The gray world considers an alternative approach to color constancy by comparing the average content of a scene with some expected values. This model assumes that the average of the perceived world is gray and that every deviation from this average is caused by the color of the illuminant. The origin of the gray world algorithm [BUC 80] goes back to Helmholtz [HEL 24] who attributed the phenomenon of human color constancy to the exclusion of the illuminant. This idea was reinforced by Helson, and it assumes that the colors are detected relative to one level of adaptation, which corresponds to a medium gray level. The average is computed as a weighted function whose the components are the reflectances of surfaces present in the visual field. Judd [JUD 40] assumed that the average chromaticity of the reflected light is equal to the chromaticity of the illuminant. Since the gray world method hypothesizes that the average of all three channels over the entire image forms a fixed ratio under the canonical illuminant, equation [2.5] implies:

$$\frac{1}{\alpha} \cdot \overline{\rho_r} = \overline{S_r} \qquad \frac{1}{\beta} \cdot \overline{\rho_g} = \overline{S_g} \qquad \frac{1}{\gamma} \cdot \overline{\rho_b} = \overline{S_b} \qquad\qquad [2.6]$$

The values $\overline{S_r}, \overline{S_g}, \overline{S_b}$ are determined empirically or based on *a priori* knowledge of the distribution of colors in the images to be corrected.

Buchsbaum [BUC 80] developed an extended model of the gray world. He assumes that spectral reflectances and illuminants can be represented with only three basic functions (which cover a non-orthogonal color space), excluding the metamerism problems and other problems associated with the use of sensors whose sensitivities overlap. His model determines the illuminant and the reflectances of surfaces by matching them with linear combinations of basic functions. The two main assumptions of Buchsbaum are as follows:

– the whole scene can be processed as a single reflectance vector (computed as a weighted average over different areas of the scene);

– the visual system adopts a standard fixed reflectance vector for the overall average of the scene.

This means that the illuminant is estimated on this basis and acts on a homogeneous surface reflectance, which is assumed to be the standard and equal to 1. After determining the illuminant, all the surfaces are corrected accordingly. In practice, it often happens that the standard average reflectance is not equal to the actual average of the visual field. In this case, the gray world algorithm has a low performance. This algorithm tends to move the surface colors toward gray, which reduces their saturation. An image containing only a blue sky will become gray since the algorithm considers that the blue reflectance is caused by the illuminant and corrects the image so that the average is gray (equal to the average standard). Choosing a slightly blue standard average improves the results for this scene, but it could give larger errors by correcting the image of a forest where the average is green. Furthermore, choosing the weighted function, which computes the average of reflectances, is also a problem since different functions give different results. Gershon *et al.* [GER 87] improved the Buchsbaum algorithm by posing some *a priori* assumptions on the reflectances and the illuminants, based on statistical measurements of reflectances and illuminants. They computed the average reflectance standard from a set of 370 reflectances determined by Krinov. They also built a 3D model for illuminants based on the Judd study. Their approach is to segment the image into a set of zones according to their chromaticity. Then, the average of the average of the zones is computed to deduce the global average reflectance of the image. This method of averaging has the advantage of representing all surfaces in an equitable manner, irrespective of their surface. This algorithm is still dependent on the assumption of a fixed reference average reflectance despite Gershon computing the illuminant using *a priori* knowledge about the world. McCann [MCC 97] conducted a series of experiments showing that the human visual system does not perform color constancy using the average tristimulus values. It recommends that color constancy should be based on a standardization process similar to the Retinex algorithm. Despite the various deficiencies of the gray world algorithm, it remains one of the simplest algorithms in terms of performance [LEE 94]. In addition, for scenes involving several surfaces and natural scenes, the algorithm yields good results that often exceed some more complex approaches [FUN 96].

2.4.2. *Retinex theory*

2.4.2.1. *Land algorithm*

The Retinex theory [LAN 77] has given rise to a great interest within the community. Although the research by Land has often been controversial [BRA 86], it has been studied and developed by many authors [FUN 92, MCC 97]. We present the basic algorithm here and give an overview of the changes that have been proposed.

Land built the Retinex algorithm based on the results of his experiments (see section 2.3.3). The method assumes that the low variations of intensity in the image are due to changes in the illuminant while large variations correspond to the boundaries between regions. The aim is therefore to remove small variations of light to estimate the color of surfaces. The basic operation is to compute, for each wavelength $\lambda \in \{L, M, S\}$, the logarithm of the ratio of the intensities of two adjacent pixels:

$$r_\lambda^x = \log \left[\frac{I_\lambda^{x+1}}{I_\lambda^x} \right] \qquad [2.7]$$

These ratios are calculated, starting from a pixel i, step by step, for all pixels of a random path p, which embodies the movements of the eye observing the scene. The combination of ratios determines the ratio of reflectances on the path in question:

$$r_\lambda^{i,p} = \sum_{x \in p} \delta \left(\log \left[\frac{I_\lambda^{x+1}}{I_\lambda^x} \right] \right) \qquad [2.8]$$

with:

$$\delta(x) = \begin{cases} x & if\ |x| > t \\ 0 & otherwise \end{cases} \qquad [2.9]$$

The function $\delta(x)$ allows us to take into account non-uniform illuminants. If the variations are greater than a specific threshold t, they are viewed as changes in the reflectance and the ratio is maintained. If the variations are lower, they are regarded as an illumination change and the ratio is set to zero. The calculation is performed on N paths starting from the pixel i. The results are averaged to obtain the average reflectance of the pixel i for the wavelength λ:

$$r_\lambda^i = \sum_{p=1}^{N} r_\lambda^{i,p} \qquad [2.10]$$

To determine the three colorimetric components of a pixel i, it is sufficient to calculate equation [2.10] for the wavelengths $\lambda \in \{L,M,S\}$.

The first problem of this algorithm is that the computational complexity increases with the number of paths used and their length. The second is the choice of the threshold t. In practice, it is difficult to find an appropriate threshold. Many variants have been proposed to improve the basic algorithm proposed by Land or decrease computing time. These examples include the use of Brownian paths [MAR 00] or their substitution by random "sprays" [PRO 07]. Rahman has proposed a multiscale approach (multiscale Retinex) of the Land algorithm [RAH 97]. The main criticism of the Land algorithm is that it is complicated to analyze and thus no result on its performance has actually been published. The Retinex theory from Land remains a reference in the field of color constancy.

2.4.2.2. White patch Retinex

The white patch Retinex algorithm [CAR 99a] is a simplified version of the Retinex algorithm described above. It assumes that the maximum values of each channel are the maximum possible reflectance of the illuminant such as the one caused by a specular reflection or an object that was originally white (white patch). Let $(\rho_r^{max}(x, y), \rho_r^{max}(x, y), \rho_r^{max}(x, y))$ be the maximum values of intensity. The system of equations [2.5] now becomes:

$$\frac{1}{\alpha} \cdot \rho_r^{max}(x, y) = S_r^{max} \tag{2.11}$$

$$\frac{1}{\beta} \cdot \rho_g^{max}(x, y) = S_g^{max} \tag{2.12}$$

$$\frac{1}{\gamma} \cdot \rho_b^{max}(x, y) = S_b^{max} \tag{2.13}$$

where the values $[S_r^{max}, S_g^{max}, S_b^{max}]$ are determined empirically or based on *a priori* knowledge. Once determined, the parameters α, β, γ allow us to perform color correction. One of the weaknesses of this algorithm is that it can be difficult to determine the maximum values given the noise and the clip due to the saturation of the sensors. The other weakness is that the maximum response of a channel may not be characteristic of the color of the illuminant. Finally, the white patch Retinex algorithm assumes in its principle that the illuminant that enlightens the scene is unique and uniform. If this condition is not satisfied, the algorithm is inefficient. To increase the reliability of the algorithm, Chambah [CHA 01] proposed the method of the modified white patch. Instead of taking the maximum values of the three RGB channels of the image, he assigned to the values $(\rho_r^{max}(x,y), \rho_r^{max}(x,y), \rho_r^{max}(x,y))$ the average of light areas that have a value greater than a specific threshold. Thus, the estimation errors due to the imperfections in the image and the possible clip of some values are minimized. He thus obtained a better estimate of the dominant color in the light areas.

2.4.3. Gamut conversion

A gamut Γ is the convex set of the responses of sensors to all physically realizable surfaces viewed under a certain illuminant. Gamut conversion algorithms (called *gamut mapping*) are based on the observation that the nature of illuminants constrains the overall plausible responses of sensors. For example, if the illuminant used in a scene is red, no surface can have a significant response on the blue channel. So, every surface in the scene introduces a new low constraint on the color of the illuminant. By considering the intersection of all these constraints, the algorithm determines a set of plausible illuminants from which it selects the best estimate. The first gamut conversion algorithm was developed by Forsyth [FOR 90]. His model assumes that the scene is composed of flat matte surfaces and that it is uniformly illuminated by a single illuminant. Another assumption concerns the overall possible illuminants, which should be "reasonable" (that is to say, configurable). The central concept of *gamut mapping* is the canonical gamut. The canonical gamut $\Gamma(C)$ is the gamut under a standard canonical illuminant. In practice, this illuminant is chosen such that the sensor responses are calibrated for that illuminant (which means, a reference white patch produces equal responses for all sensors), but other illuminants can be used. All gamuts are convex because a linear combination of two surfaces also belongs to the gamut. If $\mathbf{p_1}$ and $\mathbf{p_2}$ are two surfaces that belong to the gamut, any combination $\mathbf{p_x} = \alpha.\mathbf{p_1} + (1 - \alpha).\mathbf{p_2}$ is also in gamut because it is physically feasible. Let I be a scene observed in an unknown illuminant. For any surface $\mathbf{p_x}$, a diagonal transformation $\mathbf{D_x}$, which converts $\mathbf{p_x}$ inside the canonical gamut $\Gamma(C)$ represents a possible solution. Finding the set of all the transformations D_x is equivalent to converting $\mathbf{p_x}$ in all the points of the convex hull $H(C)$ of the canonical gamut. The set Δ of all the possible conversions $\mathbf{D_x}$, which simultaneously transforms all points of the scene I in the canonical gamut, is the intersection of all the transformations $\mathbf{D_x}$ for all the surfaces $\mathbf{p_x}$ in the scene:

$$\Delta = \bigcap_x D_x, \forall \mathbf{p_x} \qquad\qquad [2.14]$$

Since the diagonal transformations preserve the convexity of the sets, this is equivalent to computing the intersection of diagonal transformations $\mathbf{D_x}$ belonging to the surfaces defining $H(I)$ the convex hull of the scene I:

$$\Delta = \bigcap_x D_x, \mathbf{p_x} \in H(I) \qquad\qquad [2.15]$$

After the set of all possible gamut conversions has been determined, the algorithm selects the transformation that generates the gamut with the highest volume. A diagonal volume transformation consists in transforming a volume (e.g. transforming the original image gamut into the canonical gamut) by multiplying it by the trace of the transformation matrix. Finding the gamut with the highest volume is therefore equivalent to finding the transform that has the largest trace. Forsyth's algorithm exhibits good performance under controlled conditions, but the real images that usually contain specular reflections, curved surfaces and noise degrade its performances. Another problem is that the algorithm seeks to determine not only the chromaticity of the illuminant but also the intensity. Therefore, significant errors in estimating the intensity, which can darken an image or truncate the light pixels, occur if the image is not standardized. Finlayson [FIN 98a] improved Forsyth's algorithm by working in a chromaticity space instead of a 3D space and by imposing certain restrictions on the illuminant. His method, called "color in perspective" [FIN 96], uses a perspective chromaticity space: $r = R/B$ and $g = G/B$, where R, G and B are the responses of the sensors on the three color channels. Working in 2D instead of 3D reduces the complexity of the algorithm that determines the intersection of convex hulls. Visualization techniques are also simpler to implement in 2D. Finlayson added another constraint to the possible set of gamut conversions by defining an illumination gamut, composed of the set of all plausible illuminants. A gamut conversion D, described above, is considered possible if its inverse D^{-1} converts the canonical illuminant within the illumination gamut. The intersection of the set of conversions that satisfies the illumination constraint with the set of all gamut conversions Δ is taken into account. However, the selection of a conversion is always a problem. One possible solution is to select the conversion that yields the maximum surface in a manner similar to the 3D Forsyth's algorithm. Another solution is to choose a mean conversion, but both solutions are inappropriate since the calculations were made in a nonlinear perspective space that distorts distances. Finlayson *et al.* [FIN 97a] propose a novel approach to solve this problem. They rebuild the set of 3D conversions by converting the (r, g) coordinates of the hull of all the gamut conversions in 3D coordinates $(r, g, b = 1)$. These points, which are on a plane defined by $b = 1$, are then connected to the origin and form a cone. The selected gamut conversion is the average of conversions in the 3D space. As the intersections were calculated in the perspective space, the gamut conversion is obtained at the nearest scale factor. This average projected on the chromaticity space is different from the average calculated directly in the chromaticity space and gives a more accurate estimate of the chromaticity of the illuminant.

Barnard, Funt and Finlayson [BAR 97] focused on the problem of non-uniform illumination in a scene, which introduces another constraint in Finlayson's algorithm. Different conversions are calculated locally, generating a relative illumination field. This relative field is used to eliminate the change of the illuminant throughout the scene by considering it as being illuminated from an arbitrary reference point. All the relative illuminations should meet the constraints imposed on the illumination, which further reduces the number of possible solutions. Despite their complexity, the gamut conversion algorithms are considered to be among the best algorithms for color constancy under controlled conditions.

2.4.4. Probabilistic methods

The probabilistic algorithms of color constancy use stochastic models of surfaces and illuminants to derive estimates of the illuminant of the scene that have a maximum likelihood. They can be viewed as an extension of the gray world algorithm from Buchsbaum (see section 2.4.1), since they use the distribution information of reflectance functions of surfaces instead of their spatial average over the entire scene. Prior distributions of possible illuminants can help us to estimate the chromaticity of the illuminant with maximum likelihood. These stochastic algorithms can also be regarded as an extension of gamut conversion algorithms [FOR 90, FIN 95b]. Instead of calculating "strict" intersections of transformations corresponding to possible surfaces and illuminants, they find "soft" intersections of likely surfaces and illuminants. Like all algorithms that depend on *a priori* knowledge about the world, these methods depend on the precision of prior distributions on the composition of the scene, determined empirically. Let us suppose that an image contains a set of n responses of sensors (RGB) relative to n independent surfaces. The likelihood $L(A)$ that the scene is taken under an illuminant $A(\lambda)$ is given by the joint probability:

$$L(A) = \prod_{i=1}^{n} p\,(RGB_i|A) \qquad\qquad [2.16]$$

The Bayesian color constancy algorithm from Brainard and Freeman [BRA 97] is an extension of finite dimensional linear models, using stochastic models of reflectances of surfaces and illuminant spectra. Given an *a priori* model of illuminants and surfaces $p(x)$ and the observed scene y, following Bayes law the probability of each vector x can be calculated, and implicitly, the probability corresponding to each illuminant. To obtain a single estimate of the illuminant from possible illuminants, a loss function $L(\bar{x}, x)$ is introduced. The loss function specifies the penalty when an estimate $\bar{x}$ is chosen while the correct value is x. If the loss function is invariant to shift, then it depends only on the difference $\bar{x} - x$. Given a loss function L and *a posteriori* probability $p(y|x)$, the aim is to minimize the expected Bayesian loss:

$$L\,(\bar{x}|y) = \int_x L\,(\bar{x}|x)\,p\,(x|y)\,d(x) \qquad\qquad [2.17]$$

Usually, $\bar{x}$ is chosen such that it maximizes the *a posteriori* distribution or it minimizes the mean square error of the distribution. However,

Brainard and Freeman introduced a new loss function, more appropriate to perception. The local mass loss function rewards the "almost correct" answers and penalizes all estimates that produce high errors. Thus, the algorithm finds the most likely "almost correct" answer. The illuminants and surface reflectances were modeled using linear models. The reflectances of surfaces s_j were modeled by a set of weights w_j and basis functions B_s, such that $s_j = B_s w_{sj}$. The illuminants were modeled in the same way. The authors noted that the weights were not uniformly distributed, but had a density function of normal probability. If the illuminant and the surfaces of a scene are independent then $p(x) = p(w_s, w_e) = p(w_s)p(w_e)$.

Finlayson [FIN 97b] extended his "color in perspective" color constancy algorithm [FIN 95a], by using a correlation matrix to establish a stochastic relationship between the chromaticities of a scene and a set of illuminants [HUB 99]. This matrix is used as an associative memory to correlate the data of a scene with all the possible illuminants. The rows of the matrix correspond to all the chromaticities collected (determined empirically) and the columns correspond to all the possible illuminants. An element e_{ij} of this matrix is set to 1 if the chromaticity i can be seen under the illuminant j, and 0 otherwise. This matrix is calculated from *a priori* observations of the world, that is to say, derived from a large set of surfaces and illuminants. The illuminant of a scene is estimated by a voting system based on the chromaticities of the scene. The use of binary coefficients in the correlation matrix assumes that all illuminants and chromaticities have a uniform distribution. This algorithm can be improved by using *a priori* distributions of chromaticities and illuminants. In this case, the elements e_{ij} of the correlation matrix are written as the conditional probability of the illuminant j knowing the chromaticity i: $e_{ij} = p(j|i)$. As with all probabilistic approaches, this method produces not only an estimate of the illuminant, but also gives a confidence estimate in this illuminant by comparing the likelihood values of the selected illuminant with the likelihood values of other illuminants.

The Rosenberg method [ROS 00] attempts to remedy some deficiencies of basic color constancy algorithms. The method employs a parametric model of the distribution of responses of the color channels in an image, instead of pixel values, for the correction. The selected parametric model is a mixture of Gaussians, each with a diagonal covariance matrix. In this model, each 3D value of a pixel (ρ_r, ρ_g, ρ_b) is modeled as being generated by one of the Gaussians of the model with a hidden variable z_{ij}, indicating which Gaussian generated the pixel. In the following equation, the image pixels are indexed by the variable i going from 1 to m, where m is the number of pixels of the image. The variable j indexes the n Gaussians of the mixture, and the variable k indexes the color channels (the dimension):

$$P_r\left(\rho_r(i), \rho_g(i), \rho_b(i)|z_{ij}, \mu, \sigma\right) \approx$$

$$\left(\prod_{k=1}^{3}(2\pi\sigma_{jk}^2)\right)^{-\frac{1}{2}} \exp\left(-\frac{1}{2}\sum_{k=1}^{3}\frac{(\rho_k(i) - \mu_{jk})^2}{\sigma_{jk}^2}\right) \quad [2.18]$$

To build the model, the parameters of the Gaussian should be estimated, as well as the expected values of indicator variables. Rosenberg uses the *Expectation-Maximization* (EM) method to estimate these parameters. The *expectation* (E) and *maximization* (M) steps are alternated:

Step E:

$$E[z_{ij}] = \frac{\left(\prod_{k=1}^{3}\sigma_{jk}^2\right)^{-\frac{1}{2}} \exp\left(-\frac{1}{2}\sum_{k=1}^{3}\frac{(\rho_k(i)-\mu_{jk})^2}{\sigma_{jk}^2}\right)}{\sum_{c=1}^{n}\left(\prod_{k=1}^{3}\sigma_{ck}^2\right)^{-\frac{1}{2}} \exp\left(-\frac{1}{2}\sum_{k=1}^{3}\frac{(\rho_k(i)-\mu_{ck})^2}{\sigma_{ck}^2}\right)} \quad [2.19]$$

Step M:

$$\mu_{jk} = \frac{\sum_{i=1}^{m} E[z_{ij}]\rho_k(i)}{\sum_{i=1}^{m} E[z_{ij}]} \quad [2.20]$$

$$\sigma_{jk} = \frac{\sum_{i=1}^{m} E[z_{ij}]\rho_k^2(i) - (\sum_{i=1}^{m} E[z_{ij}]\rho_k(i)])^2}{\sum_{i=1}^{m} E[z_{ij}]} \quad [2.21]$$

Despite improvements made possible by this method, the estimation of the parameters of a mixture model for a set of large data is complex, especially for images (a 1280×1280 image contains 1.6 million pixels). The use of simplification techniques is therefore essential.

The gray world method based on the Expectation Maximization (EM) uses the centers of the Gaussian instead of the pixel values of the image to balance the distribution of colors in the image. Equation [2.6] becomes:

$$\frac{1}{\alpha.n} \sum_{j=1}^{n} \mu_{jr} = \overline{S_r}$$

$$\frac{1}{\beta.n} \sum_{j=1}^{n} \mu_{jg} = \overline{S_g}$$

[2.22]

$$\frac{1}{\gamma.n} \sum_{j=1}^{n} \mu_{jb} = \overline{S_b}$$

As for the white patch Retinex, the maxima of the channels is searched among the averages of Gaussian clusters, instead of the image pixels, to minimize errors due to the clip and the noise. Equation [2.11] thus becomes:

$$\frac{1}{\alpha}.\mu_{jr}^{max} = S_r^{max}$$

$$\frac{1}{\beta}.\mu_{jg}^{max} = S_g^{max}$$

[2.23]

$$\frac{1}{\gamma}.\mu_{jb}^{max} = S_b^{max}$$

Probabilistic models represent a good computational approach for color constancy. In fact, the probabilistic approaches are based on statistical methods and they are not based on the functioning of the human visual system.

2.4.5. Method based on neural networks

Hurlbert [HUR 91] implemented a neural network based on a version of the Retinex algorithm from Land. Moore [MOO 91] has implemented the Retinex algorithm using a VLSI neural network. As for Courtney [COU 95], he developed a multilayer neural network producing invariant descriptors with respect to the illuminant. Each layer corresponds to a specific step in the primate visual system, from the retina to the cortex. In all these cases, the performance of neural networks could not exceed that of the model implemented.

In contrast to approaches that simply implement an existing model, Funt [FUN 96], Cardei [CAR 00] and Barnard [CAR 99b] use a neural network to learn the relationship between the image of a scene and the chromaticity of the illumination. Each image is converted into the chromaticity space $(r, g$ where $r = R/(R+G+B)$ and $g = G/(R+G+B))$. The chromaticity space is then sampled with a fixed step; all pixels whose chromaticities are in the same interval are considered equivalent. This binary chromaticity histogram is used to feed the input neuron layer. Each sampling interval corresponds to an input neuron. The input neuron is set to 1 or 0 depending on whether a chromaticity is present or absent. The sampling reduces the resolution to chromaticity but it ensures an independence from the permutation of values. The neural network is a perceptron with one hidden layer [HER 91]. The largest layer is the input layer (depending on the sampling step); the output layer has two neurons giving the value of the chromaticity. During the learning phase, the true value of the illuminant of the scene is given to the network for back propagation. When the real illuminant of the scene is unknown, Funt and Cardei remedy this deficiency by proposing a different approach [FUN 99] for the training of the network. It consists of using the estimates of the illuminant by the gray world algorithm as feedback. The color of the illuminant is determined as follows:

$$R_i = \frac{\mu_R}{M_R}.R_w$$

$$G_i = \frac{\mu_G}{M_G}.G_w \hspace{2cm} [2.24]$$

$$B_i = \frac{\mu_B}{M_B}.B_w$$

where μ_k is the average of the channel k of the image and M_k the average of the channel k of all the images to compensate for the distribution of the color not being gray. R_w, G_w and B_w are the tristimulus of the canonical illuminant; usually we take: $R_w = G_w = B_w = 255$. The disadvantages of this approach are the significant computations that it requires (segmentation of the image and the neural network learning) and the inclusion of a single illuminant (the chromaticity of the illuminant is assumed constant throughout the whole image).

2.4.6. ACE: automatic color equalization

The ACE (Automatic Color Equalization) algorithm [RIZ 03] simulates the perception processes involved in the human visual system. The method is based on the fusion of two color constancy methods: the white patch and the gray world. This algorithm is divided into two steps: the first step is a chromatic and spatial adjustment and the second step concerns color reproduction.

The chromatic and spatial adjustment procedure produces an image R in which all pixels are processes relative to the content of the image. This process is based on two parameters: a function $r(.)$ that affects the behavior of the white patch and the contrast of the image, and a function $d(.)$ that incorporates the concept of spatial influence. Therefore, a change in shape of these functions affects the global or local effect of the ACE method. Each pixel p of the image R is processed by separately considering on each color channel $c \in \{R, G, B\}$ such that:

$$R_c(p) = \sum_{j \in I, j \neq p} \frac{r\left[I_c(p) - I_c(j)\right]}{d(p,j)} \qquad [2.25]$$

where c denotes the color channel under consideration. I_c denotes the initial image, R_c the result of the chromatic and spatial adjustment. The function $d(.)$ is a distance function that takes into account the part of the local or global contribution, and the function $r(.)$ is a function that takes into account the relative brightness of pixels. The functions $d(.)$ and $r(.)$ control the relative influence of pixels by taking into account the spatial adjustment of the brightness of the channel c. The authors state that the Euclidean distance gives the best results. The function $r(.)$ acts as a contrast modifier. The authors propose three functions: linear, saturation and signum.

The second step is to restore and enhance the colors in the output image. The output value in the intermediate matrix R varies between *min* and *max*, which are two arbitrary real values dependent on the image content. For each channel, the data should be readjusted in the range [0..255] of the final image O by choosing reference values to readjust the values. The proposed method linearly shifts the values by the following formula:

$$O_c(p) = \left[127.5 + s_c.R_c(p)\right] \tag{2.26}$$

for each pixel p, where s_c adjusts the segment $[(0, 127.5), (M_c, 255)]$ calculated by the following equation, with $M_c = max_p R_c(p)$:

$$s_c = \frac{M_c - 0}{255 - 127.5} = \frac{M_c}{127.5} \tag{2.27}$$

where M_c is used as reference white. It may happen that certain values O_c are less than zero. In this case, they are set to zero. However, for this second step, other approaches are possible. It is possible to apply the white patch Retinex algorithm or the gray world theory. It is also possible to keep the average and the reference white of the original image.

As an unsupervised algorithm requiring no *a priori* information, ACE was used for color correction of images in areas where there is no reference or *a priori* information, such as the digital restoration of colors of faded pictures [RIZ 10] and the color correction of underwater images [CHA 06].

2.4.7. *Methods combining several approaches*

Cardei and Funt have shown that by combining several color constancy algorithms, it was possible to have a better estimate of the illuminant than by using each method in isolation [CAR 99a, CAR 00]. The algorithms considered are the gray world, the white patch Retinex, and the neural network from Funt and Cardei [FUN 96]. The considered combinations are linear. One way is to take the mean of the three algorithms.

The combination can also be weighted differently. The weights are then optimized by a least squares approach and derived from the database used for the training of the neural network. A nonlinear combination was also considered to take into account higher order correlations that might exist between the various estimates. A neural network was used to model these nonlinear statistical properties. This is a multilayer perception that takes estimates of the three chosen color constancy algorithms as input. However, the linear combination has a better performance than the nonlinear combination, which suggests that there is no higher order relationship between the chromaticity estimates of the illuminant given by the different algorithms. Cardei and Funt also used a linear combination of the gray world algorithm and that of the white patch only. A simple average was considered as well as a weighted version whose weights were estimated using an approach based on least squares. The linear combination allows us to improve the performance of both algorithms. The weighted combination allows us to improve the performance of the gray world by 12% and one of the white patches by 26%. These studies show that color constancy algorithms are complementary and their combination in an appropriate manner can significantly improve the results. Chambah found that the methods of the gray world and the white patch Retinex yielded successful results in specific areas of the image. To achieve a color correction, he proposed to combine these two approaches [CHA 01]. His method consists of using a local approach rather than a global approach. A method is therefore selected for the areas in which it guarantees a good result. Therefore, the gray world method is applied only on the dark and average areas of the image, while the white patch Retinex method is applied only on light areas of the image. For this, it sets a threshold h between the light areas, which is corrected with the modified white patch Retinex approach, and for the areas to be corrected with the gray world algorithm. The results are satisfactory within each separate zone. The only inconvenience caused by this hybrid method is the lack of homogeneity of the areas with medium intensity. These areas are distributed on both sides of the threshold, each part being processed by a different algorithm. Therefore, it happens that some areas are corrected in an inadequate manner. To correct this, he performs a mixed correction in the areas of medium intensity. A new threshold $h2$ is introduced in the following section, in which we apply the gray world method. The former threshold $h2$ renamed as $h1$ defines the bright area of the image on which the modified white patch Retinex method is applied. The area between $h2$ and $h1$ is corrected by applying a combination of both algorithms to ensure a gradual transition from areas processed by the gray world to the areas processed by the modified white patch Retinex.

2.5. Comparison of color constancy algorithms

Color constancy can be constrained by the control of illumination and calibration of image sensors. However, many applications do not allow this control. Real scenes are not usually made up of only flat or Lambertian surfaces. The illuminant is rarely single and uniform. The illumination of the scene combines several interactions: halogen lamp, sunlight through a glass, shade of foliage and specular reflections. The definitions of the illuminant and reflectance spectra from the only available trichromaticity coordinates often remain a challenge since it is underdetermined. Generally, this problem is solved based on simplifying assumptions on the formation of images (single illuminant) or the content of the scene (flat or Lambertian surface, for instance), or by expressing the spectra the illuminant and the surfaces' reflectance as weighted sums of basis functions. In the case of images taken under uncontrolled illumination conditions by different devices or uncalibrated cameras, the color constancy can be improved by applying an algorithm presented in this chapter. The color correction algorithms can be classified into two categories, according to whether they operate a single color view to find the illuminant of the scene or more images and the redundancy of information they may contain. In the first category lie the presented methods of the max-RGB [LAN 71] and the gray world [BUC 80], and its latest variations [GER 87, FIN 04]. A recent version unifies these approaches by considering the statistics of increasing order [WEI 07]. These methods usually consider the illuminant as single and uniform and operate a "white balance" by applying a diagonal 3×3 linear transformation on the trichromaticity coordinates. The approaches to the second category combine several images of the scene viewed from different illuminants [FIN 04]. [DIC 01, LU 06] play on the difference between images taken with/without flash, based on the spectral power distribution of the flash. The chromagen approach exploits the difference between images with/without a colored filter knowing the filter's transmittance [HOR 06]. In both cases, we find the unknown illuminant assumed to be uniform for both the images. More general methods intend to find N illuminants from N images [DZM 94]. The reflectance unknowns of the N same surfaces observed in the different images and of the N illuminants are grouped into a system of linear equations in the form of weighted sums of basis functions. This formalization provides a bilinear model: if the characteristics (weight) of the illuminant are fixed, the resolution of reflectances is linear and vice versa. The authors propose to solve the system in two steps: they first calculate the characteristics of observed surface reflectances, and then deduce those of the N illuminants by forcing reflectances to equality in all views. This method is quite sensitive to noise and is applicable only for a specific number of illuminants and surfaces visible in all images. An improved version has recently been proposed by the resolution of several systems of linear equations in parallel [MAR 09]. The advantage of the method is that this can be applied on animated scenes (video security, for instance) also provided there are a few static objects to find the illumination.

2.5.1. *Algorithms evaluation*

The color constancy algorithms deliver various output types: characteristics of the illuminant and/or of reflectance of surfaces that are present in the scene. Several metrics are used to evaluate and compare their accuracy [HOR 06]: usually Euclidean distances or angles measure the difference between the original and the estimated illuminant. This evaluation requires the availability of images taken under standard or known illuminants.

2.5.1.1. *Test databases*

Several image databases allow the testing and comparison of algorithms [BAR 02, CIU 03]. This test data is available to the scientific community at (http://www.cs.sfu.ca/colour/data). The first includes 743 images. The fully characterized summary data and real images are acquired by a Sony DXC930 camera whose spectral responses are also provided. The images represent roughly 20 items taken on a black background in various poses under 11 different known spectral illuminants. The second offers 11,346 images and the RGB coordinates of the ambient illuminant using a neutral gray sphere attached to the camera and always in the field of view.

2.5.1.2. Metrics

The most common metric in the evaluation of color constancy is the angular difference, expressed in degrees, between the colorimetric coordinates of the estimated illuminant and those of the reference (known ground truth):

$$e_{ang} = \arccos\left(\frac{\rho^E \circ \hat{\rho}^E}{\|\rho^E\|\|\hat{\rho}^E\|}\right) \qquad [2.28]$$

This metric has the advantage of being independent of the light intensity of the source but not of the space in which the coordinates are given – usually RGB or XYZ if the spectral responses of the sensor are available. We can also use a distance to quantify the similarity between colorimetric coordinates. Distances can be applied to different color spaces. The most used is the Euclidean distance. Digital images are naturally encoded in RGB. These coordinates require a standardization to overcome the multiplicative factor related to the intensity of the source. The disadvantage of the RGB space is that it is not uniform; the human visual system is sensitive to color differences depending on the hues. A variant suggests the use of a perceptual Euclidean distance by introducing weights [GIJ 08]:

$$PED(e_e, e_u) = \sqrt{w_R(R_e - R_u)^2 + w_G(G_e - G_u)^2 + w_B(B_e - B_u)^2}$$

$$[2.29]$$

The transition to perceptual spaces defined by the CIE requires additional calculations. The RGB coordinates should be converted into the XYZ space before the transformation to L*u*v* or L*a*b* spaces. Perceptual spaces such as CIELAB are used to define the limit detectable by the human visual system through $\Delta Eab > 1$. However, a difference less than 6 is acceptable on real images [HOR 06]. Because this perceptual distance remains dependent on the brightness L*, it is common to use the chroma values C and hue values H given by:

$$C_{ab} = \sqrt{(a^*)^2 + (b^*)^2}, \quad H_{ab} = \tan^{-1}\left(\frac{b^*}{a^*}\right) \qquad [2.30]$$

Some authors prefer to use an index of color constancy or Brunswik ratio $CCI = dE/dR$, where dE is the distance between the estimated white and the ground truth and dR, the distance between the ground truth and the reference white. A final metric calculates the volume intersection between the gamut related to the estimated illuminant $\mathcal{G}_u$ and that of the ground truth $\mathcal{G}_u$:

$$d_{gamut}(e_e, e_u) = \frac{vol(\mathcal{G}_e \cap \mathcal{G}_u)}{vol(\mathcal{G}_u)} \qquad [2.31]$$

2.5.1.3. Comparative studies

Some authors analyze the least squares error (RMS) of the angular deviation over a set of test images [BAR 02]. Others suggest the use of the median because the error distribution is not normal [HOR 06]. In addition to the mean or the median, the variance or the max standard deviation is also instructive on measurement dispersion, which can be higher depending on the hues. The choice of the analysis space also plays an important role. In principle, RGB and XYZ spaces do not allow a perceptual interpretation of the gap. Two identical values may hide very different sensations. However, equivalences between the different metrics can be estimated [HOR 06]. For instance, an angular difference of 3° corresponds to a distance of about $\Delta Eab = 6.8$, which is still an acceptable difference for the human visual system. But the perception of color constancy also depends on the image content, especially the direction of the observed difference [NIK 08], which is not reflected in the angular deviation. A recent study proposes an experimental design with human observers to analyze the correlation of different metrics to each other and with a visual assessment [GIJ 08]. The results of this study show that different metrics are highly correlated. The most commonly used, the angular difference, provides on average a good correlation coefficient (around 0.9) with the perception of human observers. The Euclidean distance as well as the CCI index have a similar correlation. As strange as it may seem, the use of perceptual spaces does not improve the correlation of these metrics with the judgment of human observers. The study even observed a very significant decrease of the correlation, around 0.6, for the chroma or the hue. Other studies have also noticed a weakness of the CIELAB space in the constancy of blue hues in particular. The highest correlation scores (> 0.95) are obtained by the weighted Euclidean distance PED and the volume of intersection metric between gamuts.

2.5.2. Examples of applications with specific patterns

Color constancy research has applications in various fields, especially for the analysis or classification of objects by their color. These include the measurement of skin tones for cosmetics [MAR 07] or tissue classification in the tracking of chronic wounds [WAN 10]. In this work, image databases are taken with different types of consumer devices and without control of illumination. To overcome these difficulties, the authors recommend placing a pattern in the field of view. This pre-calibrated pattern allows us to estimate the best linear transformation to be applied by minimizing the least squares error on the hues of the pattern. An evaluation of the correction may also be performed on the colored patches of the pattern by a distance between the reference coordinates (calibrated) and those measured before and after correction. These works compare different correction modes in various spaces. They mainly point out the importance of a careful choice of colors present on the pattern to adjust at best the correction on the most relevant colors. They advocate the use of an application-specific pattern, rather than a standard pattern like the one of Macbeth. In fact, the errors are greatly reduced on the hues located inside the gamut formed by the tiles of the pattern used to estimate the correction. The results show that the best transformation depends mainly on the devices, because the observed differences between devices are generally stronger than those of correction variants applied to one device. Nevertheless, it is possible to reduce the error to around 1% in standardized sRGB and $\Delta Eab < 1$ on the tiles of the pattern that are flat and Lambertian. On real images, the corrected differences ΔEab between devices can be reduced by roughly 2 to 5. These analyses allow us to conclude that a linear transformation in the sRGB space can adequately overcome the influence of illumination and camera characteristics for a classification application, by limiting the complexity of the calculations.

2.6. Conclusion

There is no universal color constancy method. The best known basic color constancy algorithms are the gray world, the Retinex (and its various versions), and the von Kries adaptation model, which is the most ancient and widely used for color correction. Despite their extreme simplicity, a study conducted by Funt [FUN 98] has empirically shown that these methods work as well as or better than other more complex algorithms when color is used to match objects in an image database. On the other hand, these algorithms are often used as a component of more complex systems [FIN 98b, FUN 99]. In a study of different color constancy methods, Lee [LEE 94] stated that despite the rather rigid assumption made by the gray world algorithm, this assumption is true most of the time, and that the modified versions of the gray world became the best color correction algorithms for devices such as camcorders and printers. Finally, Cardei [CAR 00] showed that the combination of different constant color methods yields better results. Color constancy algorithms can also be encountered in object recognition processes. They allow us to objectively compare images that have been acquired under different illuminants [FER 12]. Color constancy algorithms aim to calculate a representation independent of the illuminant. However, the color perception of an object depends not only on the illumination conditions but also on the colors present in its immediate environment. To model these phenomena, color appearance models, dealt with in Chapter 3, have been developed.

2.7. Bibliography

[BAR 97] BARNARD K., FINLAYSON G., FUNT B., "Color constancy for scenes with varying illumination", *Computer Vision and Image Understanding*, vol. 65, no. 2, p. 311-321, 1997.

[BAR 02] BARNARD K., MARTIN L., FUNT B., COATH A., "A data set for color research", *Color Research and Application*, vol. 27, no. 3, p. 147-151, 2002.

[BER 98] BERNS R., IMAI F., BURNS P., TZENG D., "Multi-spectral-based color reproduction research at the Munsell Color Science Laboratory", *The Munsell Color Science Laboratory, Proc. SPIE 3409*, p. 14-25, May 1998.

[BRA 86] BRAINARD D., WANDELL B., "Analysis of the retinex theory of color vision", *Journal of the Optical Society of America A*, vol. 3, p. 1651-1661, 1986.

[BRA 97] BRAINARD D., FREEMAN W., "Bayesian color constancy", *Journal of the Optical Society of America A*, vol. 14, p. 1393-1411, 1997.

[BUC 80] BUCHSBAUM G., "A spatial processor model for object color perception", *Journal of the Franklin Institute*, vol. 310, no. 1, p. 1-26, 1980.

[CAR 99a] CARDEI V., FUNT B., "Committee-based color constancy", *IS&T/SID's 7th Color Imaging Conference*, Scottsdale, USA, p. 311-313, 1999.

[CAR 99b] CARDEI V., FUNT B., BARNARD K., "White point estimation for uncalibrated images", *IS&T/SID's 7th Color Imaging Conference*, Scottsdale, USA, p. 97-100, 1999.

[CAR 00] CARDEI V., A neural network approach to colour constancy, Doctoral thesis, Simon Fraser University, Canada, 2000.

[CHA 01] CHAMBAH M., Analyse et traitement de données chromatiques d'images numérisées à haute résolution. Applicatione à la restauration numérique des couleurs des films cinématographiques, Doctoral thesis, University of La Rochelle, 2001.

[CHA 06] CHAMBAH M., "More than color constancy: non-uniform color cast correction", *Computer Vision and Graphics, Computational Imaging and Vision, Chapter Color and Multispectral Image Processing*, vol. 32, p. 780-786, 2006.

[CIE 07] CIE, ISO 11664-2:2007 (CIE S 014-2/E:2006) Colorimtrie - Partie 2: Illuminants CIE normaliss, CIE, 2007.

[CIU 03] CIUREA F., FUNT B., "A large image data base for color constancy research", *IS&T/SID's 11th Color Imaging Conference*, Scottsdale, USA, p. 160-164, 2003.

[COU 95] COURTNEY S., FINKEL L., BUCHSBAUM G., "A multistage neural network for color constancy and color induction", *IEEE Transactions on Neural Networks*, vol. 6, no. 4, p. 972-985, 1995.

[DIC 01] DICARLO J., XIAO F., WANDELL B., "Illuminating illumination", *IS&T/SID's 9th Color Imaging Conference Proceedings*, Scottsdale, USA, p. 27-34, 2001.

[DZM 94] DZMURA M., IVERSON G., "General linear recovery of spectral descriptions for lights and surfaces", *Journal of the Optical Society of America A*, vol. 11, no. 9, p. 2389-2400, 1994.

[FER 12] FERNANDEZ-MALOIGNE C., MACAIRE L., ROBERT-INACIO F., *Digital Color Imaging*, ISTE, London, John Wiley & Sons, New York, 2012.

[FIN 93] FINLAYSON G., DREW M., FUNT B., "Diagonal transforms suffice for color constancy", *Proceedings of the 4th International Conference on Computer Vision*, Berlin, Germany, p. 164-171, 1993.

[FIN 95a] FINLAYSON G., "Color constancy in diagonal chromaticity space", *Proceedings of the 5th International Conference on Computer Vision*, Boston, USA, p. 218-223, 1995.

[FIN 95b] FINLAYSON G., FUNT B., BRAINARD J., "Color constancy under a varying illumination", *Proceedings of the 5th International Conference on Computer Vision*, Boston, USA, p. 431-436, 1995.

[FIN 96] FINLAYSON G., "Color in perspective", *IEEE Transactions on Pattern Analysis and Machine Intelligence*, vol. 18, no. 10, p. 1034-1038, 1996.

[FIN 97a] FINLAYSON G., HORDLEY S., "Selection for gamut mapping color constancy", *British Machine Vision Conference*, University of Essex, UK, p. 630-639, 1997.

[FIN 97b] FINLAYSON G., HUBEL P., HORDLEY S., "Color by correlation", *Proceedings of the 5th Color Imaging Conference*, Scottsdale, USA, p. 6-11, 1997.

[FIN 98a] FINLAYSON G., HORDLEY S., "A theory of selection for gamut mapping color constancy", *Proceedings of the Conference on Computer Vision and Pattern Recognition*, Santa Barbara, USA, p. 60-65, 1998.

[FIN 98b] FINLAYSON G., HORDLEY S., HUBEL P., "Recovering device sensitivities with quadratic programming", *IS&T/SID's 6th Color Imaging Conference Proceedings*, Scottsdale, USA, p. 90-95, 1998.

[FIN 04] FINLAYSON G., TREZZI E., "Shades of gray and colour constancy", *IS&T/SID's 12th Color Imaging Conference Proceedings*, Scottsdale, USA, p. 37-41, 2004.

[FOR 90] FORSYTH D., "A novel algorithm for color constancy", *International Journal of Computer Vision*, vol. 5, no. 1, p. 5-36, 1990.

[FUN 92] FUNT B., DREW M., BROCKINGTON M., "Recovering shading from color images", *2nd European Conference Computer Vision*, Santa Margherita Ligure, Italy, p. 124-132, 1992.

[FUN 93] FUNT B., "Modelling reflectance by logarithmic basis functions", *IS&T/SID's 4th Color Image Conference*, Scottsdale, USA, p. 68-71, 1993.

[FUN 96] FUNT B., CARDEI V., BERNARD K., "Learning color constancy", *IS&T/SID's 4th Color Imaging Conference Proceedings*, Scottsdale, USA, p. 58-60, 1996.

[FUN 98] FUNT B., BERNARD K., MARTIN L., "Is colour constancy good enough?", *Proceedings of the IEEE 5th European Conference on Computer Vision*, Freiburg, Germany, p. 445-459, 1998.

[FUN 99] FUNT B., CARDEI V., "Bootstrapping color constancy", *Proceedings of SPIE Conference on Electronic Imaging: Human Vision and Electronic Imaging IV*, vol. 3644, San Jose, USA, p. 421-428, 1999.

[GER 87] GERSHON R., JEPSON A.D., TSOTSOS J.K., "From [R,G,B] to surface reflectance: computing color constant descriptors in images", *IJCAI '87: Proceedings of the 10th International Joint Conference on Artificial Intelligence*, Milan, Italy, p. 755-758, 1987.

[GIJ 08] GIJSENJI A., GEVERS T., LUCASSEN M., "A perceptual comparison of distance measures for color constancy algorithms", *Proceedings of the IEEE 10th European Conference on Computer Vision, Part I*, Marseille, France, p. 208-221, 2008.

[HEL 24] VON HELMOLTZ H., "Treatise on physiological optics", (translated by J.P.C. Southall), *Optical Society of America*, 1924.

[HER 91] HERTZ J., KROGH A., PALMER R.G., *Introduction to the Theory of Neural Computation*, Boston, USA, 1991.

[HOR 06] HORDLEY S., FINLAYSON G., "Reevaluation of color constancy algorithm performance", *Journal of the Optical Society of America A*, vol. 23, no. 5, p. 1008-1020, 2006.

[HUB 99] HUBEL P., HOLM J., FINLAYSON G., "Illuminant estimation and colour correction", *Colour Imaging: Vision and Technology*, p. 73-95, 1999.

[HUR 91] HURLBERT A., "Neural network approaches to color vision", *Neural Networks for Perception: Human and Machine Perception*, vol. 1, p. 266-284, 1991.

[JUD 40] JUDD D., "Hue, saturation and lightness of surface colors with chromatic illumination", *Journal of the Optical Society of America A*, vol. 30, p. 2-32, 1940.

[LAM 60] LAMBERT J., *Photometria sive de mensura et gradibus luminis, colorum et umbrae*, Eberhard Klett, 1760.

[LAN 50] LAND E., http://web.me.com/mccanns/Color/Color_Mondrians_files/ColMond.jpg, 1950.

[LAN 71] LAND E., MCCANN J., "Lightness and Retinex theory", *Journal of the Optical Society of America A*, vol. 61, no. 1, p. 1-11, 1971.

[LAN 77] LAND E., "The retinex theory of color vision", *Scientific American*, vol. 237, no. 6, p. 108-128, 1977.

[LAN 86] LAND E., "Recent advances in Retinex theory", *Vision Research*, vol. 26, no. 1, p. 7-21, 1986.

[LEE 94] LEE H., GOODWIN R., "Colors as seen by humans and machines", *IS&T's 47th Annual Conference Proceedings*, Rochester, USA, p. 401-405, 1994.

[LU 06] LU C., DREW M., "Practical scene illuminant estimation via flash/no flash pairs", *IS&T/SID's 14th Color Imaging Conference Proceedings*, Scottsdale, USA, p. 84-89, 2006.

[LUC 00] LUCASSEN M., "Application of smoothest reflectance functions for the visualization of spectral changes due to the illuminant", *International Conference on Color in Graphics and Image Processing CGIP '00*, p. 41-44, 2000.

[MAR 07] MARGUIER J., BHATTI N., BAKER H., HARVILLE M., SÜSSTRUNK S., "Assessing human skin color from uncalibrated images", *International Journal of Imaging, Systems and Technology, Special Issue on Applied Color Image Processing*, vol. 17, no. 3, p. 143-151, 2007.

[MAR 09] MARGUIER J., BHATTI N., BAKER H., SÜSSTRUNK S., "A Home Décor expert in your camera", *IS&T/SID's 17th Color Imaging Conference Proceedings*, Albuquerque, USA, p. 85-90, 2009.

[MAR 00] MARINI D., RIZZI A., "A computational approach to color adaptation effects", *Image and Vision Computing*, vol. 18, p. 1005-1014, 2000.

[MCC 97] MCCANN J., "Magnitude of color shifts from average-quanta catch adaptation", *IS&T/SID's 5th Color Imaging Conference Proceedings*, Scottsdale, USA, p. 215-220, 1997.

[MCC 04] MCCANN J., "Mechanism of color constancy", *IS&T/SID's 12th Color Imaging Conference Proceedings*, Scottsdale, USA, p. 29-36, 2004.

[MOO 91] MOORE A., ALLMAN J., GOODMAN R., "A real-time neural system for color constancy", *IEEE Transactions on Neural Networks*, vol. 2, no. 2, p. 237-247, 1991.

[NIC 65] NICODEMUS F., "Directional reflectance and emissivity of an opaque surface", *Applied Optics*, vol. 4, no. 7, p. 767-773, 1965.

[NIK 08] NIKKANEN J., GERASIMOW T., KING L., "Subjective effect of white-balancing errors in digital photography", *Optical Engineering*, vol. 47, no. 11, p. 113201-113208, 2008.

[PRO 07] PROVENZI E., FIERRO M., RIZZI A., CARLI L., GADIA D., MARINI D., "Random spray retinex: a new retinex implementation to investigate the local properties of the model", *IEEE Transactions on Image Processing*, vol. 16, no. 1, p. 162-171, 2007.

[RAH 97] RAHMAN Z., JOBSON D., WOODELL G., "A multiscale retinex for bridging the gap between color images and human observation of scenes", *IEEE Transactions on Image Processing*, vol. 6, no. 7, p. 965-976, 1997.

[RIZ 03] RIZZI A., GATTA C., MARINI D., "A new algorithm for unsupervised global and local color correction", *Pattern Recognition Letters*, vol. 14, no. 11, p. 1663-1677, 2003.

[RIZ 10] RIZZI A., CHAMBAH M., "Perceptual color film Restoration", *SMPTE Motion Imaging Journal*, vol. 119, no. 8, p. 33-41, 2010.

[ROS 00] ROSENBERG C., "Image color constancy using EM and cached statistics", *ICML 2000*, p. 799-806, 2000.

[SMI 99] SMITS B., "An RGB to spectrum conversion for reflectances", *Journal of Graphics Tools: JGT*, vol. 4, no. 4, p. 11-22, 1999.

[TOM 91] TOMINAGA S., "Surface identification using the dichromatic reflection model", *IEEE Transactions on Pattern Analysis and Machine Intelligence*, vol. 13, no. 7, p. 658-670, 1991.

[TOR 67] TORRANCE K., SPARROW E., "Theory for off-specular refection from roughened surfaces", *Journal of the Optical Society of America A*, vol. 57, no. 9, p. 1105-1114, 1967.

[TOV 96] TOVE M., *An Introduction to the Visual System*, Cambridge University Press, Cambridge, USA, 1996.

[WAN 10] WANNOUS H., TREUILLET S., LUCAS Y., MANSOURI A., VOISIN Y., "Design of a customized pattern for improving color constancy across camera and illumination changes", *VISAPP 2010 - Proceedings of the International Conference on Computer Vision Theory and Applications*, Angers, France, p. 60-67, 2010.

[WEI 07] VAN DE WEIJER J., GEVERS T., GIJSENJI A., "Edge-based color constancy", *IEEE Transactions on Image Processing*, vol. 16, no. 9, p. 2207-2214, 2007.

[WOL 67] WOLFF L., "Diffuse-reflectance model for smooth dielectric surfaces", *Journal of the Optical Society of America A*, vol. 11, no. 11, p. 2956-2968, 1967.

[WOR 86] WORTHEY J., BRILL M., "Heuristic analysis of von Kries color constancy", *Journal of the Optical Society of America A*, vol. 3, no. 10, p. 1709-1712, 1986.

[ZEK 93] ZEKI S., *A Vision of the Brain*, Blackwell Science, Oxford, UK, 1993.

Chapter 3

Color Appearance Models

3.1. Introduction

The perception of color depends on its spectral distribution, on the size and shape of its support, as well as the surround in which it is placed and the one in which it is observed, as shown in Figure 3.1. It also depends on the human visual system (HVS) and the experience the observer has in analyzing colors under specific conditions. Basic conventional colorimetry does not take into account these different elements that are essential in cross-media reproduction of colors. This requires the development of an "aspect" model that can forecast the appearance of a color under different conditions. This is being studied in advanced colorimetry through color appearance models.

A color appearance model (CAM) tries to model how the human visual system perceives the color of an object under different illumination conditions and against different backgrounds. By developing such a model, an image that is seen under some illumination conditions and in a certain surround can be adjusted to have the same color appearance as if it were seen under completely different conditions. The ability of a CAM to perform this task properly means that it can be used to store or reproduce

---

Chapter written by Christine Fernandez-Maloigne and Alain Trémeau.

Figure 3.1. *The two patches visualized by orange circles have the same tone and yet they seem very different (example of the so-called Abney perceptual effect) (for a color version of this figure, see www.iste.co.uk/fernandez/digicolor.zip)*

the images in an optimal way, without hardware support. For example, if an image is scanned, the CAM, taking into account the characteristics of the scanner, will be able to transform the image according to its intrinsic representation. If an image is to be displayed on a monitor or printed, it is still the CAM that takes into account the specifics of the output medium and is able to transform the intrinsic representation of the image for the display or printing out. Photography, television, cinema and graphic arts in general are the many fields of application of CAM.

Various CAMs exist such as the RLAB, ZLAB, LLAB, von Kries, Nayatani, etc. Some of them have been standardized by the CIE (International Commission on Illumination, http://www.cie.co.at/) such as the CIECAM97s and the CIECAM02, presented at the end of this chapter. The "Image Technology" division of the CIE also has a technical committee devoted to CAMs: the TC8-01, "Color Appearance Models for Color Management Applications" (http://www.colour.org/tc8-01/). To fully understand the terminology and logic of the CAM, it is essential to refer to the general definitions given in the glossary of this book and to have a good knowledge of the fundamentals of colorimetry. We will introduce in section 3.2 different visual phenomena associated with the perception of color appearance by the HVS. We will insist more specifically on the key perceptual phenomena considered by various CAMs. Then, we shall be able to describe in section 3.3 the main elements of a color appearance model. We will then focus, in section 3.4, on the last standardized CAM, the CIECAM02. Finally, we will conclude with the ongoing work and perspectives by referring to the iCAM model developed at RIT (Rochester Institute of Technology) by Mark Fairchild. Moreover, we will refer to the seminal work of Fairchild to go further in the color appearance models [FAI 05].

3.2. The two perceptual phenomena of color appearance

Before describing the CAM, it is necessary to understand the perception of color by humans. Perception, from a visual sense of the term, is the ability of the human brain to interpret, or even extrapolate the raw information that it receives. This results in an analysis or interpretation error that makes us judge the color appearance of a stimulus rather than its "physical" color (wavelength, temperature). Strictly speaking, color appearance is thus not the vision but the assimilation mechanism of information at the cortical level.

If two objects with identical chromaticity coordinates, that is to say $(XYZ)_1 = (XYZ)_2$ seen by an observer (stimuli), do not exhibit the same color appearance, then just some aspects of the viewing conditions are different. To account for the different viewing conditions, we should analyze the perceptual phenomena that are taken into account for the perception of changes in the appearance of a scene by the HVS. The environment of a color, the field of view of the observer thus have an impact on its appearance, the way we perceive it. These parameters are illustrated and described in Figure 3.2.

Therefore, the appearance of stimuli depends on values taken by these different regions. The main perceptual phenomena, which are related to a color appearance model, are quickly described as follows. Most of these phenomena concern the spatial architecture of observed stimuli and the surrounding context:

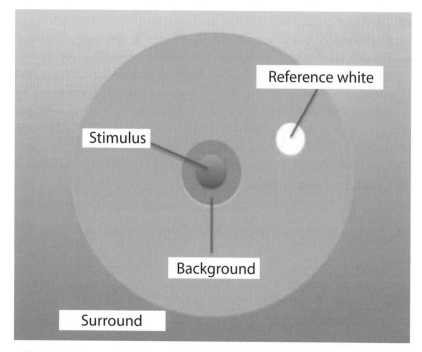

Figure 3.2. *Parameters influencing the perception of the appearance of an object*

– Hunt effect [HUN 52]: increase of the colored appearance with brightness. A stimulus appears brighter and more contrasted in full light than in shade. This effect demonstrates the importance of taking into account the absolute level of luminance of a color and not just the relative level as is done in traditional colorimetry;

– Stevens effect [STE 63]: increase of the contrast in brightness with the increase of the luminance. When the brightness increases, the dark colors appear darker and the light colors appear clearer. We often associate this effect with the Hunt-Stevens effect, mentioned in CIECAM02;

– Bartelson and Breneman effect (known as "surround" effect) [BAR 67]: increase of the apparent contrast of a stimulus associated with a change in luminance of the viewing environment. When the surrounding field goes from dark to light, the perceived contrasts seem to increase (Figure 3.3). A dark surrounding field dark patches shows as lighter

Figure 3.3. *Example illustrating Bartleson effect*

but has no pronounced effect on the clear patches. Moreover, this effect leads to a decrease in the apparent contrast between the different patches. This effect is particularly relevant especially for graphic arts applications where images are often reproduced on several media and under variable conditions of observation;

– induction or simultaneous contrast [LUO 95]: variation of the colored appearance of a stimulus based on the colorimetric characteristics of its immediate environment (proximal field). There is a simultaneous contrast between two patches of identical color and size when their color appearance differs depending on the surrounding background color (see Figure 3.4). Thus, a gray patch centered on a black background will visibly appear clearer than the same gray patch centered on a white background (see Figure 3.4a). This apparent change of color is associated

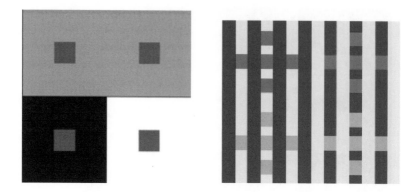

Figure 3.4. *(a) gray level; (b) color. Examples of simultaneous contrasts associated with the background color (for a color version of this figure, see www.iste.co.uk/fernandez/digicolor.zip)*

Figure 3.5. *The patterns appear to be more contrasted with the low frequencies than high frequencies*

with the phenomenon of opposite colors. This phenomenon explains that a light background induces a darker appearance while a dark background induces a clearer appearance. A red background induces a more green appearance and vice versa and a yellow background induces a more blue appearance and vice versa (see Figure 3.4b). This important effect that involves the proximal field is yet to be dealt with in the CIECAM02, described as follows;

– decrease of the sensitivity to the contrast with high frequencies ("Spreading" [BRI 06]): this effect gives the impression that the stimulus and the background blend to create a new color that tends to the tone of the background (see Figures 3.5 and 3.6).

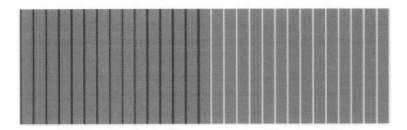

Figure 3.6. *The background color appears more blue on the left and more yellow on the right due to an assimilation effect (for a color version of this figure, see www.iste.co.uk/fernandez/digicolor.zip)*

Several studies are now being conducted to take into account this phenomenon in the CAMs, the calculations of associated color distances, such as the CIEDE2000 described below, and even in the evaluation metrics of the color quality with or without reference. These include the work of Fernandez and his team [ROS 08, FER 08]:

– Helmholtz-Kohlrausch effect [WYS 82]: increase, at constant luminance, of the perceived brightness as a function of saturation and the tone. This effect shows that the brightness cannot be considered as a function depending only on the luminance. This effect explains that a colored stimulus appears clearer than a brightness stimulus with the same lightness (see Figure 3.7), and the most saturated colors appear brighter. This phenomenon is not yet included in the standardized CAM;

– chromatic adaptation [MCC 05]: main effect to be considered by a CAM. This is the adjustment by the HVS of the color of some stimuli based on the color or brightness of the surrounding context. Chromatic adaptation allows the human observer to interpret a color according to its space-time environment. This is related to the cognitive ability of the human visual system to adapt to the color of the light source to better interpret the color of objects, irrespective of lighting conditions (see Figure 3.8). For example, under an incandescent light, a blank page appears yellow. However, the observer unconsciously models these lighting conditions and can see the page as white. The world that surrounds us would be very difficult to interpret if objects changed color each time the light source changed even slightly. Numerous models of chromatic adaptation (such as the Retinex model, Bayesian model, etc.)

Figure 3.7. *All the central patches have the same chroma and the same lightness. The saturation and the tone of surrounding patches alter the perception of central patches due to a simultaneous contrast effect (for a color version of this figure, see www.iste.co.uk/fernandez/digicolor.zip)*

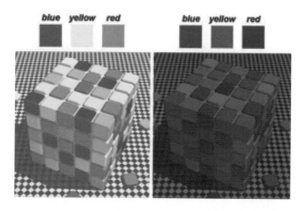

Figure 3.8. *Example of the chromatic adaptation phenomenon. When looking at the left cube and then the right cube we assign the same tone to colors yet intrinsically different (for a color version of this figure, see www.iste.co.uk/fernandez/digicolor.zip)*

based on the concept of color constancy have been proposed since the 1990s. They are found in Chapter 2.

Other perceptual phenomena related to color memory [GUL 10], to the emotion induced by colors, to color salience [TRE 06], etc. have not yet been considered so far in color appearance models. Yet these phenomena play an essential role in visual perception [WEB 02]. This is explained by these phenomena not being sufficiently well defined and modeled.

3.3. The main components of a CAM

The CAMs therefore aim to extend basic colorimetry to the prediction of appearance attributes under a large number of different viewing conditions, taking into account all or part of the phenomena described earlier. In 1976, the CIE standardized two spaces known as "perceptually uniform", the CIELAB and the CIELUV, allowing us to define consistent color distances relative to visual perception. In parallel, in the early 1980s, Hunt and Nayatani introduced the first fundamental concept for defining Color Appearance Models to predict the colored stimuli appearance under a wide variety of viewing conditions. To perform this, in any CAM, it is necessary to specify the input, the tristimulus values of the stimulus (XYZ), of the reference white (XwYwZw), the intensity of the background (Yb), the surround conditions (that can be dark, dim or average), and other factors such as the distance from the observer to the observed stimulus and the viewing angle (Figure 3.9a). On input an important factor is the adaptation field. It takes into account peripheral field, background and surround. On output, the CAMs describe the color appearance of the observed stimuli from perceptual attributes such as the brightness, the lightness, the colorfulness, the chroma, the saturation, and the hue as described in Figure 3.9b.

All the Color Appearance Models are thus based on three points:

– the Chromatic Adaptation Transform (CAT);

– a uniform color space representation and an associated distance;

– a set of descriptive color appearance attributes.

The chromatic adaptation transform (CAT) is the main element of a CAM. However, it is not enough in itself to define the color appearance of a stimulus and thus to calculate the associated attributes as output of the CAM. We can see it in the description of CAM02. The calculation of the perceptual attributes from the physical coordinates $(X_1Y_1Z_1)$ of the sample, under the initial conditions of viewing of the color, is essential to recalculate the physical coordinates $(X_2Y_2Z_2)$ that will provide the same appearance under the new conditions of reproduction and observation of the color.

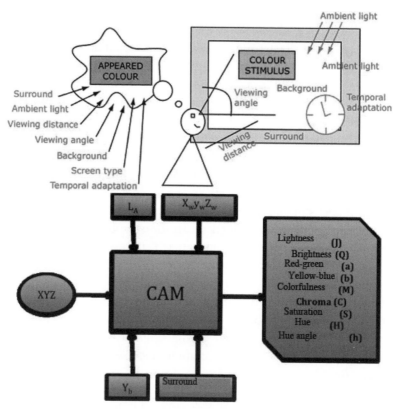

Figure 3.9. *Main parameters of a CAM. a) entries [TRE 08]; b) global diagram*

3.3.1. *Chromatic adaptation models*

The first function of a CAT is to forecast the response of the L, M and S cones during changes in viewing conditions [WRI 06]. Different models exist. The most widely used are the von Kries model and the Breneman model, which are most effective for forecasting when the luminance level of the background (surround) increases. Other models such as CIECAM97s are more efficient for the forecasting of colors that tend toward blue. But these models are more complex and not always reversible. They are generally less efficient than simple models such as the von Kries model.

A so-called chromatic adaptation transform can be summarized in a generic way by the three following steps:

– from the trichromatic coordinates $X_1Y_1Z_1$, for the initial viewing conditions (white1), we transform the coordinates $X_1Y_1Z_1$ to determine the equivalent response of the cones, $L_1M_1S_1$;

– we include information on the viewing conditions to predict the response of cones adapted to these viewing conditions (white1), e.g. La, Ma and Sa from the coordinates $L_1M_1S_1$;

– we reverse the process to the final viewing conditions (white2) to determine the response of cones L_2, M_2 and S_2, then we calculate the final trichromatic coordinates $X_2Y_2Z_2$.

The heart of a CAT therefore corresponds to Step 2 such that it can be written by the set of equations that follows:

$$La = f(L, L_{white}, ...)$$

$$Ma = f(M, M_{white}, ...) \qquad\qquad [3.1]$$

$$Sa = f(S, S_{white}, ...)$$

This generic model allows us to forecast the response of the cones (La, Ma and Sa), after taking into account all the adaptation effects. It requires the consideration of the response of the LMS cones corresponding to the luminance level of the background ($L_{white}, M_{white},$ and S_{white}). Let us recall that we move from XYZ coordinates to the LMS coordinates through a simple matrix transform.

For example, we give the first chromatic adaptation model, that of von Kries, which is based on the following set of equations:

$$La = kLL$$

$$Ma = kMM \tag{3.2}$$

$$Sa = kSS$$

The initial response of the cones is given by the L, M and S values. The coefficients k_L, k_M and k_S correspond to gains. Finally, the values La, Ma and Sa are the resulting computed responses. The following values are typically used for the gains K:

$$k_L = 1/L_{white}$$

$$k_M = 1/M_{white} \tag{3.3}$$

$$k_S = 1/S_{white}$$

Hence, the following transform, from the initial coordinates $L1, M1, S1$:

$$La = L1/L_{white1}$$

$$Ma = M1/M_{white1} \tag{3.4}$$

$$Sa = S1/S_{white1}$$

We then calculate the final coordinates $L2, M2, S2$:

$$L2 = (L1/L_{white1})L_{white2}$$

$$M2 = (M1/M_{white1})M_{white2} \tag{3.5}$$

$$S2 = (S1/S_{white1})S_{white2}$$

In a more generic way, a transform can be written using a chromatic adaptation model of von Kries type as follows:

$$\begin{bmatrix} X2 \\ Y2 \\ Z2 \end{bmatrix} = M_{CAT}^{-1}.WH_2.WH_1.M_{CAT} \begin{bmatrix} X1 \\ Y1 \\ Z1 \end{bmatrix} \tag{3.6}$$

by posing:

$$WH_1 = \begin{bmatrix} L_{white2} & 0 & 0 \\ 0 & L_{white2} & 0 \\ 0 & 0 & S_{white2} \end{bmatrix} \qquad [3.7]$$

and:

$$WH_2 = \begin{bmatrix} 1/L_{white1} & 0 & 0 \\ 0 & 1/L_{white1} & 0 \\ 0 & 0 & 1/S_{white1} \end{bmatrix} \qquad [3.8]$$

It should also be noted that according to various studies [GEG 03], the chromatic adaptation can be separated into three different time effects:

– a slow adaptation of about 20 s common to the appearance and discrimination of colors;

– a more rapid adaptation of about 40 to 70 ms, probably due to photoreceptors' adaptation, common to the appearance and discrimination of colors;

– a high-speed adaptation of about 10 ms, which is only related to the appearance color.

Other studies only distinguish two different temporal effects. These effects related to the chromatic adaptation [WHI 06], as well as other temporal effects [HAN 07], are eventually included in the analysis of color appearance, for example in the context of the spatio-temporal analysis of video sequences [FER 09].

3.3.2. *The perceptual attributes*

On output, the CAMs describe the color appearance of the observed stimulus from the attributes defined as follows:

– brightness (denoted by Q): this is an absolute measure, corresponding to the perception of lightness, of the brightness of a stimulus. This is measured on a bounded scale with zero value, corresponding to black. It should be noted that a color sample illuminated by a strong light source may appear brighter than the same sample illuminated by a dim light. This corresponds to Stevens' effect described above;

– lightness (denoted by J): this is a relative measure that corresponds to the lightness of an area considered relative to the same area illuminated by the reference white. This can be calculated by:

$$J = Q_S/Q_W$$

where Q_S and Q_W are the fragments of the lightness of the sample and the reference white, respectively. A reference white will have a value of J equals to 100;

– colorfulness (denoted M): this perceptual attribute reflects the more or less chromatic nature of a stimulus. It is measured on a bounded scale whose zero value corresponds to the grayscale. An object seen in sunlight may thus appear more colored than it was observed in the moonlight, with a ratio of 1 to 2,000;

– chroma (C): this is the colorfulness of an area considered relative to the reference white:

$$C = M/Q_W$$

– saturation (s): this is the colorfulness of an area considered relative to its own brightness:

$$s = M/Q \text{ or } s = C/J$$

– hue and hue angle (denoted H or h): the hue is the attribute that measures the proximity of a visual sensation to the red, yellow, green and blue colors. The CIECAM02 forecasts the hue with two types of measures: the hue angle between 0 degree and 360 degrees, and the hue composition from 5 basic values 0, 100, 200, 300 and 400 corresponding to the red, yellow, green and blue hues to go back to the red. For example, the orange color will be described as a mixture of red and yellow, for example 60% red and 40% yellow.

3.3.3. General architecture of CAMs standardized by the CIE

The Technical Committee TC 1-34 (Technical Committee on Color Appearance Models Testing) of the CIE (International Commission

Hunt 1994, 1996 (Hunt and Luo)	Mother of all CAM
Nayatani 1997 (Osaka, Japan)	Continuation of earlier work on chromatic adaptation
RLAB 1996 (RIT, USA)	Background in CIECAM, extension to CAT
LLAB 1996 (CII, UK)	Extension to RLAB
CIECAM97 (Hunt et Luo)	Vienna, 1996: 12 principles for CAM
CIECAM02 (Moroney, Fairchild, Hunt, Li, Luo, Newman)	

Table 3.1. *Main color appearance models (authors / research team) [FAI 05]*

on Illumination), following the intermediate works of several research teams (see Table 3.1), has standardized two color appearance models: the CIECAM97 and the CIECAM02. Both models forecast the color appearance of a stimulus depending on illumination conditions and the level of adaptation of the observer at these conditions. The CIECAM97s model, simplified version of the CIECAM97 *CIE1998* model, was the first color appearance model proposed by the CIE.

According to the TC 1-34 committee, "a color appearance model is a model that must include a chromatic adaptation transform and that includes forecasting for at least the of lightness, the chroma and the hue attributes". All standardized CAMs are therefore based on the same principle and the same general architecture [FAI 06], which is:

– a chromatic adaptation process;

– an adjustment of the cone response dynamics;

– multiple input specifications.

These different specifications are as follows:

– ambient illumination;

– luminance of the adaptation field LA (usually this is set to be 20% of the white luminance located in the adaptation field);

– XYZ trichromatic coordinates of the observed stimulus enlightened by the illumination source in question;

– XwYwZw trichromatic coordinates of the reference white enlightened by the illumination source in question;

– luminance of the white in the scene or the reproduction media;

– luminance of the peripheral field c; chromatic induction factor of the peripheral field NC; luminance contrast factor FLL, adaptation degree F; parameters used according to the type of surround (dark, dim or average); ratio $SR = LSW/LDW$ where LSW is the white luminance of the room (surround) and LDW is the white luminance of the reproduction medium (device) of the stimulus or the image;

– the transform coefficients $XYZ \leftarrow LMS$.

Table 3.2 gives examples of characteristic parameters related to the observation of a color.

Finally, it should be noted that with a CAM is necessarily associated a perceptually uniform space allowing us to calculate the distances between colors that are correlated with human perception. In the CAMs standardized by the CIE, the associated space is the L*a*b* space with the $\Delta E2000$ normalized distance. This space can be considered as a CAM, as defined by the ICE, if it is used properly, which implies that we know the reference white corresponding to the illumination conditions under which the studied stimuli were acquired. In fact, the CIELAB performs a simple modeling of the chromatic adaptation; its chromatic transform function is imprecise since it is of von Kries type. In addition, it allows calculations of *lightness*, *chroma*, and *hue* attributes, and a color difference perceptual measure. On the other hand, the CIELAB cannot forecast the effects dependent on the luminance, the *background*, and *surround* effects. Various studies have shown that this encoding space raised significant errors on the hue forecasting, especially for blue stimuli by moving from daylight illumination to an incandescent illumination. Many other models were then proposed based on different transform functions. You may refer to the book by Mark Fairchild [FAI 05] for more information. We will focus in the following section on the newest color appearance model: the CIECAM02.

Example	Ambient illumination in lux (or cd/m)	White luminance of the scene or the reproduction media	La in cd/m^2	Baseline situation	Sr	Surround type
Evaluation of a color surface in a light cabin	1,000 (318.3)	318.30 cd/m^2	60	Light cabin	1	Average
Images viewing on a TV type screen at home	38 (12)	80 cd/m^2	20	Screen display and ambient illumination	0.15	Dim
Slide projection in a dark room	0 (0)	150 cd/m^2	30	Projection	0	Dark
Images viewing on a computer screen at the office	500 (159.2)	80 cd/m^2	15	Screen display	2	Average

Table 3.2. *Parameters related to the observation of a color in some standard situations*

3.4. The CIECAM02

In 2002, the CIE has standardized its latest CAM: the CIECAM02 *CIE2004* recommended as simpler and more accurate than the CIECAM97s, an already simplified version of the CIECAM97, which is the first standardized CAM. Figure 3.10 shows the appearance calculations forecasted by the CIECAM02.

3.4.1. *Input data*

The input data of the model corresponds to the list of values given in section 3.3. The parameters related to the surround (c for the impact of the surround, chromatic induction factor Nc, and adaptation degree F) are given in Table 3.3 and illustrated in Figure 3.11.

Compared to its predecessor, the CIECAM97s, the CIECAM02 includes a compensation based on surround conditions, depending on

82   Digital Color

(a) Black background (b) White background (c) Black background
(d) White background

Figure 3.10. *Forecastings by the CIECAM02. On the left: (a) and (b) the central colors are the same but are perceived differently due to a simultaneous contrast phenomenon. On the right: (c) and (d) the colors are forecasted and corrected in order to look similar (for a color version of this figure, see www.iste.co.uk/fernandez/digicolor.zip)*

	F	C	Nc
Average	1.0	0.69	1.0
Dim	0.9	0.59	0.9
Dark	0.8	0.535	0.8

Table 3.3. *Surround parameters for the CIECAM02*

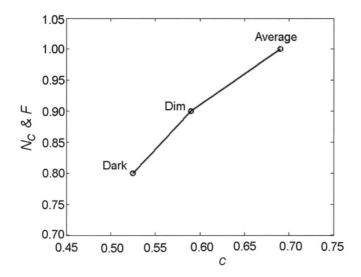

Figure 3.11. N_C *and F vary proportional with c*

whether it is average (> 20% of the luminance of the pure white, dim $(0 - 20\%)$ or dark (0%).

3.4.2. *The chromatic adaptation transform*

The Chromatic Adaptation Transform of the CIECAM02 is called the CAT02. This is used as follows in the global model:

– a first transform is to normalize and transform the trichromatic coordinates $(XYZ)_1$ of the stimulus observed in $(LMS)_1$ coordinates to match the responses of the cones:

$$\begin{bmatrix} L_1 \\ M_1 \\ S_1 \end{bmatrix} = M_{02} \begin{bmatrix} X_1 \\ Y_1 \\ Z_1 \end{bmatrix} \text{ with } M_{02} \begin{bmatrix} 0.7328 & 0.4296 & -0.1624 \\ -0.7036 & 1.6975 & 0.0061 \\ 0.003 & 0.0136 & 0.9834 \end{bmatrix} \quad [3.9]$$

– then, the following linear chromatic adaptation transform is applied:

$$\begin{bmatrix} L_a \\ M_a \\ S_a \end{bmatrix} = \begin{bmatrix} [D(Y_{white1}/Y_{white2})(L_{white2}/L_{white1}) + 1 - D] \\ [D(Y_{white1}/Y_{white2})(M_{white2}/M_{white1}) + 1 - D] \\ [D(Y_{white1}/Y_{white2})(S_{white2}/S_{white1}) + 1 - D] \end{bmatrix} \begin{bmatrix} L_1 \\ M_1 \\ S_1 \end{bmatrix} \quad [3.10]$$

with:

$$D = F[1 - \frac{1}{3.6}e^{\frac{-L_A - 42}{92}}] \qquad [3.11]$$

In fact, D is set to 1.0 for a total adaptation. If no adaptation is considered, D is set to 0. Otherwise, the intermediate values of D are calculated using equation [3.11] and correspond to various degrees of chromatic adaptation. It should be noted that if D is greater than 1 or less than 0 it will reduce it to the values 1 and 0, respectively. These initial values of the matrix CAT02 and the factor D have undergone many changes since, which are explained in [LUO 12].

– We said earlier that the chromatic adaptation was not the only phenomenon to consider. Also, in the CIECAM02, the so-called Hunt-Pointer-Estevez response is then calculated (modeling the Hunt-Stevens effect):

$$\begin{bmatrix} L \\ M \\ S \end{bmatrix} = M_{HPE}.M_{CAT02}^{-1} \begin{bmatrix} L_a \\ M_a \\ S_a \end{bmatrix} \qquad [3.12]$$

with:

$$\begin{bmatrix} 0.38971 & 0.68898 & -0.07868 \\ -0.22981 & 1.18340 & 0.04641 \\ 0.000 & 0.000 & 1 \end{bmatrix} \qquad [3.13]$$

and:

$$M_{CAT02}^{-1} = \begin{bmatrix} 1.096124 & -0.278869 & 0.182745 \\ 0.454369 & 0.473533 & 0.072098 \\ -0.009628 & -0.005698 & 1.015326 \end{bmatrix} \qquad [3.14]$$

– The responses are then recalculated after adaptation:

$$L_a' = 400.\frac{(\frac{F_L.L'}{100})^{0.42}}{(\frac{F_L.L'}{100})^{0.42} + 27.13}\%0.1 \qquad [3.15]$$

If L'_a is negative then:

$$L'_a = -400 \cdot \frac{(\frac{F_L.L'}{100})^{0.42}}{(\frac{F_L.L'}{100})^{0.42} + 27.13} \%0.1 \qquad [3.16]$$

with:

$$F_L = 0.2k^4.(5L_A) + 0.1(1 - k^4)^2.(5L_A)^{1/3} \text{ with } k = \frac{1}{5.L_A + 1} \qquad [3.17]$$

The same calculations are performed M'_a and S'_a.

	Red	Yellow	Green	Blue	Red
i	1	2	3	4	5
h_i	20.14	90.00	164.25	237.53	380.14
e_i	0.8	0.7	1.0	1.2	0.8
H_i	0.0	100.0	200.0	300.0	400.0

Table 3.4. *Values for calculating the hue composition*

3.4.3. *The appearance attributes*

– The attributes (*a* and *b*) related to the antagonistic color red-green and yellow-blue are then calculated as follows:

$$a = L'_a - 12M'_a/11 + S'_a/11 \text{ and } b = (1/9)(L'_a + M'_a - 2S'_a) \quad [3.18]$$

– Then the tone attribute (*h*):

$$h = \tan^{-1}(b/a) \qquad [3.19]$$

The eccentricity factor (e_t) and the hue composition (H) are calculated using the following table with $h' = h + 360$ if $h < h_1$, $h' = h$ otherwise. A suitable index i ($i = 1, 2, 3, 4$) should be selected such that $h_i \neq h' < h_{i+1}$. Thus:

So:

$$e_t = \frac{1}{4} \cdot \left[\cos(\frac{h'\pi}{180} + 2) + 3.8 \right] \text{ and } H = H_i + \frac{100\frac{h'-h_i}{e_i}}{\frac{h'-h_i}{e_i} + \frac{h_{i+1}-h'}{e_{i+1}}} \qquad [3.20]$$

– The brightness response (A) should also be determined for the observed sample:

$$A = [2L'_a + M'_a + (1/20)S'_a - 0.305]N_{bb} \text{ with}$$

$$N_{bb} = N_{cb} = 0.725(1/n)^{0.2}$$

[3.21]

N_{bb} and N_{cb} are the brightness and chromatic induction factors defined relative to the background and n is the induction factor of the background ($n = Y_b/Y_w$). We could also calculate the brightness response of the reference white (A_w) with the same formula.

– Then we calculate the lightness (J) from the brightness response of the sample (A) and the white (A_W):

$$J = 100(A/A_w)^{cz}$$

[3.22]

z is defined as a nonlinear exponential function $z = 1.48 + n^{1/2}$.

– Finally, the brightness (Q), amount of light coming from a stimulus, the chroma (C, not to be confused with c, luminance of the peripheral field), the colorfulness (M) level and the saturation (s) are given by:

$$Q = (4/c)(J/100)^{0.5}(A_w+4)F_L^{0.25} \text{ and } C = t^{0.9}(\frac{J}{100})^{0.5}(1.64-0.29^n)^{0.73}$$

[3.23]

with:

$$t = \frac{(\frac{50,000}{13}N_c.N_{cb})e_t(a^2 - b^2)^{1/2}}{L'_a\%M'_a\%\frac{21}{20}}\%S'_a, \quad M = C.F_L^{0.25} \text{ and } s = 100(\frac{M}{Q})^{0.5}$$

[3.24]

Since the color transform (CAT02) is linear, the CIECAM02 model is reversible. Thus, based on perceptual attributes obtained above, the inverse model will allow us to recalculate the LMS coordinates that will give the same visual appearance in different surround and stimulus observation conditions. The parameters related to these new conditions will thus be applied as in the model described above. We will refer to CIE 2004 for a description of the different steps of the inverse model.

The last step of this inverse model will consist of recalculating the XYZ coordinates in the new observation conditions known as number 2:

$$\begin{bmatrix} X_2 \\ Y_2 \\ Z_2 \end{bmatrix} = M_{CAT02}^{-1} \begin{bmatrix} L_2 \\ M_2 \\ S_2 \end{bmatrix}$$ [3.25]

So, physically, the samples viewed and observed under different conditions will not have the same trichromatic coordinates, but their perception will be similar. Figure 3.12 clearly illustrates this point that when we want to keep the same visual appearance by changing the reference illuminant, the chromatic coordinates migrate. Here, the red colors move toward the yellows, the yellows toward the greens and the greens toward the cyans when the illuminant changes from A to E.

Finally, we can say that while it is more complex, this CIECAM02 model can process all the phenomena forecast by its predecessor the CIECAM97s and improves the different luminance levels that can be considered as well as the chromatic adaptation. It thus forecasts the simultaneous contrast effects relatively well as soon as the luminance difference between the object and the background is important (see Figure 3.10). However, like the CIECAM97s, the CIECAM02

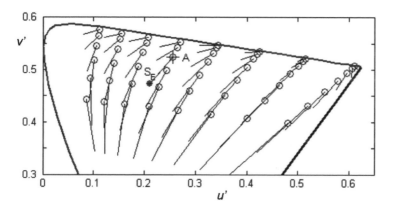

Figure 3.12. *The corresponding colors forecast by the CIECAM02 to move from illuminant A(+) to illuminant E(.), for a standard observer CIE 1931, represented in the chromaticity diagram CIE u′v′*

is not applicable in situations where the rods make a significant contribution to the vision (mesopic or scotopic conditions) or in strong light situations where the cones could be saturated. Moreover, this model, like its predecessor, is subject to the use of an empirically determined constant. The main defects of the CIECAM02 identified so far and to which researchers are currently dealing with (see [LUO 12]) are the following:

– mathematical calculation errors in CAT02 for some colors [LI 02];

– the color field of CIECAM02 is smaller than that of ICC profiles [SUS 06];

– the HPE matrix that does not fully reflect the Hunt-Stevens effects [KUO 06];

– errors, according to the saturation, in the calculation of lightness [ALE 08].

The Technical Committee of the CIE, the TC8-11, "CIECAM02 Mathematics", has been established to account for these necessary changes and extend the CIECAM02 to the largest possible number of industrial applications.

Finally, let us recall that with the two models CIECAM97s and CIECAM02, we associate the color distance CIEDE2000 [LUO 04, MEL 08], allowing us to perceptually compare color differences:

$$\Delta E_{[x,y]} = \sqrt{ \begin{array}{c} \left(\frac{\Delta L'_{[x,y]}}{K_L S_{L[x,y]}} \right)^2 + \left(\frac{\Delta C'_{[x,y]}}{K_C S_{C[x,y]}} \right)^2 + \left(\frac{\Delta H'_{[x,y]}}{K_H S_{H[x,y]}} \right)^2 \\ + R_{T[x,y]} \left(\frac{\Delta C'_{[x,y]}}{K_C S_{C[x,y]}} \frac{\Delta H'_{[x,y]}}{K_H S_{H[x,y]}} \right) \end{array} } \qquad [3.26]$$

where K_L, K_C and K_H are data-dependent constants. Generally, these constants are fixed to the value 1, but may vary in special circumstances such as those of the viewing of an image on a mobile phone. This distance allows us to better identify the latest developments on the CAMs that allow us to move toward actually perceptually uniform representation spaces. They can be certified by the famous MacAdams ellipses that are evenly distributed and that become roughly circles of equal diameter, as shown in Figure 3.13.

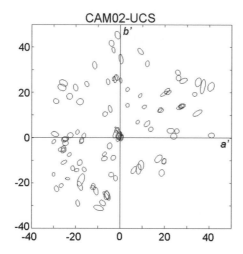

Figure 3.13. *Chromatic discrimination ellipses in the chromatic plane ab calculated from the CAM-02-UCS*

3.5. Conclusion

Color appearance models have advanced the study into the field of colorimetry and have become more and more important in the world of digital images and digital technologies, where users are increasingly demanding with respect to the reproduction quality of their color images. These models, however, remain complex and highly restrictive study frameworks. Thus, the initial model proposed by Hunt [HUN 91], which was never standardized, is probably not only the most comprehensive CAM but also one of the most complicated to implement. Many studies have been conducted to evaluate the performance of a particular CAM compared to another model [LI 02] or relative to a specific study framework [BRA 97]. Currently, a technical committee has been established at the CIEm the TC 8-08: *Testing of Spatial Color Appearance Models* (*http://div8.cie.co.at/?i_ca_id* $= 621\,pubid = 336$) whose work is ongoing. We look forward to the technical report to be published in 2012.

In an attempt to find a compromise between efficiency and implementation complexity, different lines of research are currently being pursued in different directions [KUN 09]. Let us highlight in particular the iCAM model proposed by Fairchild and Johnson based on the consideration of the spatial and temporal vision (*http://www.cis.rit.edu/mcsl/iCAM/*). Similarly, the Fernandez and Larabi team proposed extensions of the CIECAM02 by considering the sensitivity to spatial contrast [FER 08, TUL 08].

The future of CAMs definitely lies in the easy inclusion of observation situations that are even more varied, such as the scotopic and mesopic conditions, especially for digital cinema [TRE 08]. The future of CAMs will also extend to video while they currently mainly target static images and graphic art. In addition, developments regarding a better understanding of the human visual system can only enhance the CAMs that should account for even more of spatio-temporal chromatic phenomena of the Human Visual System.

3.6. Bibliography

[ALE 08] ALESSI P.J., "Pursuit of scales corresponding to equal perceptual brightness", *Personal Correspondence*, 2008.

[BAR 67] BARTLESON C., BRENEMAN E., "Brightness perception in complex fields", *Journal of Optical Society of America*, vol. 57, p. 953-957, 1967.

[BRA 97] BRAUN K.M., FAIRCHILD M.D., "Testing five color-appearance models for changes in viewing conditions", *Color Research and Application*, vol. 22, p. 165-173, 1997.

[BRI 06] BRINGIER B., RICHARD N., LARABI M.C., FERNANDEZ-MALOIGNE C., "No-reference perceptual quality assessment of colour image", *14th EUSIPCO: European Signal Processing Conference*, vol. 1, Florence, Italy, 2006.

[DEL 65] DELK J.L., FILLENBAUM S., "Differences in perceived color as a function of characteristic color", *American Journal of Psychology*, vol. 78, p. 290-293, 1965.

[FAI 05] FAIRCHILD M., *Color Appearance Models*, Wiley-IS&T, Chichester, UK, 2005.

[FAI 06] FAIRCHILD M., "Color appearance in image displays", *ICIE Pub. O. SCC/CIE Expert Symposium - 75 Years of the CIE Standard Colorimetric Observer*, p. 91-95, 2006.

[FER 08] FERNANDEZ-MALOIGNE C., LARABI M.-C., ROSSELLI V., "An extension of s-CIELAB model for predicting colour difference in images", *Industrial Symposium on Image Quality*, Taiwan, 2008.

[FER 09] FERGUSON K., "Moving image color appearance model (MICAM) for video quality ratings prediction", *Proceedings of Fourth International Workshop on Video Processing and Quality Metrics for Consumer Electronics (VPQM)*, Scottsdale, Arizona, USA, 2009.

[GEG 03] GEGENFURTNER K.R., "Cortical mechanisms of colour vision", *Nature Review, Neuroscience*, vol. 4, p. 563-572, 2003.

[GUL 10] GULICK A.V., TARR M., "Is object color memory categorical?", *Journal of Vision*, vol. 10, no. 7, p. 407, 2010.

[HAN 07] HANSEN T., WALTER S., GEGENFURTNER K.R., "Effects of spatial and temporal context on color categories and color constancy", *Journal of Vision*, vol. 7, no. 4, p. 1-15, 2007.

[HUN 52] HUNT R., "Light and dark adaptation and perception of color", *Journal of the Optical Society of America*, vol. 42, p. 190-199, 1952.

[HUN 91] HUNT R., "Revised colour-appearance model for related and un-related colours", *Color Research and Application*, vol. 16, p. 146-165, 1991.

[KUN 09] KUNKEL T., REINHARD E., "A neurophysiology-inspired steady-state color appearance model", *Journal of Optical Society of America A*, vol. 26, no. 4, p. 776-782, 2009.

[KUO 06] KUO C., ZEISE E., LAI D., "Robust CIECAM02 implementation and numerical experiment within an ICC workflow", *Color Research and Application*, vol. 22, no. 3, p. 215-219, 2006

[LI 02] LI C., MR L., RIGG B., HUNT R., "CMC 2000 chromatic adaptation transform: CMCCAT2000", *Color Research and Application*, vol. 27, no. 1, p. 49-58, 2002.

[LUO 95] LUO M., GAO X., SCIVINER S., "Quantifying colour appearance, Part V, simultaneous contrast", *Color Research and Application*, vol. 20, p. 18-28, 1995.

[LUO 04] LUO M., MINCHEW C., KENYON P., CUI G., "Verification of CIEDE2000 using industrial data", *AIC 2004 Color and Paints Interim Meeting of the International Color Association*, 2004.

[LUO 12] LUO M., LI C., *Advanced Color Image Processing and Analysis*, in FERNANDEZ-MALOIGNE C. (ed.), 2012.

[MCC 05] MCCANN J.J., "Do humans discount the illuminant?", *Proceedings of SPIE Human Vision and Electronic Imaging X*, vol. 5666, p. 9-16, 2005.

[MEL 08] MELGOSA M., HUERTAS R., BERNS R., "Performance of recent advanced color-difference formulas using the standardized residual sum of squares index", *JOSA A*, vol. 25, no. 7, p. 1828-1834, 2008.

[ROS 08] ROSSELLI V., LARABI M.-C., FERNANDEZ-MALOIGNE C., "Perceptual color difference metric based on the perception threshold", *Proceedings of IST/SPIE Image Quality and System Performance V*, vol. 6808, San Jose, CA, USA, 2008.

[STE 63] STEVENS J., STEVENS S., "Brightness functions: effects of adaptation", *Journal of Optical Society of America*, vol. 53, p. 375-385, 1963.

[SUS 06] SUSSTRUNK S., BRILL M., "The nesting instinct: repairing non nested gamuts in CIECAM02", *Proceedings of 14th SID/IST Color Imaging Conference*, 2006.

[TRE 06] TREMEAU A., TOMINAGA S., PLATANIOTIS K., "Color in image and video processing: most recent trends and future research directions", *EURASIP Journal on Image and Video Processing - Color in Image and Video*, vol. 2008, 2006.

[TRE 08] TREMEAU A., NICOLAS R., DINET E., "Influence of background in the colour appearance of images", *Journal of Colour: Design and Creativity*, no. 3, p. 1-24, 2008.

[TUL 08] TULET O., LARABI M.-C., FERNANDEZ-MALOIGNE C., "Use of spatial adaptation for image rendering based on an extension of the CIECAM02", *Proceedings of the 3rd International Conference on Computer Vision Theory and Applications, VISAPP 2008*, Funchal, Madeira, Portugal, Alpesh Ranchordas H.A., INSTICC - Institute for Systems and Technologies of Information, Control and Communication, p. 128-133, 2008.

[WEB 02] WEBSTER M. A., MALKOC G., WEBSTER S. M., "Color contrast and contextual influences on color appearance", *Journal of Vision*, vol. 2, p. 505-519, 2002.

[WHI 06] WHITE B.J., KERZEL D., GEGENFURTNER K.R., "Visually guided movements to color target", *Experimental Brain Research*, vol. 175, p. 110-12, 2006.

[WRI 06] WRIGHT W., "Why and how chromatic adaptation has been studied", *Color Research and Application*, vol. 6, p. 147-152, 2006.

[WYS 82] WYSZECKI G., STILES W., *Color Science: Concepts and Methods, Quantitative Data and Formulae*, Wiley-Interscience, New York, USA, 2nd edition, 1982.

Chapter 4

Rendering and Computer Graphics

4.1. Introduction

In computer graphics, realistic (photo) rendering is the field in which we try to produce images that are indistinguishable from photographs of the same scene. In fact, this includes simulation of the behavior of light, its propagation in the medium, and its interactions with the materials of the scene. In section 4.2 of this chapter, we describe the light sources and materials in the scene. Then, a model should be available, if possible physically correct, allowing us to simulate the propagation of the light in the scene. This model is in fact an integral equation, called the rendering equation. This model and a number of methods allow us to numerically solve this equation, which has no analytical solution. They will be described in section 4.3. Once an image of a scene is calculated using the elements described above, it should be displayed on a screen and this poses a number of problems. These will be briefly mentioned in section 4.4 of this chapter, including tone mapping, which allows us to adjust the image dynamics to that of the screen. Some perceptual aspects related to the display of images will also be touched upon.

Chapter written by Bernard PÉROCHE, Samuel DELEPOULLE and Christophe RENAUD.

4.2. Reflection and representation models of light sources

4.2.1. *Concept of luminance*

The creation of realistic images aims to provide our visual system with the illusion that what it sees could be real. Our perception of the world is related to the light energy received by the cones and rods located in the back of our retina. The main energy magnitude is called radiance. This is the energy (in watts) emitted by a surface (in square meters) in a portion of a solid angle (in steradians). It corresponds therefore to watts per square meter and per steradian ($W.m^{-2}.sr^{-1}$).

4.2.2. *Representation of the light sources*

As already noted above, the simulation of a physically realistic illumination of a scene requires knowledge of the features of the light sources and materials constituting the scene. In this section, we will focus on light sources. Generally, a light fixture is composed of one or more transmitters such as filament, neon or LED, of reflectors allowing us to direct light emission and objects disturbing the emission such as the bindings of a filament or a wire guard. It is usual for a light source to have three characteristics: its geometry, its intensity distribution, and its spectral emission.

4.2.2.1. *Geometry of a light source*

Light sources can be of the point, line, or surface type[1]. The simplest and the most used model is the point source (although it does not really exist). However, this type of source generates shadows with very sharp contours, which affect the realism of the obtained images. For soft shadows, it is necessary to use sources that emit from a line or a surface. If the geometry of a source is important when it is near an object, because it can give rise to a significant variation of illumination, it may be ignored when the transmitter is quite far away from the object. In this case, it is acceptable to use a point source. This leads to the concepts of *near-field source* and *far-field source*. This differentiation does not follow a specific

---

1 Sources such as LEDs or xenon lamps do not exhibit well-defined geometry.

law. We can adopt the Ashdown rule [ASD 93]: a source is in far-field if the distance to the source is greater than five times the largest dimension of the light fixture.

4.2.2.2. Intensity distribution

In reality, light sources do not emit light uniformly in all directions: one can think of light fixtures used in architecture or in car headlights, for example. It is therefore important to consider the intensity distribution, when it is available, to improve the quality of the illumination calculation. It should be noted that most manufacturers of light fixtures now provide this information as a *photometric solid* that represents a sampling of the light intensity emitted by the illumination device in all directions.

4.2.2.3. Spectral emission

A source can be characterized by its emission spectrum, which is the intensity of its emission at different wavelengths. Some examples are shown in Figure 4.1.

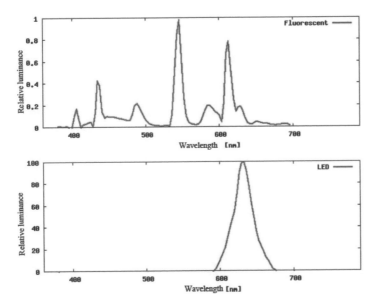

Figure 4.1. *Emission spectrum of a fluorescent source at the top and of an LED at the bottom*

4.2.2.4. *Concept of photometric solid*

The three previous properties allowing us to characterize a light source can appear as follows: a source is represented by a surface that features a luminance $L_\lambda(x, \vec{\omega})$ at any point (see section 4.2.1), depending on:

– x: the parametric position (u, v) of the point on the emitting surface;

– $\vec{\omega}$: emission direction in spherical coordinates (θ, ϕ) from the point x;

– λ: wavelength in question.

This representation of the luminance is usually called extended photometric solid (see Figure 4.2). This solid depends on five parameters and it is thus difficult to measure, store, and rebuild it. When we reduce the spatial dimension to a point, we obtain a point photometric solid model (also see Figure 4.2). This model has only 2 dimensions if a photometric projection of the monochromatic luminance is performed.

Figure 4.2. *Each of the two figures on the left represents a point photometric solid; the figure on the right represents an extended photometric solid: each point of the surface source has its own luminance distribution (for a color version of this figure, see www.iste.co.uk/fernandez/digicolor.zip)*

4.2.3. *Reflection and refraction models*

The representation of the optical properties of materials is also of great importance when one wishes to perform a realistic illumination simulation. In fact, we visually perceive the final appearance of an object only through the photons, which reach our eyes after having interacted with the material of the object: reflection on the object surface, transmission through this material, re-emission in case of phosphorescence, etc. This light-matter interaction is an extremely complex problem, which can be approached at different scales: at the microscopic level (quantum mechanics), at the mesoscopic level (electromagnetism and geometric optics), or at the macroscopic level (variable size functions). In this section, we will limit ourselves to the macroscopic level, which is the highest level used in computer graphics, and to bidirectional reflectance distribution function (BRDF). Introduced by Nicodemus *et al.* [NIC 77], the BRDF is the ratio of the luminance reflected in the direction of reflection $\vec{\omega}_r$ at a point x of an infinitesimal surface dA and the illumination incident to it in the direction of incidence $\vec{\omega}_i$[2]:

$$f_r(x, \vec{\omega}_i, \vec{\omega}_r, \lambda) = f_r(x, \theta_i, \phi_i, \theta_r, \phi_r, \lambda) = \frac{dL_r(x, \theta_r, \phi_r, \lambda)}{L_i(x, \theta_i, \phi_i, d\omega_i, \lambda)}$$

The BRDF characterizes surface reflection[3]. However, we can define similarly the notion of BTDF allowing us to characterize transparent materials. Although there are models based on the understanding of physical processes involved in light reflection (for instance, the Kubelka-Munk model [KUB 31]), most models used in computer graphics are phenomenological. We will now present the classic models.

4.2.3.1. *Lambert model*

This model assumes a perfectly diffuse surface, that is, reflecting the light with equal probability in all directions:

$$f_r(x, \vec{\omega}_i, \vec{\omega}_r, \lambda) = \pi.\rho_\lambda$$

where ρ_λ is the reflectance (or albedo) of the surface, which is the ratio between the total incident energy on the surface and the total reflected energy.

4.2.3.2. *The specular (or mirror) model*

This model assumes a perfectly specular surface, that is, reflecting the light in the direction symmetrical to the direction of incidence relative to the normal to the surface:

---

2 It should be noted that the BRDF is a dimensionless quantity.

3 As a first approximation, the BRDF assumed that the incident light energy at a point x of a surface is reflected from the same point. This is not always true as for translucent materials, for instance, and in this case we should introduce the concept of the *bidirectional sub-surface reflectance distribution function*, BSSRDF [NIC 77].

$$f_r(x, \theta_i, \phi_i, \theta_r, \phi_r) = \frac{\delta \left[cos\theta_i - \cos \theta_r \right]}{\cos \theta_i} \delta \left(\phi_i - (\phi_r \pm \pi) \right)$$

δ is the Dirac function.

4.2.3.3. Phong model [PHO 75]

This is the most commonly used model in computer graphics. It is the one proposed by the OpenGL API. It is based on the principle of a linear combination of diffuse behavior and specular behavior. If $\vec{L}$ is the direction of illumination, $\vec{V}$ the direction of reflection, and $\vec{N}$ the normal to the surface, then the BRDF is given by:

$$f_r(\vec{L}, \vec{V}) = k_d(\vec{N}.\vec{L}) + k_s F_s(\vec{L}.\vec{V})$$

The parameters k_d and k_s denote the diffuse color and the specular color of the object, which is the part of the light that is reflected in a purely diffuse way and the part that is reflected in a specular way. We should therefore have $k_d + k_s \leq 1$. The term $F_s(\vec{L}, \vec{V})$ is called *specular lobe* and it reflects the fact that the specular reflection can be performed in a non-perfect way, by allowing a more or less significant dispersion around the direction of pure specular reflection. This term can be expressed in several ways. The Blinn formulation [BLI 77] is the following:

$$F_s(\vec{L}, \vec{V}) = (\vec{N}.\vec{H})^n$$

where $\vec{H}$ is the vector bisecting vectors $\vec{L}$ and $\vec{V}$, and where n, called brightness, characterizes the surface roughness; the higher the n, the less the dispersion around the direction of specular reflection and the smoother the surface[4].

4.2.3.4. Cook-Torrance model

This model [BLI 77, COO 82, TOR 67] was the first that had a physical basis and was used in computer graphics. This model assumes a surface that consists of flat, smooth, and perfectly specular micro-facets

---

4 With this formulation, the Phong model is reciprocal, but it does not respect the energy conservation principle. To make the model physically plausible, Lewis [LEW 03] suggested a set of constraints over the parameters that must be met.

and the light source located at infinity. If da is the surface of a facet and dA the studied surface area, the model is valid if $\lambda^2 << da << dA$. The BRDF is given by:

$$fr(x, \vec{\omega}_i, \vec{\omega}_r, \lambda) = k_d \frac{\rho(\lambda)}{\pi} + k_s \frac{F(\beta, \alpha)D(\alpha)G(\theta_i, \theta_r, \alpha, \beta)}{4\pi}$$

where:

– D is the distribution function of the orientation of the facets, which models the surface roughness:

$$D(\alpha) = \frac{1}{4m^2 \cos^4 \alpha} e^{-(\frac{tan\alpha}{m})^2}$$

where the parameter m is the surface roughness (the lower the value of m, the more directional the reflection; the stronger the value of m, the more diffuse the reflection);

– G is a geometric attenuation factor ($0 \leq G \leq 1$) that modulates the BRDF to account for the self-shadowing phenomenon between facets;

– F is the Fresnel term, which corresponds to the reflection-refraction phenomenon of electromagnetic waves at the interface between two media with different refractive indices.

4.3. Simulation of light propagation

4.3.1. *Light propagation model: the rendering equation*

We can now formulate the expression of the monochromatic luminance $L(x \rightarrow \vec{\omega})$ emitted at a point x of a surface in the direction $\vec{\omega}$. At equilibrium, this luminance is the sum of the proper luminance emitted L_e from the surface (case of a light source for instance) and of the reflection L_r of all the light that reaches that surface:

$$L(x \rightarrow \omega) = L_e(x \rightarrow \vec{\omega}) + L_r(x \rightarrow \vec{\omega})$$

The energy that reaches an infitesimal surface in a portion of solid angle $d\vec{\omega}'$ is:

$$L(x \leftarrow \vec{\omega}') . \cos(\vec{N}_x, \vec{\omega}')d\vec{\omega}'$$

where $\vec{N}_x$ refers to the normal to the surface at point x.

The reflection is controlled by the BRDF (see section 4.2.3). Thus, the light equilibrium for a wavelength is defined by the following rendering equation [KAJ 86][5] in which ω represents the space of directions around point x:

$$L(x \to \vec{\omega}) = L_e(x \to \vec{\omega}) + \int_\Omega f_r(x, \vec{\omega}, \vec{\omega}\,').L(x \leftarrow \vec{\omega}\,').\cos(\vec{N}_x, \vec{\omega}\,')d\vec{\omega}\,'$$

[4.1]

In this equation, the incident luminance $L(x \leftarrow \vec{\omega}\,')$ is also unknown. It can be calculated by ray tracing. If a ray emitted from point x meets the closest surface at point y, then $L(x \leftarrow \vec{\omega}\,') = L(y \leftarrow -\vec{\omega}\,')$ (in a non-participative medium, which is a medium that does not deviate light rays and does not absorb their energy). The solid angle, under which the surface portion dy is observed, is then: $d\vec{\omega}\,' = \frac{\cos(\vec{N}_x, \vec{\omega}\,')}{d_{xy}^2}dy$. By introducing the function $V(x,y)$ specifying if x and y are mutually visible, equation [4.1] can be written as follows, S being the set of the surfaces of the objects:

$$L(x \to \vec{\omega}) = L_e(x \to \vec{\omega}) + \int_S f_r(x, \vec{\omega}, \vec{\omega}\,').L(y \leftarrow -\vec{\omega}\,').V(x,y).G(x,y)dy$$

where $G(x,y)$ is a geometric term:

$$G(x,y) = \frac{|\cos(\vec{N}_x, \vec{\omega}\,')|.|\cos(\vec{N}_y, -\vec{\omega}\,')|}{d_{xy}^2}$$

NOTE.– The energy reflected from a surface can be divided into two components: the energy that comes directly from light sources, called direct illumination, and the energy that comes from the reflection of light on other surfaces of the scene called indirect illumination. They are expressed by the following equations:

$$L_{direct}(x \to \vec{\omega}) = \int_S f_r(x, \vec{\omega} \to \vec{\omega}\,')L_e(y \to -\vec{\omega}\,')V(x,y)G(x,y)dy$$

---

5 This equation does not take into account the phenomena of fluorescence, phosphorescence, or polarization effects. However, it is more than sufficient to account for the majority of illumination effects required in realistic image synthesis.

$$L_{indirect}(x \rightarrow \vec{\omega}) = \int_S f_r(x, \vec{\omega} \rightarrow \vec{\omega}')L_r(y \rightarrow -\vec{\omega}')V(x,y)G(x,y)dy$$

$$L_r(x \rightarrow \vec{\omega}) = L_{direct}(x \rightarrow \vec{\omega}) + L_{indirect}(x \rightarrow \vec{\omega})$$

This separation can be used to facilitate and/or improve the solution of the rendering equation.

4.3.2. Solution of the rendering equation

4.3.2.1. Radiosity

This method, which was introduced in 1984 by Goral *et al.* [GOR 84], was popular for 20 years. It is hardly used nowadays. It assumes that the scene is completely diffuse. The light sources are thus assumed to emit their energy with the same intensity in all directions $L(x \rightarrow \vec{\omega}) = I(x)$ and $L_e(x \rightarrow \vec{\omega}) = L_e(x)$, and the light reflection is assumed to be identical in all directions of reflection $(f_r(x, \vec{\omega}, \omega') = \rho_x)$. The rendering equation is then simplified:

$$B(x) = B_e(x) + \pi \rho_d(x) \int_S \frac{1}{\pi} V(x,y)G(x,y)B(y)dy$$

where $B(x) = \pi L(x)$ is called *radiosity* at point x and $B_e(x)$ denotes the self-emitted radiosity at point x.

Once discretized[6], this equation takes the following matrix form:

$$B_i = B_{e,i} + \rho \sum_j F_{i,j} B_j$$

where B_i and B_j denote the radiosity of facet i and j, respectively. $B_{e,i}$ is the radiosity self-emitted by the facet i. $F_{i,j}$, known as form factor, gives the proportion of the energy emitted by a surface element S_j that is received by a surface element S_i. The calculation of these form factors (which only

---

6 In practice, all surfaces that make up the scene are cut into small pieces for which the radiosity is assumed constant at all points of their surface.

depend on the geometry of the scene) and the resolution of the above linear system allow us to obtain the radiosity of each element of the scene. Since radiosity is purely diffused, the illumination perceived at a point is independent of the observer's position. This allows an interactive exploration of the scene once the illumination calculations are performed.

4.3.2.2. *Stochastic methods*

These methods are based on the Monte Carlo integration techniques, whose principles will be recalled here. Let $I = \int_0^1 f(x)dx$ be an integral to be calculated. By performing N random uniform and independent draws θ_i over $[0, 1]$, we define a random variable $\hat{I} = \frac{1}{N}\sum_1^N f(\theta_i)$ that is called estimator of I. This estimator is unbiased (which means that the expected value of the random variable $\hat{I}$ is equal to I) and we can show that the error made by taking $\hat{I}$ instead of I is of the order $\frac{1}{\sqrt{N}}$. We can improve the previous method by using the importance sampling: if $p: [0, 1] \to \mathbb{R}$ is a probability density function ($p(x) \geq 0 \ \forall x \in [0, 1]$ and $\int_0^1 p(x)dx = 1$), then $I = \int_0^1 \frac{f(x)p(x)}{p(x)}dx$. If a random variable ξ is drawn according to the probability density p, $\hat{I} = f(\xi)p(\xi)$ is an unbiased estimator of I.

Let us consider the integral rendering equation under the form:

$$f(x) = g(x) + \int_0^1 K(x, y)f(y)dy$$

where f is unknown, g and K are known. If $p_1, p_2, \ldots, p_i$ is a series of probability densities, an estimator of f is:

$$\tilde{f}(x) = g(x) + K(x, \zeta_1)p_1(\zeta_1)\tilde{f}(\zeta_1)$$

$$\tilde{f}(x) = g(x) + \frac{K(x, \zeta_1)}{p_1(\zeta_1)}\left[g(\zeta 1) + \frac{K(\zeta_1, \zeta_2)}{p_2(\zeta_2)}\tilde{f}(\zeta_2)\right]$$

$$\tilde{f}(x) = \sum_{i=0}^{\infty}\left[\prod_{j=1}^{i}\frac{K(\zeta_{j-1}, \zeta_j)}{p_j(\zeta_j)}g(\zeta_j)\right] \text{ with } \zeta_0 = x$$

The series $\zeta_0, \zeta_1, \ldots$ is called a Random Walk.

The previous method requires an infinite number of terms for its calculation, making it intractable in practice. To simplify this method, we can use the Russian Roulette method, which is defined as follows:

Let $u\colon \mathbb{R} \to [0, 1]$ be such that $u(x) = \begin{cases} 1 & \text{for} \quad x \le 1 \\ 0 & \text{for} \quad x > 1 \end{cases}$

Let $I = \int_0^1 f(x)dx$ and P be a fixed number belonging to [0,1]:

$$I = \int_0^P f\left(\frac{y}{P}\right) dy$$

$$I = \int_0^1 \frac{1}{P} f\left(\frac{y}{P}\right) u\left(\frac{y}{P}\right) dy$$

If we apply the Monte Carlo method to the last integral with a uniform sampling on [0, 1], we obtain the unbiased estimator:

$$\tilde{I} = \begin{cases} \frac{1}{P} f\left(\frac{\zeta}{P}\right) & \text{if} \quad \zeta \le P \\ 0 & \text{if} \quad \zeta > P \end{cases}$$

By combining the Russian Roulette with the Random Walk described above, we obtain:

$$\tilde{f}(x) = \sum_{i=0}^{k} \left[\prod_{j=1}^{i} \frac{K(\zeta_{j-1}, \zeta_j)}{p_j(\zeta_j)} g(\zeta_j) \right]$$

where the stop decision of the Random Walk is obtained at the rank k using the Russian Roulette. The general method described above applies of course to the rendering equation, which is an integral equation.

4.3.2.2.1. Ray tracing

The simplest algorithm among the stochastic methods is the ray tracing, introduced in 1968 by Appel [APP 68] (as brute force method) and popularized by Whitted in 1980 [WHI 80]. The algorithm principle (shown in Figure 4.3) is the one shown above, but simplified; for each pixel of the screen, we launch a ray from the eye. We aim to intersect this ray with all the objects in the scene. If at least one intersection is found, we consider the one closest to the eye. From this intersection point, we can throw shadow rays toward each light source (assumed of point type) to see if the point is illuminated or not. If the material encountered is specular (transparent), we can launch a second reflected (refracted) ray. This method is therefore equivalent to construct, for each pixel, a tree of rays whose evaluation provides the energy reaching the pixel in the direction of the eye. This energy will allow us to compute the color of that pixel.

Figure 4.3. *Ray tracing principle. On the left, a ray (called primary) goes through a pixel of the screen and hits an object. The direct illumination of the found point is calculated by casting a shadow ray toward each source in the scene (in the center) and then the illumination through reflection is calculated by emitting a reflected ray (on the right). The process is repeated recursively (for a color version of this figure, see www.iste.co.uk/fernandez/digicolor.zip)*

4.3.2.2.2. Path tracing

The most commonly used general stochastic method is path tracing [KAJ 84]. For each pixel of the image, we trace a Random Walk $x_0, x_1, \ldots, x_i$ starting from the eye as follows: at each point x_{i-1}, we emit a ray whose direction is given by a probability density $p_i(\theta_i)$ and the first point hit by the ray defines the point x_i. The probability density p_i is associated with the BRDF of the material at the point x_{i-1}, which allows us to take into account all types of materials. When a light source is reached during a Random Walk, it contributes to the estimation of the luminous flux reaching the eye through the encountered pixel. For this method to provide reasonably accurate results, it is necessary to trace N paths for each pixel. In fact, the probability of reaching a light source during the construction of the path is relatively low, especially when the size of the sources is small compared to the size of the simulated scene or when the illumination is highly indirect. Thus, this method is expensive in computing time, because N can take values generally ranging from 64 to 4,096. In addition, it tends to provide noisy images (see Figure 4.4).

Figure 4.4. *Illustration of the noise phenomenon in the images generated by the path tracing method. The image on the left is obtained by using a single path per pixel; the image in the center uses 10 paths per pixel; the image on the right, still slightly noisy, uses 500 paths per pixel (for a color version of this figure, see www.iste.co.uk/fernandez/digicolor.zip)*

4.3.2.2.3. Light tracing

This method consists of emitting rays that carry energy (called photons) from light sources that bounce off the encountered surfaces. Whenever such a route passes through the surface of a pixel of the screen, its energy (reduced by rebounds on surfaces) is added to that of the pixel. This method suffers from the same drawbacks as those described for path tracing, since the probability that a photon emitted by a source passes through a pixel of the screen is generally very low.

4.3.2.2.4. Bidirectional methods

As has already been noted above, the path tracing or light tracing methods provide very noisy images because the probability of a light path reaching a light source or the eye is very low. A black pixel is obtained if no source has been reached, and a bright pixel is obtained in case a path of very low probability is found (due to the division by probability equation [4.2]). As an attempt to solve this problem, bidirectional methods [LAF 93] have been introduced: the rays are sent both from light sources and from the eye, then combined, thus increasing the correlation between the light sources and the eye. The combination of paths starting from the eye or light sources is achieved by a *Multiple Importance Sampling* (MIS): let $\omega_1(x)$, $\ldots$, $\omega_N(x)$ be real numbers such that $\omega_i(x) \geq 0, \forall i, \sum_{i=1}^{N} \omega_i(x) = 1$.

Let $X_{i,j}$ be independent random variables of density p_i. Then:

$$\tilde{I} = \sum_{i=1}^{N} \frac{1}{N_i} \sum_{j=1}^{i} \omega_{i,j}(Xi,j) \frac{f(X_{i,j})}{p_i(X_{i,j})} \qquad [4.2]$$

is an unbiased estimator of I.

4.3.2.2.5. Other methods

Stochastic methods have been an area of active research for several years. Therefore, there are many algorithms allowing us to solve the rendering equation. It is not possible to develop these methods in the context of this chapter. We can only mention them by referring interested readers to the bibliography: *Instant radiosity* [KEL 98], *Metropolis* [VEA 97], *Metropolis Instant Radiosity* [SEG 07], etc. and finally a very popular yet biased method in the field of computer graphics: *photon mapping* introduced by Jensen [JEN 01].

4.4. Display of results

4.4.1. *LDR and HDR Images*

We can define the *dynamic range* of an image as the ratio between the largest and smallest representable intensity in the same image. The conventional encoding of images is done in 32 bits of which 24 are used for color, which represents 8 bits per channel (red, green and blue)[7]. This 8-bit encoding implies a strong restriction; the dynamic range of representable intensities thus consists of only 256 values. This is relatively low compared to the discriminatory ability of the human eye whose dynamic range is at least 1:100,000 (and even more if the time adaptation is taken into account). The 32-bit encoded images are referred to as LDR (or *low dynamic range*). To represent a wider range of intensities, the *high dynamic range images* were introduced (HDRI or HDR only). The RGBe format was proposed by GW Larson [LAR 91]. It allows us to represent each RGB channel (red, green and blue) according to a real number using a 32-bit encoding: 3 channels on 8 bits and a shared

---

7 The remaining 8 bits can encode the transparency according to the formats.

exponent, which allows us to represent luminances within a range from 10^{-38} to 10^{38}. Other HDR formats have been proposed (LogLuv TIFF developed by SGI, which uses a CIE L*u*v* model to approximate the human perception, OpenEXR by IML [KAI 02] with 16 or 32 bits per channel and Log format by Pixar). However, it is not enough that the file format covers a wide range of luminances to perform an accurate rendering computation. The HDRR (High Dynamic Range Rendering) covers all rendering applications that incorporate a high dynamic range in illumination computations. The computations for the intensity of light sources and light exchanges are performed very accurately. This allows the preservation of details that are due to significant light contrasts. This is the case, for instance, of halo effects, diffusion of light in participative media, refraction in almost transparent materials, and so on. However, these algorithms have to take into account the fact that display devices (monitors in particular) also have their own range of illumination. That is, among other things, the role of *tone mapping* algorithms.

4.4.2. *Tone mapping*

The luminance values that can be measured in the real world range from $10^{-5}cd.m^{-2}$ (soil of a forest illuminated by the stars) to $10^{5}cd.m^{-2}$ (sun reflected by the snow). But a CRT or LCD type of screen can only display luminances ranging from 1 to $10^{2}cd.m^{-2}$. It is therefore essential to transform the images that we want to display to control the changes that they will experience. Such a transformation is called a *tone mapping operator*. In this section, we present some of the operators that have been proposed in the literature of computer graphics. Readers interested in more information on this subject can refer to the state of the art by Devlin *et al.* [DEV 02]. There are two classes of tone mapping operators: the global operators (or spatially uniform) that apply the same transformation to all the pixels of the image and the local operators (or spatially variable) that apply a different transformation to different parts of the image.

4.4.2.1. *Global operators*

4.4.2.1.1. Linear compression

The simplest transformation is linear compression:

$$L_d(i,j) = a.L_w[i,j] + b$$

with:

$$a = \frac{L_d^{max} - L_d^{min}}{L_w^{max} - L_w^{min}}$$

$$b = \frac{L_d^{max} L_w^{min} - L_d^{min} L_w^{max}}{L_w^{max} - L_w^{min}}$$

$L_d(i,j)$ is the displayed luminance on the screen for pixel (i,j), and $L_w(i,j)$ is the actual luminance at the point projecting in pixel (i,j).

This method is equivalent to uniformly compress the contrasts. This transformation would be efficient if the contrasts were perceived in the same way irrespective of the ambient light level. But this is not the case, as shown by the *threshold versus intensity* functions for the rods and cones [FER 96].

4.4.2.1.2. Ward operator

This operator [WAR 94] uses a contrast perception model to convert the luminances of the real scene in displayable luminances. This model is based on the assumption of a linear operator m such that a contrast at the perception threshold in the real scene becomes a contrast threshold in the displayed scene:

$$L_d = m.L_w$$

$$\Delta L(L_{da}) = m.\Delta(L_{wa})$$

The value L_{da} denotes the average luminance of the scene assuming that the visual system has adapted to the luminance. In practice, the computation of $\Delta L(L_{da})$ is performed using the psychophysical model of contrast sensitivity by Blackwell [CIE 81]:

$$\Delta L(L_{da}) = 0.05(1.219 + L_a^{0.4})^{2.5}$$

Ward suggested that we consider $L_{dmax}/2$ as L_{da} and the average of the logarithms of luminances in the scene be displayed (excluding the light sources) as L_{wa}.

This operator is used to compress the contrasts while maintaining contrast ratios.

4.4.2.1.3. Larson *et al.* operator [LAR 97]

This operator is based on histogram adjustment. A histogram, showing the rate of representation within the real scene of each level of adaptation, is first computed. Such a level of adaptation is obtained by taking the logarithm of the average of luminances in a unit area of one degree (corresponding to the foveal adaptation). The least frequent level ranges are compressed, and then the cumulative histogram is thresholded. The compression tends to increase the contrast excessively.

NOTE.– Before adjusting the histogram, the image is processed; the perception of blur is added and the sensitivity of the color is simulated.

4.4.2.2. *Local operators*

4.4.2.2.1. Pattanaik *et al.* operator [PAT 98]

This operator takes into account the sensitivity of the human visual system to patterns, luminance and color. It uses the known physiological and psychophysical data on the chromatic and achromatic adaptation. This operator is divided into two parts: a visual model and a display model. The visual model uses a multiscale representation of patterns of the image and extracts from it the local contrasts at different spatial frequencies after having split chromatic and achromatic channels. A gain is applied to each of these contrasts according to a local adaptation luminance. The display model consists of reversing the visual model; a new gain is applied taking into account the extremal luminances of a standard screen; then the channels are reassembled and the image is reconstructed.

4.4.2.2.2. Reinhard *et al.* operator [REI 02]

This operator re-uses the "dodging and burning" technique of photographers. One area is chosen to represent the average gray. Then, the exposure time that is determined from this area is applied to the entire image to maximize the information captured. Applied to computer graphics, the method is thus as follows: the dynamics of the image are determined and an average gray is selected. The authors then match the average luminance of the scene to the average gray with a scale factor that leads to a normalized luminance image. A spatially uniform operator ensures that the dynamics of luminances lie between 0 and 1:

$$\overline{L_w} = \frac{1}{N} exp \left(\sum log(\delta + L_w(i,j) \right)$$

$$L(i,j) = \frac{a.L_w(i,j)}{\overline{L_w}}$$

$$L_d(i,j) = \frac{l(i,j)}{1 + V_1(i,j,s_m(i,j))}$$

where N is the number of pixels, δ is a very small arbitrary numerical value (to avoid having an infinite value with the logarithm if $L_w(i,j)$ has a zero value), and a takes values ranging between 0.045 and 0.72 and corresponds to the average gray. By default, it is set to 0.18. V_1 is a local average around pixel (i,j), and $s_m(i,j)$ is the optimal size of the area over which this average is computed.

4.4.3. *Management of spectral aspects*

4.4.3.1. *Problems with RGB rendering*

The final image generated by the rendering algorithm is necessarily in RGB, since this representation mode of color is the standard of display devices[8]. The most common technique is to perform the entire illumination computation using this encoding. It is therefore considered that the emission spectrum of sources and the material properties are available only on these three wavelengths (red, green and blue). Furthermore, the path of the light is assumed to be identical for all three wavelengths, usually for reasons of computation speed. All these simplifications introduce, however, many problems when one wishes to perform an illumination simulation as precisely as possible:

– the light/matter interaction functions (BRDF, BRTDF, BSSRDR, etc.) are generally not identical for the three wavelengths considered,

---

8 We do not consider here other types of devices such as printing devices, knowing the transition from the RGB mode to their also simplified representation mode, such as the CYMK that is processed in the "Color Management" chapter.

which, on the one hand, limits the accuracy sought, and on the other hand, reduces the possibility of simulating specific phenomena. These phenomena, such as refraction, induce a different path of the light depending on its wavelength (classical experiment of white light refraction through a prism glass);

– illumination computation not only aims at photo-realism, but also at simulating and forecasting the amount and the composition of light received at one point. For some applications, it is thus necessary to obtain physically accurate results, or even not to be restricted to the visible spectrum (infrared or ultraviolet radiations);

– some visual effects are not taken into account by the RGB; this is the case of metameric objects. Objects are called metameric if their appearance under a certain illumination condition is the same for an observer. The perception of metameric objects varies according to illumination conditions. Two objects may seem to have the same hue under a given illumination, yet they are very different under other conditions. This behavior is impossible to reproduce with an RGB encoding because two objects that are characterized by the same RGB triplet will always be reproduced as identical even if the composition of the light source varies;

– other phenomena related to light/matter interactions cannot be taken into account accurately in the RGB model. This is the case of the fluorescence, dispersion and interferences.

4.4.3.2. *Spectral rendering*

In the case of spectral rendering, more wavelengths are considered for the representation of light sources and materials. The photometric solids of light sources and the reflectance functions should include information on the wavelength. Illumination computations then take into account all these parameters: a ray from a given source will then be characterized by either its spectral composition or by the fact that it has only one wavelength. This spectral composition is changed during the interaction with the materials. We should then have as many rays as simulated wavelengths since the wavelength carried by a ray can possibly be modified during its propagation. Another problem is therefore to represent the spectral functions continuously in the illumination computations. The most traditional approach is to sample these functions. For instance, the visible spectrum can be divided into 81 values (every 5 nm between 380 and 780 nm). However, the number of values to be represented may be important and furthermore, some functions may exhibit rapid variations, which produce a spectral aliasing problem. Another approach [MEY 88] is to decompose the BRDF in a small number of basic functions (polynomial, Gaussian, etc.). At the end of the illumination simulation, there is, for each pixel of the generated image, a color represented by a spectral distribution. It therefore remains to convert this information to recode the final image according to the RGB primaries.

4.4.3.3. *Problems with spectral rendering*

The major drawback of this technique is a significant increase in computation time for a change in color rendering, which is not always noticeable. This is why some methods are designed to limit this problem. It is thus possible to use the information on the wavelengths only for direct illumination [JOH 99].

Another problem may arise from the variety of samplings of different functions. Some materials or light sources may have been recorded with different accuracies. Should we restrict ourselves to the smallest sampling (the one with the lowest values)? Is it possible to re-include some information available only in RGB? Smits [SMI 99] suggested a method to interpolate the missing values.

4.4.4. *Computer graphics and perception*

The aim of photo-realistic rendering methods is to produce images of a scene that are indistinguishable from a photograph of the same scene. However, the observer sees the image using his visual system that has its own characteristics, limitations, etc. Several questions may then arise: is it necessary to do all the illumination calculation to produce photo-realistic images? How can we guide the algorithm to eliminate unnecessary parts of the calculation by taking into account the human visual system? We know part of how vision works and we are able to model it.

4.4.4.1. *Concept of contrast sensitivity*

One of the key factors of the perception in an image is related to its contrast. We can define the contrast c of a region [MIC 27] by:

$$c = \frac{Y_{max} - Y_{min}}{Y_{max} + Y_{min}}$$

Y_{max} and Y_{min} are respectively the maximum and minimum luminance of the area in question.

It is easy to show experimentally that there is a contrast threshold below which the area is perceived as uniform (the signal is no longer received). However, the contrast sensitivity is variable and depends on the structure of the signal of the image. In the case of a sinusoidal signal, the contrast sensitivity is determined by the spatial frequency (f), which is defined as the number of cycles per unit angle.

Campbell and Robson [CAM 68] showed that the contrast sensitivity function (CSF) has an optimum (from 1 to 10 cycles per degree depending on the conditions). For larger or smaller values, there is a decline following a Gaussian law on a logarithmic scale. That is why Sakrison and Manos [MAN 74] suggested we model the contrast sensitivity by the following equation:

$$A(f) = a(b + c.f).e^{-(c.f)^d}$$

Experimentally, we find the following variable values:

$$\begin{cases} a &= 2.6 \\ b &= 0.0192 \\ c &= -0.114 \\ d &= 1.1 \end{cases}$$

The modeling of the CSF function and other mechanisms of the human visual system lead to models that quantify the visual difference between two images. This is the case, among others, of the VDP by Daly [DAL 93].

4.4.4.2. *Exploitation of global illumination algorithms*

The use of the VDP for photorealistic computer graphics has been validated [MYS 98]. The perceptual criteria can be used in the calculation of image rendering either as stopping criterion of calculations, or as control factor of the algorithm.

4.4.4.2.1. Stopping criterion

As highlighted above (section 4.3.2.2), the estimate through Monte Carlo methods is potentially infinite. This requires that we stop the calculation when the number of samples reaches a threshold. It appears that the perceptual quality of produced images is related to the number of samples used. When the image is calculated with an insufficient number of samples, it appears noisy. Beyond a number of samples, the produced image, although still containing an error, becomes indistinguishable from a reference image (calculated with a very large number of samples). It is thus possible to use the VDP to compare two successive reports to determine if the calculation brings a perceptible change in the image. If so, the calculation is pursued; otherwise, it can be stopped [TAK 09].

4.4.4.2.2. Rendering algorithm control

Another application of perceptual models is to guide computer graphics algorithms. The general principle is to focus the calculations in the areas where errors are highly visible. Conversely, in some parts of the image, the quality can be degraded. This decision may be used at the geometry level (the use of an adaptive mesh whose accuracy is guided by the VDP [VOL 00]) or at the rendering algorithm level (progressive perceptual rendering [FAR 02]).

4.5. Conclusion

This chapter on rendering in computer graphics is rather unusual for a book on color. Not because color plays no role in rendering, on the contrary, performing realistic (photo) rendering without color does not make sense. Thus, as we have seen, this chapter is mainly devoted to algorithmic aspects related to the production of photo-realistic images. However, the use of color in realistic rendering poses some problems (which are not all solved currently) as we have attempted to show, including the handling of the spectral representation of the light, the display of images, or the consideration of perceptual concepts.

At present, the application of these methods, which are based on the simulation of the behavior of the light, remains confined to specific applications (high-quality rendering, simulation of energy exchanges). However, these methods cannot be used in real time. The research efforts in this field focus therefore on their acceleration (using all the computing power of GPU in particular, algorithms optimization, etc.).

4.6. Bibliography

[APP 68] APPEL A., "Some techniques for shading machine renderings of solids", *AFIPS 1968 Spring Joint Computer Conference*, vol. 32, p. 37-45, 1968.

[ASD 93] ASDOWN I., "Near-field photometry: a new approach", *Journal of the Illuminating Society*, vol. 22, p. 163-180, 1993.

[BLI 77] BLINN J.F., "Models of light reflection for computer synthesized pictures", *Computer Graphics (SIGGRAPH '77 Proceedings)*, vol. 11, no. 2, p. 192-198, 1977.

[CAM 68] CAMPBELL F.W.C., ROBSON J., "Application of fourier analysis to the visibility of gratings", *Journal of Physiology*, vol. 197, p. 551-566, 1968.

[CIE 81] CIE, An analytic model for describing the influence of lighting parameters upon visual performance, Report no. Report 19/2.1, Commission internationale de l'éclairage, 1981.

[COO 82] COOK R.L., TORRANCE K.E., "A reflectance model for computer graphics", *ACM Transactions on Graphics*, vol. 1, no. 1, p. 7-24, 1982.

[DAL 93] DALY S., "The visible differences predictor: an algorithm for the assessment of image fidelity", *Digital Images and Human Vision*, p. 179-206, MIT Press, 1993.

[DEV 02] DEVLIN K.A., CHALMERS A., WILKIE A., PURGATHOFER. W., "Tone reproduction and physically based spectral rendering", *Proceedings of Eurographics 2002*, p. 101-123, 2002.

[FAR 02] FARRUGIA J.P., Modèles de vision et synthèse d'images, PhD thesis, University Jean Monnet Saint-Étienne, 2002.

[FER 96] FERWERDA J.A., PATTANAIK S.N., SHIRLEY P., GREENBERG D.P., "A model of visual adaptation for realistic image synthesis", *Computer Graphics (SIGGRAPH '96 Proceedings)*, vol. 30, no. 3, p. 249-258, 1996.

[GOR 84] GORAL C.M., TORRANCE K.E., GREENBERG D.P., BATTAILE B., "Modelling the interaction of light between diffuse surfaces", *Computer Graphics (SIGGRAPH '84 Proceedings)*, vol. 18, p. 212-22, 1984.

[JEN 01] JENSEN H.W., *Realistic Image Synthesis Using Photon Mapping*, A.K. Peters, Natick, USA, 2001.

[JOH 99] JOHNSON G.M., FAIRCHILD M.D., "Full-spectral color calculations in realistic image synthesis", *IEEE Transactions on Computer Graphics and Applications*, vol. 19, no. 4, p. 47-53, 1999.

[KAI 02] KAINZ F., BOGART R., HESS D., OpenEXR image file format, 2002.

[KAJ 84] KAJIYA J.T., HERZEN B.P.V., "Ray tracing volume densities", *Computer Graphics (Proceedings of SIGGRAPH '84)*, vol. 18, p. 165-174, 1984.

[KAJ 86] KAJIYA J.T., "The rendering equation", *SIGGRAPH '86: Proceedings of the 13th Annual Conference on Computer Graphics and Interactive Techniques*, New Orleans, USA, ACM, p. 143-150, 1986.

[KEL 98] KELLER A., Quasi-Monte carlo methods for photorealistic image synthesis, PhD thesis, University of Kaiserslautern, Kaiserslautern, Germany, 1998.

[KUB 31] KUBELKA P., MUNK F., "Ein beitrag zur optik der Farbanstriche", *Zeitschrift für Technische Physik*, vol. 12, p. 593-601, 1931.

[LAF 93] LAFORTUNE E.P., WILLEMS Y.D., "Bi-directional path tracing", *Proceedings of Third International Conference on Computational Graphics and Visualisation Techniques (COMPUGRAPHICS '93)*, p. 145-153, 1993.

[LAR 91] LARSON G.W., "Real pixels", *Graphics Gems II*, p. 80-83, Academic Press, 1991.

[LAR 97] LARSON G.W., RUSHMEIER H., PIATKO C., "A visibility matching tone reproduction operator for high dynamic range scenes", *IEEE Transactions on Visualization and Computer Graphics*, vol. 3, p. 291-306, 1997.

[LEW 03] LEWIS R., "Making shaders more physically plausible", *Fourth Eurographics Workshop on Rendering*, p. 47-62, June 2003.

[MAN 74] MANNOS J.L., SAKRISON D.J., "The effects of a visual fidelity criterion on the encoding of images", *IEEE Transactions on Information Theory*, vol. 20, no. 4, p. 525-536, 1974.

[MEY 88] MEYER G.W., "Wavelength selection for synthetic image generation", *Computer Vision, Graphics, and Image Processing*, vol. 41, no. 1, p. 57-79, 1988.

[MIC 27] MICHELSON A., Studies in optics, PhD thesis, University of Chicago, 1927.

[MYS 98] MYSZKOWSKI K., "The visible differences predictor: applications to global illumination problems", in DRETTAKIS G., MAX N.L. (eds), *Rendering Techniques*, p. 223-236, 1998.

[NIC 77] NICODEMUS F., RICHMOND J., HSIA J., GINSBERG I., LIMPERIS T., Geometric considerations and nomenclature for reflectance, Report no. Monograph 161, National Bureau of Strandards (US), October 1977.

[PAT 98] PATTANAIK S.N., FERWERDA J.A., FAIRCHILD M.D., GREENBERG D.P., "A multiscale model of adaptation and spatial vision for realistic image display", *SIGGRAPH '98 Conference Proceedings*, Annual Conference Series, ACM SIGGRAPH, Addison Wesley, p. 287-298, July 1998.

[PHO 75] PHONG B., "Illumination for computer generated pictures", *Communication of ACM*, vol. 18, no. 6, p. 311-317, 1975.

[REI 02] REINHARD E., STARK M., SHIRLEY P., FERWERDA J., "Photographic tone reproduction for digital images", *ACM Transactions on Graphics*, vol. 21, no. 3, p. 267-276, ACM, 2002.

[SEG 07] SEGOVIA B., IEHL J.-C., PÉROCHE B., "Metropolis instant radiosity", *Computer Graphics Forum*, vol. 26, no. 3, p. 425-434, Blackwell Publishing, September 2007.

[SMI 99] SMITS B., "An RGB-to-spectrum conversion for reflectances", *Journal of Graphics Tools*, vol. 4, no. 4, p. 11-22, A.K. Peters, Ltd., 1999.

[TAK 09] TAKOUACHET N., Utilisation de critères perceptifs pour la détermination d'une condition d'arrêt dans les méthodes d'illumination globale, PhD thesis, University of the Littoral Opal Coast, 2009.

[TOR 67] TORRANCE K., SPARROW E., "Theory for off-specular reflection from roughened surfaces", *Journal of the Optical Society of America*, vol. 57, no. 9, p. 1105-1114, 1967.

[VEA 97] VEACH E., Robust monte carlo methods for light transport simulation, PhD thesis, Stanford University, Stanford, California, December 1997.

[VOL 00] VOLEVICH V., MYSZKOWSKI K., KHODULEV A., KOPYLOV E.A., "Using the visual differences predictor to improve performance of progressive global illumination computation", *ACM Transactions on Graphics*, vol. 19, p. 122-161, 2000.

[WAR 94] WARD G., *A Contrast-based Scale Factor for Luminance Display*, p. 415-421, HECKBERT P. (ed.), Boston, Academic Press Edition, 1994.

[WHI 80] WHITTED T., "An improved illumination model for shaded display", *Communications of the ACM*, vol. 23, no. 6, p. 343-349, 1980.

Chapter 5

Image Sensor Technology

This chapter deals with electronic structures dedicated to the perception of color images. In section 5.1, some elements of physics on light/matter interactions are revisited. In section 5.1.1, the different types of pixels allowing us to collect light are presented through a brief review of microelectronics. Finally, the notion of color imaging is introduced in section 5.4. In this way, the key characteristics of these devices are highlighted through various commercial achievements.

5.1. Photodetection principle

The "solid" electronic imaging technologies[1] are based on photon detection in silicon. This detection is performed through the creation of electrical charges (electrons and holes) as a result of radiation. This is the photoelectric effect. The principle of this photoelectric effect is to "collect" the charges released when a semiconductor is subjected to a radiation of wavelength λ. The appearance of an electron/hole pair is due to a band transition caused by the photon energy of the light $E = h.\nu$ (Figure 5.1). When the energy of a photon is greater than the energy

Chapter written by François BERRY and Omar AIT AIDER.
1 In contrast to systems implemented from vacuum tubes.

difference between the valence band and the conduction band (band gap is $E_g=E_c-E_v$eV for silicon), a silicon atom can create an electron/hole pair by "absorbing" the photon. That band transition is associated with photodetection in silicon.

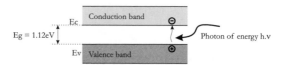

Figure 5.1. *Photoelectric effect in silicon*

In other words, when a silicon atom is illuminated by a radiation whose wavelength is sufficient[2], this atom can liberate charge carriers and thus create an electric current. However, each photon that has sufficient energy does not automatically create an electron/hole pair. In fact, according to their wavelength (thus "their color"), the photons penetrate more or less in the material and therefore have a different quantum efficiency. The efficiency denoted as η is expressed by the number of electron-hole pairs generated per incident photon:

$$\eta(\lambda) = \frac{I_p}{q}\frac{P_{opt}(\lambda)}{h.v}$$

where I_p is the current photogenerated by absorption of the optical power P_{opt} at the wavelength λ corresponding to the energy $h.v$, and q is the electron charge such that $q = 1.6 \times 10^{-19}C$.

This efficiency depends on the wavelength of the light and the design parameters of the device and will specify a spectral range of use of the detector. This range is limited:

– the upper bound consists of the fundamental absorption threshold of the semiconductor material used. In fact, for a photon to contribute to a current, its energy should be greater than the band gap (also called gap);

2 The energy gap of silicon is 1.12 eV, which gives a maximum wavelength of 1.1 μm. It should thus be noted that silicon is sensitive to infrared radiation.

– the lower bound consists of the absorption of light near the illuminated surface. In this case, the penetration depth is very low. In fact, if the photon creates an electron hole pair at the interface, this pair will recombine immediately and will not contribute to a photocurrent. This property is directly related to the recombination parameter at the surface.

There is another quantity that derives from η; this is the responsivity (in A/W), which is expressed by the ratio of the photocurrent to the optical power such that:

$$R = \frac{I_p}{P_{opt}} \frac{\eta q}{h.\nu} = \frac{\eta.\lambda}{1.24} (en \; \mu m)$$

In most cases, this light/electricity transduction is carried out either by a photodiode or by a capacitive structure of the PhotoMOS type.

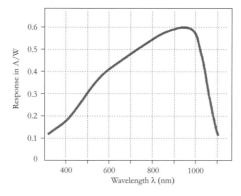

Figure 5.2. *Responsivity of silicon traditionally used in the manufacture of photo-elements. It should be noted that the silicon allows an absorption peak around 1 μm which corresponds to the wavelength of the infrared. For this reason, most image sensors made of silicon incorporate an IR filter (bluish color) in front in order to avoid blooming*

5.1.1. *The photodiode*

The principle employed in a photodiode is to use the depletion region (space charge region) to separate the carriers created by the incident photons. In fact, when a photon is absorbed, there is an appearance of a hole due to the release of an electron. However, these electron/hole pairs should be subjected to an electric field to separate the electron from the hole. Without an electric field, the electron and the hole will recombine immediately. As part of the photodiode, this electric field is generated within the junction that will be polarized in reverse. This polarization allows us to extend the Space Charge Region (SCR or depletion region) and thus create a region where an electric field exists (Figure 5.3). This electric field is due to the ionized dopant atoms (N and P) in the SCR.

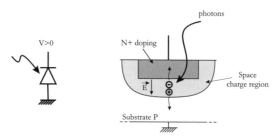

Figure 5.3. *Structure of a photodiode pixel*

A silicon photodiode can be represented by a current source I_{ph} in parallel with an ideal diode. The current source represents the current generated by the incident radiation, and the diode represents the p-n junction. In addition, a *junction capacitance* (C_j) and a *shunt resistance* (R_{SH}) are in parallel with the other components. *Series resistance* (R_S) is connected in series with all components in this model:

– R_{sh}: the *shunt* resistance of an ideal photodiode is infinite. In fact, this resistance ranges between 100 KΩ and 1 GΩ depending on the quality of the photodiode. This resistance is used to calculate the leakage current (or noise) in the photovoltaic mode, which means without polarization of the photodiode;

– C_j: this capacitor is due to the charge region (SCR). This is inversely proportional to the space charge width (W): $C_j = \frac{\varepsilon_{Si} A}{W}$, where A is the section surface of the photodiode, W is proportional to the reverse polarization and ε_{Si} denotes the permittivity of silicon. This capacitor varies from 100 pF for low polarizations to several tens of pF for high polarizations;

– R_s: this resistance is mainly due to the resistance of the substrate and to the contact resistances. R_s can vary between 10 Ω and 500 Ω depending on the surface of the photodiode.

5.1.2. *The photoMOS*

The photoMOS is based on a capacitor of the MOS type. The term MOS stands for Metal-Oxide-Semiconductor and derives from the physical structure of the capacitor. In fact, the latter (Figure 5.4) consists of the superposition of a P-doped silicon substrate, then a thin oxide layer (SiO$_2$ silica), and finally a thin layer of metal or of heavily doped polysilicon[3]. This blend of two more or less conductive materials (semiconductor substrate and metal or polysilicon grid) separated by an insulator forms a capacitive structure.

The application of a voltage on the grid of the cell reveals a potential well beneath it, which is used to collect and retain photon charges. Subjected to the electric field present in that region, the photoelectrons are attracted under the grid of the PhotoMOS detector. Such a structure can therefore be considered a capacitor whose charge is proportional to the illumination.

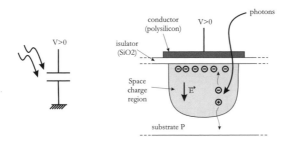

Figure 5.4. *PhotoMOS detection structure*

These two phototransduction structures (Photodiode and PhotoMOS) are the basis of the CMOS and CCD imaging technologies. They operate within array architectures that allow a spatial and temporal sampling of the luminous flux. Equipped with a reading circuit of information, these components thus form an imager. The CMOS and CCD imaging technologies differ both by the nature of the photodetecting cells used and by the mode of access to the light information.

---

3 This layer is relatively thin and appears to be virtually transparent to light radiations.

5.2. Imagers

The term imager is used when we work with integrated electronic structures that include a set of photosensitive cells. These cells can be arranged in a linear or array form.

(a)   (b)

Figure 5.5. *(a) Linear imagers; (b) array imager*

The linear or array arrangement depends primarily on the targeted type of applications. The linear sensors are widely used in "bar code" type readings or in scanning systems. They are also often found in production lines when the dimensions of components that are moving along the belt need to be checked. These imagers deliver only one (or sometimes two or four) line of pixels at relatively high frequencies (several Mpixels/s). In the case of linear color imagers, three pixels are added side by side with a red, green or blue colored filter for each.

The array distribution of pixels can be found in most image sensors both for shooting photographs and for video applications. In section 5.4, different methods are presented to explain how it is possible to capture "color" information in array structures.

5.2.1. *CMOS and CCD technologies*

In the visible range, there are nowadays two major technological trends: the CCD (Charge Coupled Devices) structure and the CMOS (Complementary Metal Oxyde Semiconductor) technology. We will not deal with the case of CID (Charge-Injected Devices) structures, which remain confidential and restricted to very specific applications.

The CCD and CMOS technologies are two approaches that are regularly in direct competition. Historically, the first attempts to acquire electronic images date back to the 1960s. CMOS technology was available during the period 1966–1970, but the imagers were beset with the problem of fixed pattern noise (FPN). The first charge transfer imager also known as CCD appeared in 1970. This imager was born following the work of Willard Boyle and George E. Smith in 1969 at AT&T Bell Labs. They were working on a new type of memory based on shift registers and the implemented principle allowed the development of the first CCDs. A history tracing the evolution of CCD and CMOS technologies can be found in the reference article by Eric Fossum [FOS 97].

When it first appeared in 1970, the CCD sensor [BOY 70] exhibited a low fixed pattern noise compared to the CMOS structure. This advantage allowed it to become the electronic image sensor of choice until 1980. It was widely used in all types of commercial and scientific applications. Despite the success of CCD imagers, research on CMOS imagers has continued because this type of sensor has several advantages:

– ability to integrate the processing electronics directly on the imager;

– ease of manufacture and at lower cost;

– more or less random access to pixels allowing windowing, binning, or sub-sampling.

In fact, in contrast with CCD structures, CMOS imagers are fully compatible with the technologies of conventional CMOS micro-electronics, which allow us to integrate electronics to the imager (readout electronics, digital conversion, image preprocessing, etc.) and thus reduce integration costs[4]. Thus, when the first CMOS sensors exhibiting performances comparable to CCD sensors appeared, they were well received. Currently, CMOS imagers are used in multiple applications. In the consumer sector, they are found in digital camcorders, cameras, webcams or even mobile phones. In the scientific field, CMOS sensors are exploited to develop fast cameras [CAS 03, ERC 02, KLE 01] or for applications that require a high measurement dynamic where the logarithmic characteristic of the photodiode pixel in current mode is interesting [HUA 02, JOS 02].

---

4 It is this consistency that explains why these imagers are known as CMOS type.

5.2.2. CCD (charge coupled device) imager principle

The imagers called CCD are composed of a photosensitive region of photoMOS type. After an accumulation time of photocharges, they are transferred from site to site before being read by a reading diode. This gradual charge transport is achieved through the electrons property of being accumulated in the deepest potential well (Figure 5.6).

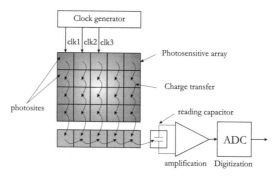

Figure 5.6. *General principle of a CCD structure*

The circuit that performs the reading includes a reverse-biased diode and a transistor operating as a switch controlled by a *reset* signal (Figure 5.7). A follower transistor provides the impedance adjustment between the read bus and the photo-detector. The reading requires three phases to measure the amount of charge present in the diode: a *reset*, an integration, and a measurement phase.

During the *reset* phase, the switch transistor is used to initialize the voltage across the internal capacity C_D of the diode. When the voltage across the capacitor reaches a certain reference value V_{ref}, the switch isolates the diode voltage V_{cc}, and the diode is said to be floating. The integration phase begins at this point. During integration, the capacitor C_D of the diode discharges and the voltage at its terminals V is expressed as a function of the current that comes from the accumulation of photon charges:

$$V = V_{ref} - \frac{1}{C_D} \int_{t_d^i}^{t_f^i} I_{photon}(t)\, dt$$

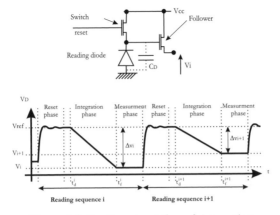

Figure 5.7. *Reading circuit through integration*

By considering that the light remains constant during the integration phase, the photocurrent I_{photon} can be considered a constant. Thus, the voltage variation during the integration phase is directly proportional to the photocurrent for a given integration time $\delta t = t_f^i - t_d^i$:

$$\delta V_i = \frac{\delta t}{C_D} . I_{photon}$$

After the integration time δt, the voltage variation δV_i is measured during the measurement phase. This measurement technique is known as *Correlated Double Sampling*. The major advantage of this method is the elimination of the noise in "KTC" of the capacitor from a differential measurement. A detailed description of this traditional reading technique is proposed in the thesis by C. Cavadore [CAV 98] or by M. Tabet in [TAB 02].

However, the CCD structure intrinsically requires an electronic or mechanical shutter to execute the transfer and reading with no illumination. Otherwise, if the reading time of the array is not negligible compared to the time of shifting the pixel lines, the illumination measurement will be distorted. In fact, during the integration phase (Figure 5.7), the latest read pixels would have been exposed longer than the first, and thus the amount of accumulated charges is no longer significant. The problem then is to separate the photodetection stage and the transport stage, and to explain why there are three types of CCD sensors.

5.2.2.1. *Full-frame CCD*

The simplest structure for a CCD sensor is known as "full frame". In this device, during exposure, the pixel constitutes the site of generation and collection of electrons. Then, during the transfer phase, it also constitutes the memory element, which allows the transport of charges. Thus, in such a structure, the entire surface of the pixel is photosensitive. The fill factor[5] is close to 100%.

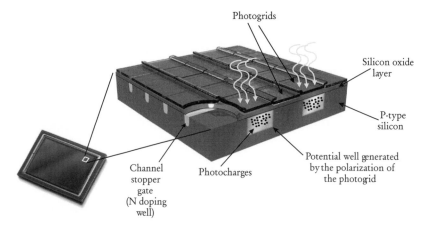

Figure 5.8. *Structure of a full frame CCD*

The "full frame" structure consists of a P-doped silicon substrate on which a layer of silicon oxide (SiO_2 or silica) is deposited. On this oxide layer, the photogate consists of either polysilicon or a thin layer of indium oxide (ITO for Indium Tin Oxide). ITO is often preferred because it is more transparent than the polysilicon in the blue and purple, and turns out to be completely opaque (acts like a mirror) in infrared light. However, the ITO is not part of the standard technology processes, making it less

---

5 The fill factor is the ratio of the effective photosensitive surface to the total surface of the pixel. As part of pixels integrating electronics (case of CMOS imagers), this ratio rarely exceeds 60%.

frequent when we are in a non-dedicated production line. The stopping channels are used to separate the photocharges in the same column.

In this structure (Figure 5.8), the photo-gate is polarized positively to create a potential well in the substrate. In this way, there is a gathering of photocharges. After a given time (integration time), the polarization is shifted from one electrode, which has the effect of transferring the photocharges step by step up to the reading circuit (Figure 5.9).

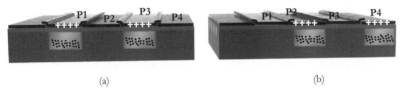

(a)   (b)

Figure 5.9. *(a) The photogrids P1 and P3 are polarized positively, which generates potential wells. After a given time, (b) the photogrid potentials are applied to neighboring photogrids (here P2 and P4), which shifts the potential wells. In this way, the photocharges are moved gradually*

However, during the transfer phase and especially the reading phase (which is very long compared to the transfer phase) in this full-frame device, the photons continue to arrive and charge the potential wells that are not yet read. There is therefore a problem of non-constant integration time depending on where one is located on the array. To resolve this problem, two solutions were proposed:

– the frames transfer structure;

– the interline structure.

5.2.2.2. *Frame transfer CCD*

This first solution known as CCD frame transfer aims to achieve an array twice as large in width and then to mask half of the array through a metal section. The masked part is used as a memory area. In fact, when the illuminated part has completed the integration of the photons of the image, the photo-charges are shifted toward the masked portion to be read. During this reading time, the illuminated part can simultaneously continue to collect photons. The capture and reading process is then performed in parallel as a *pipeline*.

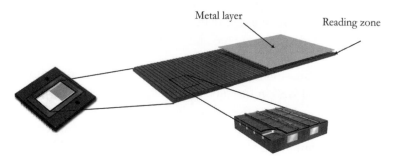

Figure 5.10. *Structure of a CCD frame transfer*

This solution is optimal, but is also the most expensive since it requires a surface twice as sensitive. An alternative solution consists of inserting a memory column between each column of pixels. This is the interline structure.

5.2.2.3. *Interline CCD*

Another solution is to add a protected transport register of light within the pixel (Figure 5.11). This type of structure called "Interline CCD" allows us to replace the PhotoMOS cell by a photodiode at the expense of the fill factor (~25%).

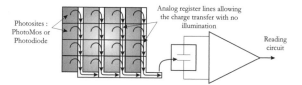

Figure 5.11. *Principle of an "interline" CCD array*

The capture of photocharges is performed through the photodiode and the storage is performed by operating on the control line of the register (Figure 5.12).

5.2.2.4. *Limitations of CCD imagers*

5.2.2.4.1. Blooming

By nature, the pixels of the CCD imagers (either full frame, interline, or frame transfer) are not electrically insulated against each other.

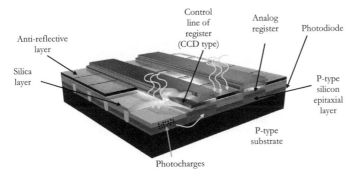

Figure 5.12. *Structure of "interline" CCD pixels*

The stopping channels (Figure 5.8) avoid too strong an overflow of charges between the columns and only the photo-gate potentials may maintain the charges in the substrate. However, when the amount of light is excessive, the number of photocharges generated can become excessive for the potential well and then there is overflow on neighboring pixels. This overflow occurs initially in the direction of the column since the stopping channels prevent the pollution of other columns. If the amount of light is really too much, the stopping channels can no longer contain all the charges and then there is overflow on the other columns (Figure 5.13).

Figure 5.13. *Blooming effect on a CCD array*

5.2.2.4.2. Smearing

The reading of the image takes place without shutter, through translation along a column. At the passage of a highly illuminated pixel, the information of the above pixels, whose reading passes through this illuminated pixel, is altered by the superposition of additional photocharges. This gives a smearing effect from that pixel (Figure 5.14).

Figure 5.14. *Smearing effect on a CCD array*

5.2.2.4.3. Use constraints, fragility

The use of CCD sensors requires the generation of complex clock signals as well as high voltage levels (not always compatible with current digital electronics 1.2 V, 3.3 V, 5 V) to ensure an efficient charge transfer, which leads to a high consumption. Moreover, it happens that the array has a defective pixel. Unlike CMOS technology, the transmission of information is performed through shifting, and this type of defect penalizes a part of the column (Figure 5.15).

However, CCD technology has become very mature. These arrays provide very high optical and electrical performances leading to excellent image quality. This technology is essential for scientific applications that require radiometric performances. In addition, this is still widely used in the field of digital photography.

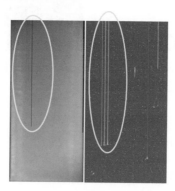

Figure 5.15. *The defective pixels condemn all the rest of the above column*

5.2.3. *CMOS imagers principle*

The first sensors derived from CMOS technology were simple photodiode arrays interconnected to a multiplexing system. This type of sensor also called CMOS PPS (for *Passive Pixel Sensor*) had a very bad signal/noise ratio and did not provide a large picture. In fact, when several tens of thousands of pixels are interconnected, the energy generated by the photodiodes is not sufficient to "load" the metal interconnects[6] allowing the information to be conveyed outside of the sensor.

To remedy this problem, the APS (for *Active Pixels Sensor*) concept aims to integrate within the pixel, in the photodiode, a circuit performing the impedance matching between the read bus and photosensitive cell (Figure 5.16).

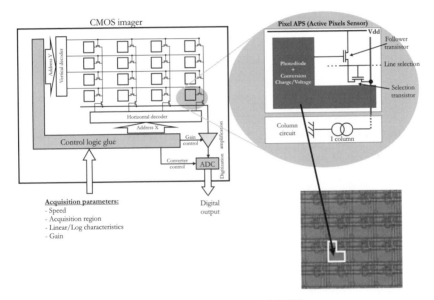

Figure 5.16. *Principle of a CMOS APS imager*

The major difference between a CMOS imager and a CCD imager lies in the independence of pixels in a CMOS structure. In fact, in the latter

---

6 We speak of charging in the sense that the interconnects have a resistance and especially an important parasite capacitor inducing significant RC constants.

case, the pixels are all independent of each other and can (in absolute terms) be totally separately controlled. In this approach, an array should be able to be addressed in a completely random manner, thus allowing the selection of any region of interest (ROI). In reality, this possibility is often largely constrained for two main reasons:

– most commercial CMOS imagers are designed for the "low cost" embedded market (webcam, laptop etc.) and we aim to minimize the number of input/output pins by using serial protocols (I2C classically) to specify the acquisition parameters. Thus, the glue logic (in gray in Figure 5.16) decodes the I2C frames and automatically generates regions to be acquired as well as the speeds and the characteristics of gain, conversion, etc. Thus, this makes it easy to understand that there is no direct access to the addressing of the array and, in most cases, only certain types of addressing are already configured (Figures 5.17, 5.18, 5.19);

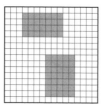

Figure 5.17. *Rectangular ROI: a rectangular region often configurable only in row or column (for pre-charge reasons – see below)*

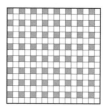

Figure 5.18. *Sub-sampling: the selection of a pixel over n (usually a multiple of 2)*

– in Figure 5.16, the reading structure of the pixel consists of a follower transistor and a selection transistor. The connection line wiring all the pixels of the same column to the column amplifier circuit is much longer when there are many pixels. This length induces a parasitic capacitor that constitutes one of the major limitations of the sensor in terms of bandwidth. To optimize the reading, the connection line *Vdd* is

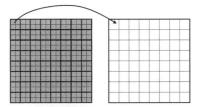

Figure 5.19. *Binning: the gathering of neighboring pixels allowing us to make macro pixels. In most cases, the value of the macro pixel is the average of the initial pixels*

pre-charged to prevent the follower transistors from having to provide all the current to bring the line to the right potential. This pre-charging takes time compared to the reading time of a pixel and that explains why it is faster to read in one direction rather than another. That is why purely random ROIs are difficult to maintain in terms of acquisition time.

The APS concept is not really new, but the realization of performant CMOS APS sensors has only been made possible much later. In fact, the photodetection surface is reduced compared to the total surface of the pixel (Figure 5.20) and the fill factor decreases the sensitivity of the pixel and thus the quality of the image. The integration of the APS pixel, keeping a reasonable fill factor, has become possible due to the increase in the accuracy of etching of the CMOS technology (0.35 μm technology).

The main pixel structures that are currently being used are the photodiode pixel in current mode or in integration mode and the PhotoMOS pixel.

Many types of CMOS pixels of varying complexity are found in the literature. The two simplest types (called Pixel 3T for 3 transistors) that are used as the basis for most of the more complex assemblies are presented below.

5.2.4. *Photodiode pixel in current mode*

This type of pixel is based on the measurement of the photocurrent generated by the displacement of photocharges. The major advantage of this reading mode is its wide measurement dynamic [HUA 02, JOS 02]. The sensors based on this type of pixel are easily able to measure

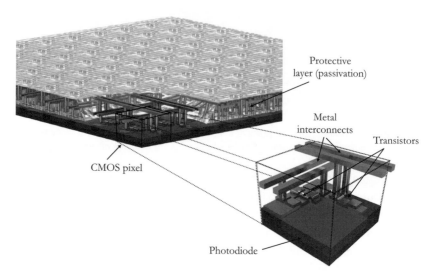

Figure 5.20. *Structure of a CMOS APS imager*

variations in light intensity of more than 120 dB (10^6) which is more than the difference in brightness between day and night. To exploit this measurement dynamic, the photocurrent flowing in the diode is converted into voltage from the conversion structure in Figure 5.21.

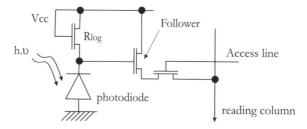

Figure 5.21. *Photodiode pixel in current mode*

This reading structure uses a charge transistor R_{log} (in weak inversion) that admits a logarithmic current/voltage characteristic. The follower transistor then carries out the impedance matching between the read bus and the photodetector. The response of this pixel can be written as:

$$V = V_{cc} - \frac{kT}{q} \ln \left(\frac{I_p}{I_0} \right)$$

where V_{cc} is the supply voltage; I_p is the photon current proportional to the light flux; I_0 is the current of strong inversion; $\frac{kT}{q}$ is a variable proportional to the temperature.

This pixel exhibits a good fill rate (40 to 60%) because it has only three transistors. The main drawback of this type of pixel is the disparity of the charge transistors R_{log} and the follower circuit. The etching accuracy of the manufacturing process of the sensor induces a disparity of the characteristics of the pixels. The differences in threshold voltages V_{th} of the charge transistors R_{log} induce a distinct response characteristic for each pixel. Thus, this type of sensor displays a significant *Fixed Pattern Noise* that requires a correction. In addition, the term $\frac{kT}{q}$ generates a response sensitive to temperature variations. Finally, the imagers based on this type of structure are relatively noisy but admit a large dynamic range.

Figure 5.22. *(a) Significant column fixed pattern noise due to the presence of column amplifiers (Fuga 1000 - Cypress); (b) image with no correction of the fixed pattern noise (NC1802 - Neuricam); (c) image after correction of the fixed pattern noise (NC1802 - Neuricam)*

5.2.5. Photodiode pixel in integration mode

In this type of pixel, the parasitic capacitor of the photodiode is used. The principle here is to pre-charge the photodiode (reverse polarized) using the *reset* transistor (switch in Figure 5.23). Once charged, this capacitor is discharged by the photocharges and the measurement of the light intensity simply consists of measuring the discharge after a given time (the integration time).

The presence of the *reset* bus in the structure of this pixel reduces its fill rate and its design requires a more accurate technology. Its sensitivity

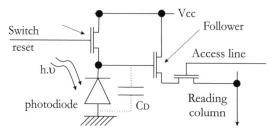

Figure 5.23. *Photodiode pixel in integration mode*

is lower than that of the photodiode pixel in the photocurrent mode. Moreover, for this type of pixel, the measurement time of the amount of photon charges depends on the integration time while this is almost instantaneous in the photocurrent mode. The main advantages of imagers based on this type of pixel, on the one hand, are its high signal-to-noise ratio and, on the other hand, its linear response.

5.3. Spectral sensitivity of imagers

It is relatively tricky to give absolute spectral sensitivities of CMOS or CCD imagers. In fact, each manufacturer often uses dedicated technologies inducing different spectral responses. However, as an illustration, Figure 5.24 provides a comparison of normalized spectral sensitivity for CMOS and CCD sensors. From these curves, we can see that each sensor has its own spectral range (Max. of CCD: 900 nm, Max of CMOS: 600 nm) and in both cases, the response in the infrared is far from being negligible.

To avoid blooms of the sensor through infrared radiations, it is common to add a filter to the sensor, which appears as a bluish glass in the surface (Figure 5.25).

5.4. Color acquisition systems

The "color" perception of a scene through a camera requires the capture of three components, whether the red, green, and blue primaries or the cyan, yellow and magenta complementaries. However, if the "gray level" capture appears to be relatively immediate with a single CCD or

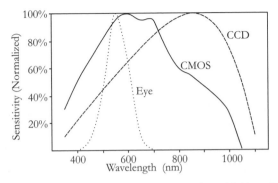

Figure 5.24. *Comparison of normalized spectral sensitivities of CMOS and CCD sensors*

Figure 5.25. *Nikon sensor (a) with and (b) without IR filter*

CMOS imager, the color case is still more complex. Generally, there are 4 techniques to acquire a color scene:

– through the use of color filters in front of a monochrome camera;

– through a triple sensor: tri-CCD camera;

– through subsampled filtering directly on a single sensor (typically a Bayer type filter);

– through a semiconductor structure with buried triple-junction.

Naturally, these techniques are quite diverse and specific to very special applications. Let us explore their scope in the following sections.

5.5. Through monochrome camera

The color image capture using a monochrome camera is done by adding to the camera a set of filters, which are mounted on a rotating disk to allow us to scroll through them. Such a multispectral acquisition system is proposed in Figure 5.26, where a set of interference filters scrolls successively in front of the camera lens [HAN 06, KNI 98].

(a)   (b)

Figure 5.26. *Multispectral acquisition system used in astronomy. Solutions proposed by (a) QSI and by (b) Orion. On the photo (QSI), it is possible to notice the reflection made by the filters: for example, the filter that passes red reflects cyan (for a color version of this figure, see www.iste.co.uk/fernandez/digicolor.zip)*

Such a device is based on a mechanical component that successively moves a series of filters in front of the camera lens. This type of system has the same disadvantages as the previous one to cope with dynamic scenes and adds a more or less important mechanical component.

To overcome the "heavy mechanics" problem, prototypes based on liquid crystal filters have been proposed. These filtering systems named LCTF (Liquid Crystal Tunable Filter) allow a selection of wavelengths with narrow and adjustable bandwidths (bandwidths 5–50 nm) over a wide range of wavelengths [HAR 02]. Figure 5.27 proposes a camera equipped with such a filtering system.

Figure 5.27. *LCTF filter mounted on a CCD camera*

The "varispec" filtering system through liquid crystals (Figure 5.27) implemented by CRI (www.cri-inc.com) has a switching time of 50 ns over spectra ranging from the visible (400–720 nm) to the infrared (850–1800 nm) with bandwidths varying from 5 nm and 20 nm. The latter system has two obvious advantages: the removal of the mechanical component and the possibility of computationally controlling the wavelengths to be perceived. These systems are widely used in microscopy, where the fluorophore protein labeling allows us to easily discern different bodies.

5.6. Tri-sensor systems

This system consists of three monochrome sensors (CCD or CMOS) for each of the RGB primary colors: red, green, and blue. This type of camera is considered as a *"must"* for color cameras and is primarily found in the professional world of video production. Separating the three components using a system of prisms and filters (Figure 5.28) provides an improved image quality and removes interferences.

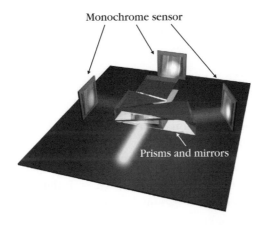

Figure 5.28. *Structure of a tri-sensor color camera (for a color version of this figure, see www.iste.co.uk/fernandez/digicolor.zip)*

The rays entering the separator prisms pass through the first prism and are filtered at its output by a blue dichroic mirror. The latter will reflect only the blue rays and let the others go through. The blue rays will then be reflected by a semi-transparent mirror toward the blue sensor. The same applies in the second prism for the red rays. Only the green rays remain and they pass through the three prisms without being deflected.

(a)   (b)

Figure 5.29. *Separator prisms block with 3 CCD sensors by (a) Panasonic and (b) Philips*

The main difficulty in this type of device lies at the implementation level, where we will seek to have a very good alignment of the three imagers. Moreover, it should be noted that this system compared to single-sensor structures (see next section) does not address the definition of the image but the quality of colored shades instead (there are Tri-CCD cameras with a Full-HD resolution, that is 1920×1080, in the market). In fact, in this case, the separation of the three primaries is almost perfect.

5.7. Color camera based on color filter arrays

Although the tri-sensor systems provide a high quality color image, they still remain relatively expensive devices. It thus became necessary to design systems based on a single imager, easily produced in series, inexpensive and avoiding the alignment problem of tri-CCD.

In this context, it has therefore been necessary to perform the filtering system directly on the imager. This is done in most cases by placing a color filter over each pixel CFA: Color Filter Array (Figure 5.30). Each pixel thus receives only a given wavelength, which implies a color sub-sampling and therefore a "demosaicing" step detailed in Chapter 6.

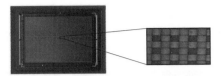

Figure 5.30. *Detail of a color imager with Bayer filter (for a color version of this figure, see www.iste.co.uk/fernandez/digicolor.zip)*

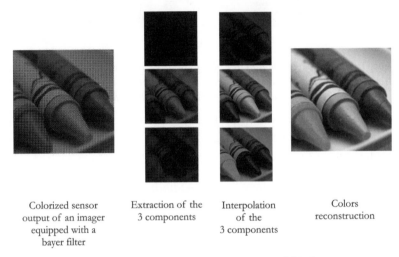

| Colorized sensor output of an imager equipped with a bayer filter | Extraction of the 3 components | Interpolation of the 3 components | Colors reconstruction |

Figure 5.31. *Bayer filtering (for a color version of this figure, see www.iste.co.uk/fernandez/digicolor.zip)*

5.7.1. *Types of filters*

Many color filters were used to try to optimize color rendering. Among the more conventional filters include the RGB Bayer and the RGBC (Red Green Blue Cyan) Bayerfilters.

In most cases, the tricolor RGB filter is used. However, we can also note the use of the three complementaries or primary/complementary or primary/white blends. In the conventional RGB filter (Figure 5.32a), twice as many green filtered pixels as red and blue should be noted. This allows us to take into account the greater sensitivity of the human eye to the green component.

The use of more than four colors (Figure 5.32c) can help us improve the accuracy of tones at the expense of a prohibitive computing time. Also, it should be noted that the use of blends of primaries, complementaries, and white colors poses additional problems of saturation, which limits their use to a "dark" color.

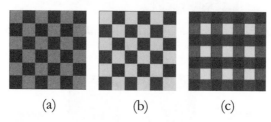

(a)   (b)   (c)

Figure 5.32. *(a) Conventional RGB Bayer filter; (b) Bayer filter in complementaries; (c) variant of the filter of complementaries with the green (for a color version of this figure, see www.iste.co.uk/fernandez/digicolor.zip)*

According to observations, a filter of primaries would be equivalent to a filter of complementaries. According to some, the filter of complementaries would improve the sensitivity.

The second aspect to consider in the filtering is the respective position of colors. Again, a number of proposals have emerged as shown in Figure 5.33.

In all these proposals, the Bayer filters are among the best adapted considering the distribution of colors. Some artifacts related to the vertical or diagonal repetition are thus avoided. Let us note the existence of pseudo-random filter with good response against the moiré, but with the drawback of repetition of basic patterns.

5.8. Variants of integrated sensors

5.8.1. *Backside illumination: Sony, Omnivision*

In 2009, Sony was the first to introduce the BSI (for BackSide Illumination or illumination through the back of the array) as a commercial product. The principle is to prevent the light rays from passing through the oxide layers and reflecting on the metal lines before reaching the photodiode. The idea was therefore to return the sensor by placing the control electronics on one side and the sensitive surface on the other (Figure 5.34).

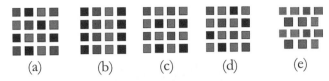

Figure 5.33. *(a) Diagonal RGB filter; (b) column RGB filter; (c) conventional Bayer RGB filter; (d) modified Bayer RGB filter (diagonal); (e) Rockwell RGB filter (for a color version of this figure, see www.iste.co.uk/fernandez/digicolor.zip)*

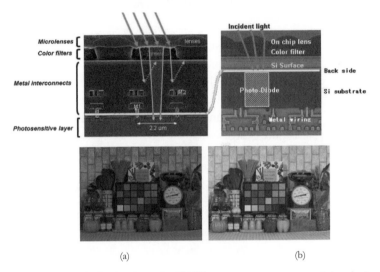

Figure 5.34. *Back illumination of a CMOS sensor: top – structure of the pixels, middle – microphotographic section, bottom – comparison of a Sony imager (Sony source) (for a color version of this figure, see www.iste.co.uk/fernandez/digicolor.zip)*

This technology was quickly followed by Omnivision, and it has found a way to significantly reduce the size of these sensors and cameras. In fact, with this technology, the fill factor increases to 100% and we get a surface gain from 33 to 45%.

5.8.2. *BDJ or buried double junction*

In the mid-1990s, university research had developed a process for perceiving different wavelengths on the same pixel by using a buried double junction. This technique was based on the fact that when radiation penetrates into the silicon, the penetration depth of this radiation is directly related to its wavelength (Figure 5.35). Therefore, the method is to use the silicon depth as a filter.

Figure 5.35. *Filtering of wavelengths in silicon (for a color version of this figure, see www.iste.co.uk/fernandez/digicolor.zip)*

The perception of each color is therefore performed by stacking two junctions and by comparing the currents of each of them. This technology has been used and patented by Foveon and is called X3 technology (Figure 5.36).

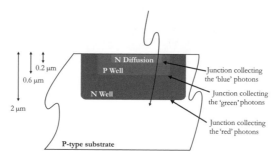

Figure 5.36. *Details of the Foveon X3 technology (for a color version of this figure, see www.iste.co.uk/fernandez/digicolor.zip)*

Some studies lead us to believe that not only is this technology not standard, but also that it would not provide sufficient sensitivity. However, this is the best alternative to the tri-sensor in terms of integration [FER 08].

5.9. Conclusion

This chapter presented the various microelectronic structures designed to capture color images. The first part of the chapter presented the semiconductor detection elements through the sensors of CMOS and CCD type. In the second part, we discussed approaches allowing us to capture the "color" information. As a conclusion, a brief comparison is made on the different techniques of color perception mentioned below:

	Advantages	Disadvantages
Sequential filtering	Use of a standard monochrome sensor	Slow, Controlled environment, Restricted to static scenes
Tri-CCD	Resolution and Acquisition frequency	Alignment of the complex sensors
Color filters network (CFA)	Affordable and integrated	Only one color per pixel: demosaicing necessary
Buried triple Junctions	All colors are within the pixel	Non-standard CMOS process

5.10. Bibliography

[BOY 70] BOYLE W., SMITH G., Charge-coupled semiconductor devices, Report no. 49, Bell Systems Techical Journal, 1970.

[CAS 03] CASSADEI B., Conception et réalisation d'un capteur en technologie CMOS pour l'observation d'impulsions lumineuses brèves voisines de 1ns, PhD thesis, University Louis Pasteur, Starsbourg, 2003.

[CAV 98] CAVADORE C., Conception et caractérisation de capteurs d'image à pixels actifs CMOS-APS, PhD thesis, SUPAERO, 1998.

[ERC 02] ERCAN X., XIAO F., WANDELL B., "Experimental high speed CMOS image sensor system and Applicaions", *Proceedings of IEEE Sensors*, vol. 1, p. 15-20, 2002.

[FER 08] FERUGLIO S., LU G.-N., GARDA P., VASILESCU G., "A review of the CMOS buried double junction (BDJ) photodetector and its applications", *Sensors*, vol. 8, p. 6566-6594, 2008.

[FOS 97] FOSSUM E., "CMOS image sensors: electronic camera on a chip", *IEEE Transactions on Electron Devices*, vol. 44, no. 10, p. 1689-1698, 1997.

[HAN 06] HANEISHI H., MIYAHARA S., YOSHIDA A., "Image acquisition technique for high dynamic range scenes using a multiband camera", *Wiley's Color Research and Application*, vol. 31, p. 294-302, 2006.

[HAR 02] HARDEBERG J.Y., SCHMITT F., BRETTEL H., "Multispectral color image capture using a liquid crystal tunable filter", *Optical Engineering*, vol. 41, p. 2532-2548, 2002.

[HUA 02] HUANG Y., Current-mode CMOS image sensor, PhD thesis, University of Waterloo, 2002.

[JOS 02] JOSEPH D., Modeling and calibration of logarithmic CMOS image sensors, PhD thesis, University of Oxford, 2002.

[KLE 01] KLEINFELDER S., LIM S., LIU X., GAMAL A.E., "A 10 000 frames/s CMOS digital pixel sensor", *IEEE Journal of Solid-State Circuits*, vol. 36, p. 2049-2059, 2001.

[KNI 98] KNIG F., PRAEFCKE W., *The Practice of Multispectral Image Acquisition*, vol. 3409, p. 34-41, 1998.

[TAB 02] TABET M., Double sampling techniques for CMOS Image Sensors, PhD thesis, University of Waterloo, 2002.

Chapter 6

From the Sensor to Color Images

6.1. Introduction

In Chapter 5, we saw how color sensors convert a light radiation into an electrical signal to build a digital image. It describes the two currently most widespread sensor technologies (CCD and CMOS) as well as the emerging technologies offered by some manufacturers. These color sensors are nowadays ubiquitous in the objects of everyday life, but the acquisition devices equipped with three sensors are overwhelmingly confined to the professional sectors and to very specific applications. Owing to the complexity of their manufacture, these devices are costly and largely unaffordable by the public. A whole range of so-called "hi-tech" products such as digital cameras, mobile phones and computers are thus equipped with a single sensor to form a color image, as are many professional devices such as quality control cameras and video surveillance cameras. One reason for this is the dramatic advances in the operation aiming to obtain a color image from the sensor data. The operation in question, known as *demosaicing*, is the subject of this chapter.

Chapter written by Olivier Losson and Eric Dinet.

Devices equipped with a single sensor form a color image by estimating it from the so-called *raw* image or color filter array (CFA) image, which contains only one color component level per pixel. Specifically, the filter mosaic of the CFA samples a single color component (red, green or blue) at each photoreceptor, and demosaicing aims to estimate the two missing components at the corresponding pixel. This is a far from trivial operation, and the colors estimated are thus less consistent with the color stimuli of the observed scene than those provided by a three-sensor camera. Improving the fidelity of the color image is still a topical issue, on which scientists and engineers are working. To obtain an image rendering the colors of the scene as accurately as possible, other processings are typically integrated into the acquisition system, foremost among which are calibration and color correction.

In the following pages, we look at the formation of color images from the data delivered by the sensor, and at the fidelity of these images to the observed scene. The first three sections, largely inspired by the work of Yanqin Yang [YAN 09], deal with the problem of demosaicing, while the last part tackles the problem of color camera calibration. After setting a few notations, in the first section, we present two principles used by the majority of demosaicing methods. The second section presents the key ideas of the main demosaicing algorithms. The issue of fidelity of the estimated image is discussed in the third section, which presents both the main measurement criteria and some results allowing us to select a demosaicing method. Finally, we examine the need for and the implementation of the processing known as *white balance*, usually done before demosaicing, to obtain a color image that is faithful to the scene regardless of illumination conditions.

6.2. Presentation and formalization of demosaicing

After identifying the need for the demosaicing operation within single-sensor cameras, a formalization is proposed to introduce the notations useful in the following. Then, we introduce the problems associated with color estimation, from a study based on a very simple method using the interpolation of the available levels. This allows us to set the fundamental principles generally used in demosaicing methods, which is discussed in the next section.

6.2.1. *Need for demosaicing*

As was seen in Chapter 5, single-sensor color cameras use a mosaic of spectrally selective color filters to sample a single color component at each pixel (see Figure 6.1a). The camera manufacturers have developed several types of filters, but the most widely used remains that of Bayer [BAY 76]. This filter is the subject of most studies and is considered in the following. It features twice as many green filters (*G*) as red (*R*) or blue (*B*) filters, to properly estimate the luminance to which the green component is often equated[1]. The data delivered by the sensor is preprocessed to obtain the CFA image, which therefore contains twice as many pixels whose levels represent the green as pixels representing the red or the blue component. The *demosaicing* operation must then estimate the levels of the two color components missing at each pixel of the CFA image to obtain the final color image.

As shown in Figure 6.1b, other operations are typically performed after demosaicing within a single-sensor color camera [LUK 08]. They aim, for instance, to correct the colors, to increase the image sharpness, and to reduce the noise, to render a visually satisfactory color image to the user. All these processes contribute to the quality of the rendered image, and, ultimately, they are the important difference between the different models of digital cameras, as manufacturers and sensor models are few in number. Although the underlying algorithms have some common features, the adjustment of their parameters determines the more or less significant presence of residual errors (or *artifacts*) that characterize each camera model.

---

1 The assimilation of the luminance to the component *G*, used especially to design the Bayer CFA and in the early demosaicing methods, is based on the observation that the curve of the luminous efficiency function of the human visual system in daylight (or *photopic*) vision is similar to that of the colorimetric function of the green primary proposed by the CIE for the reference observer.

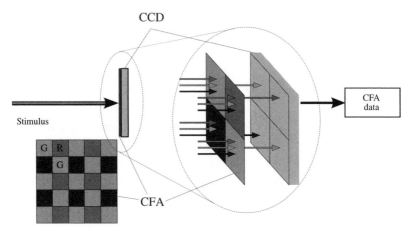

(a) Single-CCD technology (simplified), with filters arrangement according to the Bayer CFA

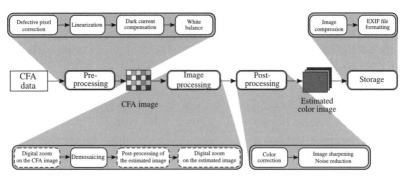

(b) Image acquisition in a single-CCD color camera (detailed diagram). Dotted steps are optional

Figure 6.1. *Structure of a single-CCD color camera (for a color version of this figure, see www.iste.co.uk/fernandez/digicolor.zip)*

6.2.2. *Formalization*

A digital image is represented by an array of pixels that we individually note $P(x, y)$, where x and y are the coordinates of the pixel P in the image of size $X \times Y$, with $(x, y) \in \mathbb{N}^2$, $0 \leq x \leq X - 1$ and $0 \leq y \leq Y - 1$. A single-plane image is written I, and $I(P)$ is the level of each of its pixels. A color image, denoted **I**, consists of three component planes, and **I**(P) is a color point in a 3D color space. In the case of the *RGB* space that interests us, the three components of this vector are $\mathbf{I}(P) = \left(I^R(P), I^G(P), I^B(P)\right)$, where $I^k(P)$, $k \in \{R, G, B\}$, is the level of the color component k at the pixel P. To simplify the notations used for demosaicing and to clarify the spatial coordinates, we similarly adopt in the remainder one of the following simplified notations: $\mathbf{I}(P) = (I^R_{x,y}, I^G_{x,y}, I^B_{x,y}) = (R_{x,y}, G_{x,y}, B_{x,y})$.

To establish a formalism for demosaicing, let us consider the acquisition process of a color image as whether the camera features three sensors or only one sensor (see Figure 6.2). A three-sensor camera (Figure 6.2a) combines the data delivered by the three sensors to form the color image of a scene. This color image $\mathbf{I}$ consists of three component planes I^k, $k \in \{R, G, B\}$. In a single-sensor camera (Figure 6.2b), the formation of a color image is quite different. The CFA image delivered by the sensor has only one plane of levels, and can therefore be represented by a 2D array of integer values (usually between 0 and 255). This image I^{CFA} is demosaiced (taking into account the known configuration of the CFA) to estimate the three component planes of the color image $\hat{\mathbf{I}}$.

Considering the Bayer CFA whose arrangement is shown in Figure 6.3a, the CFA image is defined at each pixel of coordinates (x, y) by the single color component associated with it:

$$I^{CFA}_{x,y} = \begin{cases} R_{x,y} & \text{if } x \text{ is odd and } y \text{ even} \\ G_{x,y} & \text{if } x \text{ and } y \text{ are of the same parity} \\ B_{x,y} & \text{if } x \text{ is even and } y \text{ odd} \end{cases} \qquad [6.1]$$

Let $\mathcal{I}^k$, $k \in \{R, G, B\}$, be the subset of pixels of I^{CFA} at which the available component is k (see Figures 6.3b to d):

$$\mathcal{I}^R = \{P(x, y) \in I^{CFA} \mid x \text{ odd and } y \text{ even}\} \qquad [6.2]$$

$$\mathcal{I}^G = \{P(x, y) \in I^{CFA} \mid x \text{ and } y \text{ of the same parity}\} \qquad [6.3]$$

$$\mathcal{I}^B = \{P(x, y) \in I^{CFA} \mid x \text{ even and } y \text{ odd}\} \qquad [6.4]$$

so that $I^{CFA} \equiv \mathcal{I}^R \cup \mathcal{I}^G \cup \mathcal{I}^B$. To determine the color at each pixel $P(x, y)$ of the estimated color image, the demosaicing process (denoted $\mathcal{D}$) generally keeps the color component available at the same coordinates in I^{CFA} and estimates the other two components:

$$I^{CFA}(P) \xrightarrow{\mathcal{D}} \hat{\mathbf{I}}(P) = \begin{cases} \left(I^{CFA}(P), \hat{I}^G(P), \hat{I}^B(P) \right) & \text{if } P \in \mathcal{I}^R \\ \left(\hat{I}^R(P), I^{CFA}(P), \hat{I}^B(P) \right) & \text{if } P \in \mathcal{I}^G \\ \left(\hat{I}^R(P), \hat{I}^G(P), I^{CFA}(P) \right) & \text{if } P \in \mathcal{I}^B \end{cases} \quad [6.5]$$

In this equation, each triplet of color components contains the one available at the pixel P in I^{CFA} (i.e., $I^{CFA}(P)$) and the other two components estimated by demosaicing (two among $\hat{I}^R(P)$, $\hat{I}^G(P)$, and $\hat{I}^B(P)$).

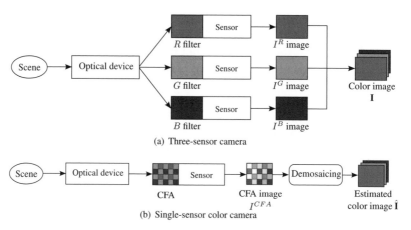

Figure 6.2. *Acquisition of a color image according to the type of camera (simplified diagrams) (for a color version of this figure, see www.iste.co.uk/fernandez/digicolor.zip)*

6.2.3. *Implemented principles*

In the CFA image (see Figure 6.3a), there are four different spatial neighborhood structures, shown in Figure 6.4 for a size of 3×3 pixels. These are denoted here by the color components available on the center line containing the central pixel of analysis, namely $\{GRG\}$, $\{GBG\}$, $\{RGR\}$ and $\{BGB\}$. Demosaicing aims to estimate the two color components missing at the central pixel of each of these four structures, by taking into account the levels of neighboring pixels and the components that are available there. Note that {GRG} and {GBG} are structurally similar, with the exception that the components R and B are swapped. They can thus be treated in the same way, which also applies to the {RGR} and {BGB} structures. To denote the levels in these neighborhood structures, we use the notation in relative coordinates of Figure 6.4. Thus, $R_{\delta x, \delta y}$ denotes the level (a red level, in this case) of the pixel at coordinates $(\delta x, \delta y)$ with respect to the central pixel. The coordinates of the central pixel $(0, 0)$ are omitted to alleviate notations in the following.

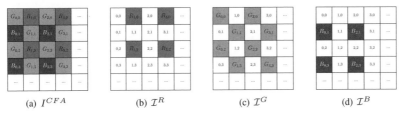

(a) I^{CFA} (b) $\mathcal{I}^R$ (c) $\mathcal{I}^G$ (d) $\mathcal{I}^B$

Figure 6.3. *CFA image and pixel subsets $\mathcal{I}^k$, $k \in \{R, G, B\}$. To clarify the picture, the pixels are colorized with the color component associated with them (for a color version of this figure, see www.iste.co.uk/fernandez/digicolor.zip)*

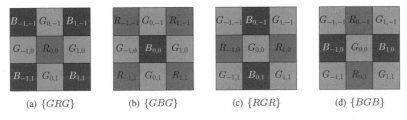

(a) {GRG} (b) {GBG} (c) {RGR} (d) {BGB}

Figure 6.4. *3×3 neighborhood structures of pixels in the CFA image. The spatial coordinates are here relative to those of the central pixel (for a color version of this figure, see www.iste.co.uk/fernandez/digicolor.zip)*

To introduce the principles generally used in demosaicing methods, let us examine one of the oldest and simplest methods that uses bilinear interpolation, as well as the artifacts it produces. Implemented as an embedded processing since the mid-1980s [COK 86], demosaicing by bilinear interpolation estimates the missing levels at a pixel by averaging the levels available at the nearest neighboring pixels. This is achieved in each of the two main directions of the image plane and on each color plane separately. More explicitly, the values of the missing components at the central pixel are estimated using the following equations, according to the structure in question:

$$- \text{for } \{GRG\}: \quad \begin{cases} \hat{B} & = \quad \frac{1}{4}\left(B_{-1,-1} + B_{1,-1} + B_{-1,1} + B_{1,1}\right) \\ \hat{G} & = \quad \frac{1}{4}\left(G_{0,-1} + G_{-1,0} + G_{1,0} + G_{0,1}\right) \end{cases} \qquad [6.6]$$

$$- \text{for } \{RGR\}: \quad \begin{cases} \hat{R} & = \quad \frac{1}{2}\left(R_{-1,0} + R_{1,0}\right) \\ \hat{B} & = \quad \frac{1}{2}\left(B_{0,-1} + B_{0,1}\right) \end{cases} \qquad [6.7]$$

Figure 6.5 is an example of results obtained by bilinear interpolation. To assess the demosaicing quality, a reference color image is used (typically, an image that comes from a three-sensor camera such as the one in Figure 6.5a). Its color components are sampled according to the CFA mosaic to form the CFA image (Figure 6.5b). This is then demosaiced, and the obtained estimated image (Figure 6.5c) can then be compared to the reference image. Demosaicing by bilinear interpolation is simple and fast, but although it provides satisfactory results in image regions of homogeneous colors, it generates erroneous colors at many pixels in regions with high spatial frequencies.

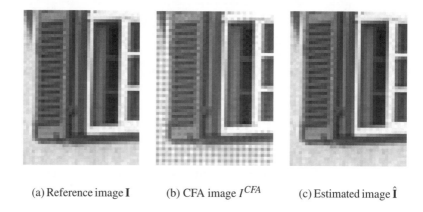

(a) Reference image **I**   (b) CFA image I^{CFA} (c) Estimated image $\hat{\mathbf{I}}$

Figure 6.5. *Example of demosaicing by bilinear interpolation on a sample taken from the "Houses" image from the Kodak database [KOD 91] (for a color version of this figure, see www.iste.co.uk/fernandez/digicolor.zip)*

To precisely investigate the causes of these artifacts, let us simulate their generation using a synthetic image, like Chang and Tan [CHA 06]. In the reference image shown in Figure 6.6a, two homogeneous regions are separated by a vertical transition, which reproduces the boundary between two real objects characterized by different shades of gray. The three color components of each pixel are thus equal. The levels of pixels (labeled as l) representing the dark object on the left are lower than those of pixels (labeled as h) representing the bright object on the right. Demosaicing the corresponding CFA image by bilinear interpolation yields the result illustrated in Figure 6.6b. On the color planes R and B, this algorithm produces a column of pixels of intermediate levels, whose values are the averages of the levels representing the two objects. On the green plane, however, it generates an alternating pattern of pixels with two intermediate levels around the boundary, one of low value $\frac{3}{4}l + \frac{1}{4}h$ and the other of high value $\frac{1}{4}l + \frac{3}{4}h$. Comparison of the marginal profiles of the center line of pixels of both images reveals that the transition located at the same horizontal positions for the three components of the reference image is not reproduced identically for the three components of the estimated image. This inconsistency generates false colors in the estimated image. On each color plane of the reference image, the transition corresponds to a sudden break of homogeneity along its normal direction. After bilinear interpolation, averaging the component levels of pixels located on both sides of the transition has the effect of making it less sharp. Although established on an achromatic image, these findings help to highlight two fundamental properties of color images that must be respected to improve the result of demosaicing: *spectral correlation* and *spatial correlation*.

The property of *spectral correlation* has been studied by Gunturk *et al.* [GUN 02]. These authors show that the levels of the three components are highly correlated in a natural color image, and especially in areas of high spatial frequencies. To exploit this spectral intra-pixel correlation for demosaicing, two principles are mainly used in the literature: the local constancy of the *ratio* of color components, and the local constancy of their *difference*. Historically, the first method implementing spectral correlation is that of Cok [COK 87], which uses the principle of local constancy of the "hue" (understood as the ratio

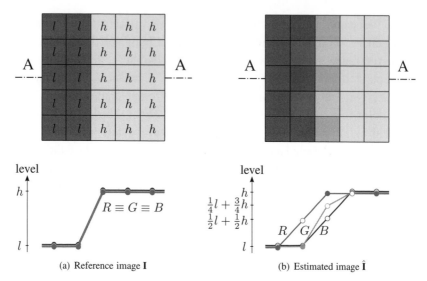

Figure 6.6. *Marginal images and profiles of levels of pixels located on the center line A-A, for a reference image (a) and the corresponding image estimated by bilinear interpolation (b). In the profiles, the solid dots denote available levels and the hollow dots denote estimated levels (for a color version of this figure, see www.iste.co.uk/fernandez/digicolor.zip)*

of the chrominance and luminance and equated to R/G or B/G). After estimating all the missing green levels by bilinear interpolation, this method estimates the missing red (respectively blue) levels by weighting the green level with the average "hue" values of neighboring pixels where the red (respectively, blue) component is available. For instance, to interpolate the blue level at the center of the $\{GRG\}$ structure (see Figure 6.4a), the following equation is applied. It uses the four diagonal neighbors at which the blue component is available:

$$\hat{B} = \hat{G} \cdot \frac{1}{4} \left[\frac{B_{-1,-1}}{\hat{G}_{-1,-1}} + \frac{B_{1,-1}}{\hat{G}_{1,-1}} + \frac{B_{-1,1}}{\hat{G}_{-1,1}} + \frac{B_{1,1}}{\hat{G}_{1,1}} \right] \qquad [6.8]$$

Such a bilinear interpolation of the color component ratios is based on the fact that this ratio is locally constant in a homogeneous region, which is justified by Kimmel [KIM 99] under the assumption of Lambertian observed surfaces. Another simplified model of the inter-channel correlation, also widely used in the literature, is based on the local constancy principle of the *difference* of color components (see justification in [LIA 07]). The interpolation step of the chrominance by Cok's method is then rewritten using the component difference average, equation [6.8] becomes:

$$\hat{B} = \hat{G} + \frac{1}{4}\left[(B_{-1,-1} - \hat{G}_{-1,-1}) + (B_{1,-1} - \hat{G}_{1,-1})\right.$$
$$\left. +(B_{-1,1} - \hat{G}_{-1,1}) + (B_{1,1} - \hat{G}_{1,1})\right] \tag{6.9}$$

The two local consistency principles of the ratio and of the difference of color components are generally consistent, but that using the ratio is more prone to generate artifacts, particularly in the image regions where the components R and/or B are saturated.

The *spatial correlation* property is easily understood by considering a color image as composed of juxtaposed homogeneous regions. Within a homogeneous region, all pixels are characterized by similar levels, and this, for each color component. To estimate the missing levels of each pixel in question, it is thus possible to use the levels of neighboring pixels. However, that is more difficult at pixels located near transitions between two distinct regions, where the local variation of color components is strong. In such cases, the missing components should be interpolated using only neighboring pixels that belong to the same homogeneous region. The spatial correlation principle is implemented in that way in many demosaicing methods, and the next section presents a few examples. It is typically used – sometimes combined with that of spectral correlation – in a first step of estimating the green component, since the green information is the most dense in the CFA image and represents the luminance of the image to be estimated (following Bayer's idea). The estimation of the red and blue components (considered the chrominance according to Bayer) is done only in a second step, using the already interpolated luminance and the spectral correlation property.

6.3. Demosaicing methods

The problem of estimating the levels missing in the CFA image arose in the late 1970s, right after the invention of the first filter mosaics for single-sensor color cameras. Numerous demosaicing algorithms have been developed since then, and it is impossible to draw up an exhaustive list here. Highly comprehensive inventories are available in the literature (such as [LI 08, LUK 08, LOS 10]) and online[2]. After the explanation of the basics in the previous section, we now introduce some of the most significant methods using a spatial analysis. Section 6.3.2 focuses on the principle of frequency analysis, used by the currently most efficient algorithms. We briefly present other approaches proposed for demosaicing, as well as post-processing typically implemented to improve the quality of the estimated image.

6.3.1. *Methods based on a spatial analysis*

Noting that the method based on the hue constancy suffers from serious estimation errors in regions of high spatial frequencies (see Figure 6.9b), Cok proposed the first edge-sensitive demosaicing algorithm [COK 94]. Based on pattern recognition, this method improves the green-level estimation by classifying (as *edge*, *stripe* or *corner*) the 3 × 3 neighborhood of pixels where that level is missing, then by adapting the interpolation formula according to the neighborhood class. The criterion used to distinguish the three classes, which compares the neighboring levels to their average, is very simple and not always sufficient to correctly identify the actual shape. However, the criterion was improved later [CHA 06], and the idea marks a milestone because it opens the way to methods adapting themselves to the local properties of the image.

Many methods thus implement the property of spatial correlation in demosaicing. Most of them exploit the principle of interpolating only levels whose pixels belong to the same homogeneous region. In other words, when the neighborhood of a pixel in question is located on the transition between two homogeneous regions, it is necessary to estimate the values missing at this pixel *along* the transition and not through it. A key point is thus to correctly determine the transition direction from the samples available in the CFA image. Computing a gradient

---

2 http://www.danielemenon.netsons.org/top/demosaicking-list.php.

is a straightforward solution to this problem. The method proposed by Hibbard [HIB 95] uses horizontal and vertical gradients to determine the direction along which the interpolation provides the best estimation of the green level. As an example, let us consider the $\{GRG\}$ structure again (see Figure 6.4a), in which the green level $\hat{G}$ of the central pixel is estimated in two steps. The first is to compute an approximation of the gradient norm (hereafter referred to as *gradient* for simplification purposes) according to the horizontal and vertical directions:

$$\Delta^x = \left| G_{-1,0} - G_{1,0} \right| \qquad\qquad [6.10]$$

$$\Delta^y = \left| G_{0,-1} - G_{0,1} \right| \qquad\qquad [6.11]$$

The second step is to interpolate the green level using the equation:

$$\hat{G} = \begin{cases} (G_{-1,0} + G_{1,0})/2 & \text{if } \Delta^x < \Delta^y & [6.12a] \\ (G_{0,-1} + G_{0,1})/2 & \text{if } \Delta^x > \Delta^y & [6.12b] \\ (G_{0,-1} + G_{-1,0} + G_{1,0} + G_{0,1})/4 & \text{if } \Delta^x = \Delta^y & [6.12c] \end{cases}$$

Laroche and Prescott [LAR 93] propose a variant of this method that takes into account the levels available in a 5×5 neighborhood to determine the transition direction, for example $\Delta^x = \left| 2R - R_{-2,0} - R_{2,0} \right|$. Hamilton and Adams [HAM 97] combine the two previous approaches, using a first-order differentiation for the green component and a second-order differentiation for the red and blue components. For instance, to estimate the green level in the case of the $\{GRG\}$ structure (see Figure 6.7a), this method first computes the following horizontal and vertical differences:

$$\Delta^x = \left| G_{-1,0} - G_{1,0} \right| + \left| 2R - R_{-2,0} - R_{2,0} \right| \qquad\qquad [6.13]$$

$$\Delta^y = \left| G_{0,-1} - G_{0,1} \right| + \left| 2R - R_{0,-2} - R_{0,2} \right| \qquad\qquad [6.14]$$

then interpolates the green level using the equation:

$$\hat{G} = \begin{cases} (G_{-1,0} + G_{1,0})/2 + (2R - R_{-2,0} - R_{2,0})/4 & \text{if } \Delta^x < \Delta^y & [6.15a] \\ (G_{0,-1} + G_{0,1})/2 + (2R - R_{0,-2} - R_{0,2})/4 & \text{if } \Delta^x > \Delta^y & [6.15b] \\ (G_{0,-1} + G_{-1,0} + G_{1,0} + G_{0,1})/4 & \\ \quad + (4R - R_{0,-2} - R_{-2,0} - R_{2,0} - R_{0,2})/8 & \text{if } \Delta^x = \Delta^y & [6.15c] \end{cases}$$

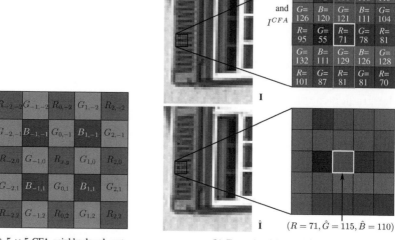

	$R=$ 121	$G=$ 72	$R=$ 101	$G=$ 110	$R=$ 115
and I^{CFA}	$G=$ 126	$B=$ 120	$G=$ 121	$B=$ 111	$G=$ 104
	$R=$ 95	$G=$ 55	$R=$ 71	$G=$ 78	$R=$ 81
	$G=$ 132	$B=$ 111	$G=$ 129	$B=$ 126	$G=$ 128
	$R=$ 101	$G=$ 87	$R=$ 81	$G=$ 81	$R=$ 70

$R_{-2,-2}$	$G_{-1,-2}$	$R_{0,-2}$	$G_{1,-2}$	$R_{2,-2}$
$G_{-2,-1}$	$B_{-1,-1}$	$G_{0,-1}$	$B_{1,-1}$	$G_{2,-1}$
$R_{-2,0}$	$G_{-1,0}$	$R_{x,y}$	$G_{1,0}$	$R_{2,0}$
$G_{-2,1}$	$B_{-1,1}$	$G_{0,1}$	$B_{1,1}$	$G_{2,1}$
$R_{-2,2}$	$G_{-1,2}$	$R_{0,2}$	$G_{1,2}$	$R_{2,2}$

$\hat{I}$ $(R = 71, \hat{G} = 115, \hat{B} = 110)$

(a) 5×5 CFA neighborhood centered in R (b) Example of demosaicing result

Figure 6.7. *Hamilton and Adams' method [HAM 97]. (a) One of the CFA neighborhood structures used by this method (size 5×5 pixels, centered at R). (b) Example of demosaicing result, on the same image sample as in Figure 6.5. The 5×5 detail has the CFA neighborhood structure of figure and the corresponding levels in the CFA image are represented at the upper right, superimposed on the reference image. This detail highlights the failure of the method to correctly determine the interpolation direction: at its central pixel, since $\Delta^x = 57 > \Delta^y = 48$, the vertical neighboring pixels are erroneously used to estimate $\hat{G}$ according to equation [6.15b] (see detail of the estimated image at the lower right) (for a color version of this figure, see www.iste.co.uk/fernandez/digicolor.zip)*

This algorithm yields much better results than Hibbard's method, not only because it computes the gradient more accurately by combining the information from two color components, but also because it exploits the spectral correlation to interpolate the green component[3]. However, the criterion used to determine the interpolation direction may be inappropriate and may provide unsatisfactory results in regions

---

3 The horizontal estimation of the green level (equation [6.15a]) can be rewritten as the average of an interpolation term on the left $\hat{G}^l = G_{-1,0} + \frac{1}{2}(R - R_{-2,0})$ and of an interpolation term on the right $\hat{G}^r = G_{1,0} + \frac{1}{2}(R - R_{2,0})$. Each of these terms expresses the local constancy of the component difference, since and $\hat{G}^l - R = G_{-1,0} - \frac{1}{2}(R_{-2,0} + R)$ and $\hat{G}^r - R = G_{1,0} - \frac{1}{2}(R + R_{2,0})$.

containing thin objects or textures. For instance, Figure 6.7b shows that the approximation of horizontal and vertical differences (Δ^x and Δ^y) does not always lead to the right decision for the interpolation direction.

Wu and Zhang [WU 04] propose an approach to determine this direction more reliably, again using a local neighborhood. Two candidate levels are computed to interpolate the missing green value at a pixel: one is determined with the horizontal neighbors, and the other with the vertical neighbors. Then, the missing value R or B is estimated according to the horizontal and vertical directions with each of these two candidates for the G. Finally, the selected interpolation direction is that for which the component differences $(R-G)$ and $(B-G)$ show minimal variations. This interpolation direction is used to select the levels (previously computed) to take into account when estimating the missing components of the pixel, thus ensuring the consistency of interpolation directions between these components. Wu and Zhang's method uses the same formula as that of Hamilton and Adams to interpolate the missing color levels, but improves the determination of the interpolation direction by using a 3×3 neighborhood rather than a single row or column, and by measuring the gradient of the component *differences* over this neighborhood.

Other authors attempt to refine the selection of the interpolation direction to still more accurately estimate the pixels representing the observed scene. For example, Hirakawa and Parks [HIR 05] propose a selection criterion using the number of pixels with homogeneous colors in the neighborhood of a given pixel. They compute the distances between a pixel's color and its neighbors' in the CIE space $L^*a^*b^*$, which better represents the human perception of colors than RGB. Then, they use an adaptive homogeneity threshold, which allows them to reduce the color artifacts due to an improper selection of the interpolation direction. Chung and Chan [CHU 06] show that the interpolation of the green plane is crucial to the quality of the estimated image. They hence propose to estimate the variance of the color component difference in a neighborhood to evaluate the local homogeneity, and to choose the direction corresponding to the minimum variance. This criterion is used to refine the estimation of the green component, especially in textured regions.

The methods mentioned above, whether Cok's based on pattern recognition or those using a directional gradient, require a classification step of the neighborhood to perform the interpolation. Kimmel [KIM 99] proposes a linear interpolation with adaptive weights that merges these two steps. With each available level of the neighborhood, this method associates a normalized weight that depends on a directional gradient. The direction of that gradient is specific to each neighboring pixel. For instance, to interpolate the green level at the center of the {GRG} or {GBG} structure, the equation is the following:

$$\hat{G} = \frac{w_{0,-1} \cdot G_{0,-1} + w_{-1,0} \cdot G_{-1,0} + w_{1,0} \cdot G_{1,0} + w_{0,1} \cdot G_{0,1}}{w_{0,-1} + w_{-1,0} + w_{1,0} + w_{0,1}} \quad [6.16]$$

where the coefficients $w_{\delta x, \delta y}$ are the weights computed over the neighborhood of the pixel in question. To exploit spatial correlation, these weights are adjusted to reflect the shape found in the neighborhood. Thus, the interpolation automatically adapts to the transition present in the image. Of course, the determination of these weights is crucial to the quality of results provided by this method, and several authors [LU 03, LUK 05] propose improvements to the formula originally used by Kimmel for their computation.

Finally, another interpolation method without neighborhood classification is worth mentioning. This original method is based on the fact that demosaicing by interpolation exhibits strong similarities with the super-resolution problem approach. With Orchard, Li [LI 01] achieves demosaicing by adapting the algorithm he proposes in his PhD thesis [LI 00] to increase the resolution of a grayscale image. In both problems, conventional approaches by interpolation (bilinear and bicubic) smooth the transitions and produce artifacts in regions of high spatial frequencies. Li's method exploits spatial correlation by evaluating a local covariance of the levels to interpolate the missing values with no directional gradient computation. To achieve demosaicing, each subset $\mathcal{I}^k$, $k \in \{R, G, B\}$, from the CFA image is considered as a sub-sampling of the corresponding plane $\hat{I}^k$ of the image to be estimated. The main problem is to locally compute the covariance of the levels in the high-resolution image from the known levels in the low-resolution image. This is possible by exploiting the *geometric duality* principle: since the covariance is computed over a local neighborhood in the low-resolution image, the equivalent high-resolution covariance is estimated by geometric duality by considering pairs of pixels at the two resolutions according to the same direction of the image plane.

To close this section about methods based on spatial analysis, let us recall that the green plane is often interpolated first. This estimation is essential because the green component generally carries most of the high-frequency information, particularly in edges or texture regions of natural images. Once the green plane is completely determined, it is used to estimate the chrominance. Hence, there is the need to select a method that successfully exploits spatial correlation. A detailed study of the methods mentioned above [LOS 10] shows, in addition, that those estimating the missing green levels only from CFA green levels (case of Cok's [COK 86], Li and Orchard's [LI 01], and bilinear interpolation methods) generally yield poorer results than others. The estimation of the green plane is improved when using the information from the R and B components. A powerful demosaicing method should therefore make the most of spatial and spectral correlations, simultaneously and for each color component.

6.3.2. *Methods based on a frequency analysis*

A demosaicing approach using the frequency domain[4] is proposed by Alleysson *et al.* [ALL 05]. This is the origin of a particularly important family of demosaicing algorithms, as they are currently the most efficient (see next section). Their principle is to represent a CFA image as a combination of a luminance[5] component at low spatial

---

4 The frequency mentioned here is the *spatial* frequency (in cycles/pixel) that is defined as the inverse of the number of adjacent pixels representing the same series of levels, along a preferred direction in the image (typically, the horizontal or vertical direction).

5 The "luminance" term denotes the achromatic component. It is re-used here from publications about demosaicing methods by frequency analysis.

frequencies and of two chrominance components modulated at high spatial frequencies[6], and then to estimate the color image by adequately selecting the frequencies. To outline such an approach, we retain the formalism proposed by Dubois [DUB 05].

Let us assume that each component $k \in \{R, G, B\}$ of a color image corresponds to an underlying signal f^k. Demosaicing then involves computing an estimation $\hat{f}^k$ (coinciding with $\hat{I}^k$) at each pixel. Let us also assume that there exists a signal, denoted as f^{CFA} and called *CFA signal*, underlying the CFA image (i.e. coinciding with I^{CFA} at each pixel). The CFA signal value at each pixel of coordinates (x, y) can be expressed as the sum of the spatially sampled signals f^k:

$$f^{CFA}(x, y) = \sum_{k=R,G,B} f^k(x, y) m^k(x, y) \qquad [6.17]$$

where $m^k(x, y)$ is the sampling function of the component k corresponding to the Bayer CFA shown in Figure 6.3a:

$$m^R(x, y) = \tfrac{1}{4}\left[1 - (-1)^x\right]\left[1 + (-1)^y\right] \qquad [6.18]$$

$$m^G(x, y) = \tfrac{1}{2}\left[1 + (-1)^{x+y}\right] \qquad [6.19]$$

$$m^B(x, y) = \tfrac{1}{4}\left[1 + (-1)^x\right]\left[1 - (-1)^y\right] \qquad [6.20]$$

By setting $\begin{bmatrix} f^L \\ f^{C_1} \\ f^{C_2} \end{bmatrix} = \begin{bmatrix} \frac{1}{4} & \frac{1}{2} & \frac{1}{4} \\ -\frac{1}{4} & \frac{1}{2} & -\frac{1}{4} \\ -\frac{1}{4} & 0 & \frac{1}{4} \end{bmatrix} \begin{bmatrix} f^R \\ f^G \\ f^B \end{bmatrix}$, the expression of f^{CFA} becomes:

$$f^{CFA}(x, y) = f^L(x, y) + f^{C_1}(x, y) \underbrace{(-1)^{x+y}}_{e^{j2\pi(x+y)/2}} + f^{C_2}(x, y) \underbrace{\left[(-1)^x - (-1)^y\right]}_{e^{j2\pi x/2} - e^{j2\pi y/2}}$$

$$[6.21]$$

---

6 Bayer's hypothesis is not used in this representation. Luminance is not assimilated to the green component, nor chrominance to the red and blue components.

The CFA signal can then be interpreted as the sum of a luminance component f^L at baseband, of a chrominance component f^{C_1} modulated at spatial frequencies (horizontal and vertical) $(u = 0.5, v = 0.5)$, and of another chrominance component f^{C_2} modulated at spatial frequencies $(u = 0.5, v = 0)$ and $(u = 0, v = 0.5)$[7]. If it is possible to estimate the functions f^L, f^{C_1} and f^{C_2} from the CFA signal at each pixel, the estimated levels of the color components R, G, and B are then simply found as:

$$
\begin{bmatrix} \hat{f}^R \\ \hat{f}^G \\ \hat{f}^B \end{bmatrix} = \begin{bmatrix} 1 & -1 & -2 \\ 1 & 1 & 0 \\ 1 & -1 & 2 \end{bmatrix} \begin{bmatrix} \hat{f}^L \\ \hat{f}^{C_1} \\ \hat{f}^{C_2} \end{bmatrix}
\qquad [6.22]
$$

The Fourier transform of the CFA signal can be expressed from equation [6.21] as:

$$
\begin{aligned}
F^{CFA}(u, v) = {} & F^L(u, v) + F^{C_1}(u - 0.5, v - 0.5) \\
& + F^{C_2}(u - 0.5, v) - F^{C_2}(u, v - 0.5)
\end{aligned}
\qquad [6.23]
$$

where the terms are the Fourier transforms of $f^L(x, y)$, of $f^{C_1}(x, y)(-1)^{x+y}$, as well as of the two signals defined as $f^{C_{2a}}(x, y) = f^{C_2}(x, y)(-1)^x$ and $f^{C_{2b}}(x, y) = -f^{C_2}(x, y)(-1)^y$.

Observing the energy distribution of a CFA image in the frequency plane (see example in Figure 6.8a) reveals a concentration in nine quite distinct regions, centered on the spatial frequencies corresponding to equation [6.23]. In particular, the energy of $F^{C_2}(u - 0.5, v)$ lies on the horizontal frequency axis u and that of $F^{C_2}(u, v - 0.5)$ lies on the vertical frequency axis v. The energy of $F^L(u, v)$ is mainly concentrated at the center of the frequency plane, while that of $F^{C_1}(u - 0.5, v - 0.5)$ is located in the diagonal regions (called "corners") of the plane. The key of methods based on frequency selection thus lies in the design of filters able to effectively separate the components of luminance L and of chrominance C_1 and C_2. The bandwidth of these filters should be

---

7 It is easy to verify that, on a grayscale image for which $f^R = f^G = f^B$, the two chrominance components of the CFA signal are zero.

adjusted with particular care, given the mutual overlapping (*aliasing*) of the three signal spectra.

Various proposals of selective filters have emerged. For instance, the original article of Alleysson *et al.* [ALL 05] uses the filter whose spectrum is reproduced on the upper part of Figure 6.8b to isolate the luminance component. Dubois [DUB 05] proposes to form the estimation of f^{C_2} by giving more weight to the subcomponent (C_{2a} or C_{2b}) that is less prone to aliasing with the luminance. In a local region of the image, such aliasing occurs mainly in either the horizontal direction or the vertical direction.

Lian *et al.* [LIA 05] show that the estimation of the luminance by these methods is sensitive to the bandwidth of the selective filters. Yet, the parameters of these filters (r_1 and r_2 in Figure 6.8b) depend on the image content and are difficult to adjust. In addition, the luminance selection by low-pass filtering the CFA image causes the loss of the high-frequency information located along the horizontal and vertical directions, to which the human visual system is particularly sensitive.

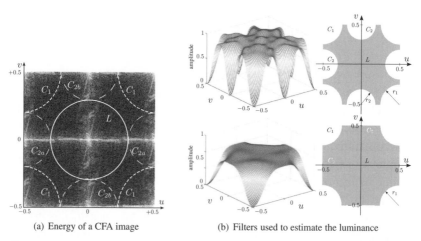

(a) Energy of a CFA image   (b) Filters used to estimate the luminance

Figure 6.8. *Frequency analysis of a CFA image (frequencies in cycles/pixel). (a) Distribution, in the frequency plane, of the normalized energy (Fourier transform module) of the "Lighthouse" CFA image (number 19 of the Kodak database) [ALL 05]. (b) Filters (spectrum and bandwidth) used to estimate the luminance, proposed by Alleysson et al. [ALL 05] (top) and Lian et al. [LIA 07] (bottom) (for a color version of this figure, see www.iste.co.uk/fernandez/digicolor.zip)*

The same authors [LIA 07] point out that along these directions, the spectrum associated with the filter used to estimate the component C_2 is zero if the G locations of the CFA are solely considered. At these locations, they hence apply a filter (see bottom of Figure 6.8b) whose spectrum is zero in the "corners" of the frequency plane where the energy of C_1 is concentrated, which provides the spectrum of the luminance F^L at these G locations. The advantage of doing so is that L exhibits less spectral overlapping with C_1 than with C_2, as can be seen in the example in Figure 6.8a. To estimate the luminance at R and B locations of the CFA, as it is difficult to isolate the component C_2, the authors use a spatial analysis based on the component difference constancy (exploiting spectral correlation) and a linear interpolation with adaptive weighting (exploiting spatial correlation).

6.3.3. *Other methods and post-processing*

This section is a supplement to the presentation of demosaicing methods. We very briefly talk about some classical post-processings performed by the algorithms already mentioned to remove demosaicing artifacts, as well as alternative approaches.

A post-processing is often performed on the estimated image to correct the estimated colors, usually by increasing iteratively the spectral correlation among the three color components. The median filter, typically used to remove impulse noise in a grayscale image, was historically often used due to its ability to effectively remove false colors without damaging the local variations. Freeman [FRE 88] is the first to take advantage of this filter by applying it to the estimated planes of component differences $R - G$ and $B - G$ (that generally contain few high spatial frequencies), which improves the bilinear interpolation estimation quite significantly. Several authors also include this filter to remove the demosaicing artifacts, such as Hirakawa and Parks [HIR 05], Lu and Tan [LU 03] or Chang and Tan [CHA 06]. A common approach to these last two works is to pre-identify the image regions that may contain artifacts, then to apply the median filter only on those regions. Among other interesting corrective procedures, the reader can refer to that incorporated into (previously described) Kimmel's method [KIM 99], or to that of Menon *et al.* [MEN 06] taking into account the local edge direction.

Demosaicing methods known as "by regularization" may be viewed as sophisticated correction approaches of the estimated colors. They indeed require an initial estimation $\tilde{\mathbf{I}}$ generated by a simple method (for example, Hamilton and Adams'), that is then iteratively improved by exploiting the spectral correlation principle. In this way, Keren and Osadchy [KER 99] apply a regularization by minimizing (with a finite element method) a cost function that includes a spatial smoothing term and a color correlation term:

$$\text{Cost} = \int \int \sum_{k=R,G,B} \left[\left(\frac{\partial^2 \tilde{I}^k}{\partial x^2} \right)^2 + 2 \left(\frac{\partial^2 \tilde{I}^k}{\partial x \partial y} \right)^2 + \left(\frac{\partial^2 \tilde{I}^k}{\partial y^2} \right)^2 \right] dxdy$$

$$+ \gamma \int \int \left(\tilde{\mathbf{I}}_{x,y} - \bar{\mathbf{I}}_{x,y} \right) \mathbf{C}_{x,y}^{-1} \left(\tilde{\mathbf{I}}_{x,y} - \bar{\mathbf{I}}_{x,y} \right)^t dxdy \qquad [6.24]$$

where $\bar{\mathbf{I}}_{x,y}$ and $\mathbf{C}_{x,y}$ are the average color and the color covariance matrix respectively at pixel (x, y), and where γ is a positive constant. Gunturk *et al.* [GUN 02] propose a method that gradually homogenizes the high-frequency characteristics among the three component planes, while keeping the data available in the CFA image. These objectives are fulfilled thanks to two convex sets of constraints on which the algorithm alternately projects the estimated data. The first set, called "Observation", ensures the consistency with the data available in the CFA image. The second, called "Detail", is based on a decomposition of each plane R, G and B into four frequency sub-bands resulting from the filter bank approach. This algorithm yields excellent demosaicing results, and it has been considered as a performance comparison benchmark for many years. However, it is complex and relatively expensive in computing time (see Table 6.1), and the final quality partly depends on that of the original estimation. A summary of existing regularization approaches is available in the article of Menon *et al.* [MEN 09].

A last important family of methods, following Taubman's idea [TAU 00], considers demosaicing as a generalized inverse problem [RIB 08]. Here, we take up Chaix de Lavarène's [CHA 07] formulation and notations, considering images as random variables in this Bayesian framework. The CFA image X is viewed as the transform of the reference color image $\mathbf{Y}$ by the sampling process, represented as a projection operator $\mathbf{Pr}$, that is $X = \mathbf{Pr}\,\mathbf{Y}$. Assuming that the reference data is a linear combination of the acquired CFA data, and that the acquisition process is spatially invariant, the estimation problem can be solved by a Wiener approach. The demosaicing problem thus boils down to finding a matrix $\mathbf{D}$ to estimate the color image $\hat{\mathbf{Y}} = \mathbf{D}\,X$ from the CFA image X, while minimizing the mean square error to the reference image $e = E[\|\mathbf{Y} - \hat{\mathbf{Y}}\|^2]$. Wiener's solution is written as:

$$\mathbf{D} = \left(E[\mathbf{Y}\,X^t]\right)\left(E[X\,X^t]\right)^{-1} \qquad [6.25]$$

where $E[\cdot]$ represents the mathematical expectation. Note that this equation requires a dataset of reference images $\mathbf{Y}$ that are representative of images that will be demosaiced later using the matrix $\mathbf{D}$. This inverse problem approach also allows us to perform other operations in parallel with the demosaicing. For instance, Condat [CON 10] uses it to perform a demosaicing–denoising by a variational approach that minimizes the total variation under the constraint of consistency with the acquired data. Soulez and Thiébaut [SOU 09] jointly achieve deblurring and demosaicing. To be as complete as possible on the resolution of this underdetermined problem of demosaicing, let us finally mention that some methods use neural networks [KAP 00] or Hidden Markov fields [MUK 01].

6.4. Quality of the estimated image

Evaluating the quality of the estimated image (and thus the performance of the demosaicing method used) can be achieved in various ways: subjectively or objectively, with or without reference, using different metrics, etc. (see Chapter 9 on the evaluation of the quality of color images). We focus here on the objective evaluation of the estimated image by assuming the availability of the reference image, as it is performed in the vast majority of articles on demosaicing[8]. Several metrics have been proposed for this evaluation according to the objective. In addition to conventional fidelity metrics based on the *RGB* color space, there are:

– metrics based on perceptually uniform spaces, designed to better reflect the quality of an image as the human visual system perceives it [CHU 06, ZHA 97];

– metrics based on the analysis of the artifacts generated in the estimated image, designed to assess their impact on low-level processing applied later on this image [LU 03, YAN 09].

In the context of color image formation, we are solely interested in *fidelity* metrics of the estimated image relative to the reference image. Section 6.4.1 presents the usual procedure and criteria used to carry out this evaluation. Results are presented in section 6.4.2, before we discuss the performance of the different demosaicing methods detailed in this chapter.

6.4.1. *Fidelity criteria of the estimated image*

To objectively assess the quality of the demosaicing result, the experimental protocol already mentioned in the previous section is still followed. The CFA image is first simulated from the reference color image by selecting only one color component among the three according to the CFA mosaic arrangement. A demosaicing method is next applied to the CFA image to provide the estimated image. The objective evaluation of the demosaicing quality is then based on the pixel-to-pixel comparison between the reference image and the estimated image. Classically, objective evaluation metrics sum up the errors between the pixel levels in both images. At each pixel, the error between the reference image and the estimated image is quantified using a color distance between two color points in a 3D space.

---

8 To our knowledge, only the article of Longère *et al.* [LON 02] describes the experiment of a subjective assessment of the demosaicing quality, involving human observers and regulated by a series of experimental protocols.

Classical fidelity criteria are restricted to the *RGB* space. The demosaicing literature uses three main criteria, the last being deduced from the second:

1) Mean absolute error (*MAE*).

The *MAE* criterion estimates the mean absolute error between the reference image **I** and the estimated image **Î** as:

$$MAE(\mathbf{I}, \hat{\mathbf{I}}) = \frac{1}{3XY} \sum_{k=R,G,B} \sum_{x=0}^{X-1} \sum_{y=0}^{Y-1} \left| I_{x,y}^k - \hat{I}_{x,y}^k \right| \qquad [6.26]$$

Let us recall that $I_{x,y}^k$ denotes the level of the color component k at the pixel located at spatial coordinates (x, y) in image **I**, X and Y being the numbers of columns and rows of that image. The value of the *MAE* criterion varies between 0 and 255, and the lower it is, the better the demosaicing.

2) Mean square error (*MSE*).

The *MSE* criterion estimates the mean square error between the reference image **I** and the estimated image **Î** as:

$$MSE(\mathbf{I}, \hat{\mathbf{I}}) = \frac{1}{3XY} \sum_{k=R,G,B} \sum_{x=0}^{X-1} \sum_{y=0}^{Y-1} (I_{x,y}^k - \hat{I}_{x,y}^k)^2 \qquad [6.27]$$

The value range for this metrics is $[0, 255^2]$ and the interpretation of its values is identical to that of the *MAE* criterion: the optimal demosaicing quality corresponds to the zero value of the *MSE* criterion.

3) Peak signal-to-noise ratio (*PSNR*).

The *PSNR* is a distortion metrics particularly used in image compression. It quantifies the encoder performance by measuring the reconstruction quality of the compressed image relative to the original image. Many authors (e.g. [ALL 05, HIR 05, LIA 07, WU 04]) apply this criterion to quantify the demosaicing performance. Usually expressed in decibels, its definition is:

$$PSNR(\mathbf{I}, \hat{\mathbf{I}}) = 10 \cdot \log_{10} \left(\frac{d^2}{MSE} \right) \qquad [6.28]$$

where d is the maximum possible level for the two compared images. In the standard case of an image whose color components are coded on 8 bits, d equals 255. The better the demosaicing quality, the higher the *PSNR* value. The *PSNR* value of images estimated by classical demosaicing methods usually varies between 30 and 40 dB, which corresponds to values between 65.03 and 6.50 for the *MSE* criterion.

Note that these three criteria can also be used to measure the errors on each color component plane. On the green plane, for instance, the mean square error is expressed as:

$$MSE^G(\mathbf{I}, \hat{\mathbf{I}}) = \frac{1}{XY} \sum_{x=0}^{X-1} \sum_{y=0}^{Y-1} (I_{x,y}^G - \hat{I}_{x,y}^G)^2 \qquad [6.29]$$

The peak signal-to-noise ratio on the green plane is then computed by using MSE^G in equation [6.28]. These marginal criteria are useful for assessing the degradation due to demosaicing on each component, especially on the green plane (often estimated first, thus crucial to estimate the red and blue planes).

6.4.2. Fidelity results and discussion

To give an insight into the performance of demosaicing methods, we select the main ten among those presented in sections 6.2 and 6.3. These are listed in the caption of Figure 6.9 and repeated in Table 6.1[9]. The images used for these tests are those commonly encountered in the

---

9 The source code is available online for some of these methods:

– Bilinear, C. hue, Cok and Hamilton (by Ting Chen): http://scien.stanford.edu/pages/labsite/1999/psych221/projects/99/tingchen/main.htm,

– Li, Gunturk: http://www.csee.wvu.edu/ xinl/demo/demosaic.html,

– Dubois   (with   [VAN 07]):   http://lcavwww.epfl.ch/reproducible_research/VandewalleKAS07.

demosaicing literature, namely the 12 natural images from the Kodak database [KOD 91][10].

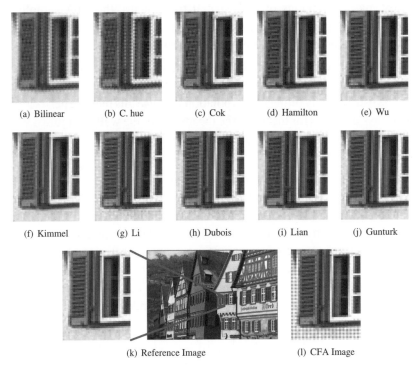

(a) Bilinear   (b) C. hue   (c) Cok   (d) Hamilton   (e) Wu

(f) Kimmel   (g) Li   (h) Dubois   (i) Lian   (j) Gunturk

(k) Reference Image   (l) CFA Image

Figure 6.9. *Demosaicing results obtained by ten demosaicing methods on a sample of the image "Houses"(k) (number 8 of Kodak database): (a) by bilinear interpolation [COK 86], (b) under the assumption of constant hue [COK 87], (c) by pattern recognition [COK 94], (d) using a gradient [HAM 97], (e) using component consistency of interpolation directions [WU 04], (f) with adaptive weighting [KIM 99], (g) using the local covariance [LI 01], (h) by frequency selection [DUB 05], (i) by frequency and spatial analyses [LIA 07], (j) by alternating projection of components [GUN 02] (for a color version of this figure, see www.iste.co.uk/fernandez/digicolor.zip)*

Figure 6.9 gives a visual overview of the results provided by the ten methods on a sample of the image "Houses". We can first note that all the estimated images display demosaicing artifacts. No method is

10 The Kodak database is available at http://www.math.purdue.edu/ lucier/PHOTO_CD, and the selected 12 images show a significant diversity of colors and textured regions.

able to perfectly reproduce the reference image shown in Figure 6.9k. Indeed, the presence of fine details makes this image particularly difficult to estimate: in regions of high spatial frequencies, the CFA sampling causes aliasing, which means an inevitable loss of information under the Nyquist-Shannon theorem. Demosaicing artifacts are of three main types.

– the blurring effect is characterized by an attenuation of transitions and a loss of very fine details. This effect is especially marked for the image estimated by bilinear interpolation because this method performs a low-pass filtering (for instance, see the texture of the wall in Figure 6.9a), but it is also found in most of the other methods (see the attenuation of the transoms of the opened window side);

– the *zipper effect* is a typical demosaicing artifact. It appears as a repeating (high and low levels alternation) and colored (cyan or orange) pattern that mainly occurs along the horizontal, vertical or diagonal transitions. The main cause of this artifact is an interpolation of levels that belong to homogeneous regions representing different objects. It is particularly noticeable in the images estimated by bilinear interpolation (Figure 6.9a) and under the assumption of constant hue (Figure 6.9b), along the uprights and the lower edge of the window;

– the *false color* artifact corresponds to a high deviation between the estimated and reference colors of a pixel. Occurring as a visually aberrant color, this effect typically derives from a loss of correlation among the color components (see section 6.2.3 and Figure 6.6b), leading in particular to a poor estimation of the components R and/or B. This artifact can be interpreted in the frequency domain as related to the mutual overlapping of the estimated luminance and chrominance spectra, due to a bad design of the selective filters used to estimate these components. All demosaicing methods tend to generate false colors, sometimes jointly with the zipper effect. Such aberrant colors are visible in the shutter slats, or at the upper-left corner of the window (notably in Figures 6.9 c, d, f and i).

The fidelity criteria described in section 6.4.1 allow us to objectively assess the demosaicing quality and to compare the relative performance of the methods. Table 6.1 shows the numerical results of fidelity obtained by the ten demosaicing methods under the *PSNR* criterion. The results under the *MSE* (whose *PSNR* is the logarithmic form) and *MAE* criteria

Method \ Image	6	7	8	9	11	16	19	20	21	22	23	24	Rank sum	PSNR (dB)	Operations
Bilinear	10	10	10	10	10	10	10	10	10	10	9	10	119	30.89	6
C. hue	9	9	9	9	9	9	9	9	9	9	8	8	106	33.26	11
Cok	8	7	7	7	7	8	8	7	7	7	7	6	86	34.58	43
Hamilton	5	4	5	5	4	5	5	4	5	4	5	5	56	38.20	21
Wu	4	5	4	4	5	4	4	5	4	5	4	4	52	38.62	80
Kimmel	6	6	6	6	6	6	6	6	6	6	10	6	76	35.61	300
Li	7	8	8	8	8	7	7	8	8	8	7	9	93	34.39	>1300
Dubois	1	2	1	2	1	1	2	3	2	2	2	1	20	41.16	145
Lian	3	1	3	1	3	3	3	1	3	1	1	2	25	40.49	65
Gunturk	2	3	2	3	2	2	1	2	1	3	3	3	27	40.82	384

Table 6.1. *Evaluation of the demosaicing fidelity under the peak signal-noise ratio (PSNR) criterion for twelve color images from Kodak database. In addition to the average values in the penultimate column, the table shows the performance ranks achieved by the same ten demosaicing methods as those in Figure 6.9. The last column shows the average number of operations required to estimate the color of a pixel*

are not reported here, but it should be noted that the latter provides very similar rankings. The relative performances of the methods are given as their rank for each image, rather than the actual *PSNR* values that are less synthetic. The average actual values are, however, given in the penultimate column of the table, and it is possible to note that their classification coincides with that provided by the rank sum computed in the previous column.

We find that the two methods taking advantage of the frequency domain (i.e. those of Dubois and Lian *et al.*) consistently provide better results than methods using only a neighborhood in the image plane. Moreover, the method proposed by Dubois on the basis of the work of Alleysson *et al.* is often classified in the first two, and achieves the highest scores on average over the 12 images. Gunturk *et al.*'s method by alternate projection of components also provides excellent results. In contrast, the "historical" methods (by bilinear interpolation and using hue constancy) achieve scores well behind, which confirms the visual assessment of Figure 6.9. Moreover, globally, those rankings obtained for the 12 images coincide both with each other and roughly with the subjective quality found on image number 8 alone. A reservation concerns the ranking of Kimmel's method for image number 23, whose highly saturated colors cause the generation of artifacts during the iterative correction phase based on a component ratio.

In the perspective of an implantation of one of these algorithms, *a fortiori* for an embedded processing of real-time demosaicing, we think it useful to add an overview of their respective complexity in the last column of Table 6.1. Due to the variety of implementations that we have (Matlab, C, etc.) and being unable to assess their optimization level, we estimate the computational complexity of the methods as the number of operations required rather than their execution time[11]. Observed in conjunction with those of fidelity, these results suggest a quality/speed compromise. We can notably point out that Hamilton and Adams' method yields satisfactory results despite its simplicity, while Li and Orchard's method is prohibitive due to the extremely high computational cost of the matrix inversion used. Iterations, such as those integrated into Kimmel's and Gunturk *et al.*'s methods[12], are highly detrimental in terms of computational complexity. Finally, Lian *et al.*'s method probably provides the best balance between the result fidelity and the computation time.

6.5. Color camera calibration

The signals emitted by an acquisition system should be transformed appropriately to match a faithful representation of the colors as they appear to the human observer. Such a transformation is often called *calibration* and is based on a more or less sophisticated color model whose role is to make the connection between the output of the sensor(s) (after demosaicing in the case of single-sensor color cameras) and the color information of the acquired scene.

In general, such a color model is different from one acquisition system to another, mainly due to the variability of spectral sensitivities

---

11 For simplicity, all the basic operations (addition, multiplication, comparison, and absolute value) are accounted equally.

12 Let us note, however, that an implementation of Gunturk *et al.*'s method requiring only one pass was recently proposed [LU 10].

of the device channels and of all the nonlinearities that may arise. In addition, we should not forget that the spectral characteristics of the illuminant used is directly involved in the acquisition process. This suggests that, ideally, a different color model per illuminant should be used. Except under very controlled illumination, the huge diversity of concrete situations makes it unrealistic to have as many color models as possible acquisition configurations. In practice, most systems address the problem by adjusting the gain values of each channel during a process commonly known as *white balance*.

As suggested by its name, a white balance adjusts the output signals of the different channels depending on the spectral characteristics of the light sources, so that achromatic regions of the acquired scene are actually represented as such. For instance, with an incandescent lamp, it is necessary to increase the sensitivity of the channels dedicated to low wavelengths of the visible spectrum relative to that of channels dedicated to high wavelengths, to prevent white objects from appearing artificially yellowish.

The major difficulty in white balancing is to determine which parts of the acquired scene can be considered achromatic. The reliable way is of course to use a Lambertian test pattern of the same reflection coefficient for all wavelengths in the visible spectrum. However, if this approach is ideally suited in a professional context, it is much more difficult to implement in a general public context. In the latter case, methods are deployed to estimate the color temperature of the illuminant.

One of these methods uses a set of photodiodes typically coated with RGB filters. The photodiodes are placed in the acquisition device so that they directly receive the incident light [HAN 83]. Unfortunately, this approach may provide incorrect results due to spurious reflections from colored areas of the scene. Furthermore, additional components may induce a significant additional cost.

Better results are usually obtained by estimating the white balance adjustment from the raw data of the sensor(s). The acquired image is divided into a more or less significant number of regions (typically at least 20). For each region, the average signal value of each channel is computed. The obtained average values are then differentiated according to a given algorithm to search for specific signatures allowing us to select, within a set of previously identified light sources, the most likely to illuminate the acquired scene [MOR 90, LIU 95, SPA 98]. Once the most likely source is selected, the different channels are weighted accordingly to adjust their relative contributions to the spectral distribution of energy of the incident light.

Whatever the method used to perform white balance, this operation is not in itself a complete color model [LAM 05]. The color information captured should be correlated with what an observer perceives. In other words, care should be taken to minimize the differences between digital colors and perceived colors. This refers to the problems of color appearance that has been dealt with in Chapter 3 of this book. In practical terms, the color model can be built following a white balance by performing an acquisition of a set of reference colors under the same shooting conditions as the scene to be imaged. The issue is then to determine the transformation(s) required to correlate the output values of the acquisition system with the reference colors.

The general principle is to match the observations of the selected samples with their values in a standardized color space such as *XYZ*. The underlying assumption is that the knowledge of the correspondence between a number of well-chosen colors in two spaces linked by a transformation allows us to deduce an approximation of the transformation for a richer and more extensive colors set. This implies that a linear transformation exists between the acquisition space and the selected normalized space [HOR 84]. In practice, such a condition is generally not strictly fulfilled, but the general approach, however, gives satisfactory results.

The color model aims to link the values provided by the sensor(s) and the colors perceived by the observer. The values it provides can be encoded in multiple ways in color spaces that are dependent or independent of the material, depending on the applications and devices with which the acquisition system is related.

6.6. Conclusion

This chapter focuses on one of the fundamental processings performed in a single-sensor color camera: demosaicing. We have seen why and how the color image is estimated from the raw data sampled from the sensor. The main principles underlying most demosaicing methods are presented here along with the outstanding algorithms that implement them. Among these, we mainly identify two families: methods based on a spatial analysis of the image, and those using the frequency domain. Other recently proposed approaches are also mentioned briefly.

The multiplicity and diversity of demosaicing methods reflect the acuteness of this problem, while the latest ones show its topicality. The steady expansion of research into this topic for over 30 years has allowed significant progress in the quality of the estimated image, and more precisely in its fidelity to the observed scene. The brief fidelity study presented here, which is performed on a representative sample of the methods mentioned and on a representative set of images, highlights the superiority of approaches analyzing the CFA signal in the frequency domain. Indeed, these provide the most accurate results under the signal-to-noise ratio criterion, for a relatively low computational cost.

In the context of color image formation within single-sensor color devices, we have strictly confined ourselves here to a fidelity study of the estimated image. It would be interesting to extend the quality study of this image in the context of its display or reproduction. This requires complete control over the acquisition conditions and the use of other quality metrics, better correlated with the human visual perception, as well as subjective quality tests.

6.7. Bibliography

[ALL 05] ALLEYSSON D., SÜSSTRUNK S., HÉRAULT J., "Linear demosaicing inspired by the human visual system", *IEEE Transactions on Image Processing*, vol. 14, no. 4, p. 439-449, April 2005.

[BAY 76] BAYER B.E., Color imaging array, U.S. patent 3,971,065, to Eastman Kodak Co., Patent and Trademark Office, Washington D.C., July 1976.

[CHA 06] CHANG L., TAN Y.-P., "Hybrid color filter array demosaicking for effective artifact suppression", *Journal of Electronic Imaging*, vol. 15, no. 1, p. 013003,1-17, January 2006.

[CHA 07] CHAIX DE LAVARÈNE B., ALLEYSSON D., HÉRAULT J., "Practical implementation of LMMSE demosaicing using luminance and chrominance spaces", *Computer Vision and Image Understanding*, vol. 107, no. 1-2, p. 3-13, July 2007.

[CHU 06] CHUNG K.-H., CHAN Y.-H., "Color demosaicing using variance of color differences", *IEEE Transactions on Image Processing*, vol. 15, no. 10, p. 2944-2955, October 2006.

[COK 86] COK D.R., Signal processing method and apparatus for sampled image signals, U.S. patent 4,630,307, to Eastman Kodak Co., Patent and Trademark Office, Washington D.C., December 1986.

[COK 87] COK D.R., Signal processing method and apparatus for producing interpolated chrominance values in a sampled color image signal, U.S. patent 4,642,678, to Eastman Kodak Co., Patent and Trademark Office, Washington D.C., February 1987.

[COK 94] COK D.R., "Reconstruction of CCD images using template matching", *Proceedings of the IS&T's 47th Annual Conference, Physics and Chemistry of Imaging Systems (ICPS '94)*, vol. 2, p. 380-385, Rochester, New York, USA, May 1994.

[CON 10] CONDAT L., "A simple, fast and efficient approach to denoisaicking: joint demosaicking and denoising", *Proceedings of the IEEE International Conference on Image Processing (ICIP '10)*, p. 905-908, Hong Kong, China, September 2010.

[DUB 05] DUBOIS E., "Frequency-domain methods for demosaicking of Bayer-sampled color images", *IEEE Signal Processing Letters*, vol. 12, no. 12, p. 847-850, December 2005.

[FRE 88] FREEMAN W.T., Median filter for reconstructing missing color samples, U.S. patent 4,724,395, to Polaroid Co., Patent and Trademark Office, Washington D.C., December 1988.

[GUN 02] GUNTURK B.K., ALTUNBASAK Y., MERSEREAU R.M., "Color plane interpolation using alternating projections", *IEEE Transactions on Image Processing*, vol. 11, no. 9, p. 997-1013, September 2002.

[HAM 97] HAMILTON J.F., ADAMS J.E., Adaptive color plan interpolation in single sensor color electronic camera, U.S. patent 5,629,734, to Eastman Kodak Co., Patent and Trademark Office, Washington D.C., May 1997.

[HAN 83] HANMA K., MASUDA M., NABEYAMA H., SAITO Y., "Novel technologies for automatic focusing and white balancing of solid state color video camera", *IEEE Transactions on Consumer Electronics*, vol. CE-29, no. 3, p. 376-382, August 1983.

[HIB 95] HIBBARD R.H., Apparatus and method for adaptively interpolating a full color image utilizing luminance gradients, U.S. patent 5,382,976, to Eastman Kodak Co., Patent and Trademark Office, Washington D.C., January 1995.

[HIR 05] HIRAKAWA K., PARKS T.W., "Adaptive homogeneity-directed demosaicing algorithm", *IEEE Transactions on Image Processing*, vol. 14, no. 3, p. 360-369, March 2005.

[HOR 84] HORN B.K.P., "Exact reproduction of colored images", *Computer Vision, Graphics, and Image Processing*, vol. 26, no. 2, p. 135-167, May 1984.

[KAP 00] KAPAH O., HEL-OR Z., "Demosaicing using artificial neural networks", *Proceedings of the SPIE - Applications of Artificial Neural Networks in Image Processing V*, vol. 3962, p. 112-120, San Jose, CA, USA, January 2000.

[KER 99] KEREN D., OSADCHY M., "Restoring subsampled color images", *Machine Vision and Applications*, vol. 11, no. 4, p. 197-202, December 1999.

[KIM 99] KIMMEL R., "Demosaicing: image reconstruction from color CCD samples", *IEEE Transactions on Image Processing*, vol. 8, no. 9, p. 1221-1228, September 1999.

[KOD 91] KODAK, Kodak photo CD PCD0992, access software & photo sampler, final version 2.0, [CD-ROM, Part No. 15-1132-01], 1991.

[LAM 05] LAM E.Y., "Combining gray world and retinex theory for automatic white balance in digital photography", *Proceedings of the 9th IEEE International Symposium on Consumer Electronics (ISCE '05)*, Hong Kong, China, p. 134-139, June 2005.

[LAR 93] LAROCHE C.A., PRESCOTT M.A., Apparatus and method for adaptively interpolating a full color image utilizing chrominance gradients, U.S. patent 5,373,322, to Eastman Kodak Co., Patent and Trademark Office, Washington D.C., June 1993.

[LI 00] LI X., Edge directed statistical inference and its applications to image processing, PhD thesis, Princeton University, New Jersey, USA, November 2000.

[LI 01] LI X., ORCHARD M.T., "New edge-directed interpolation", *IEEE Transactions on Image Processing*, vol. 10, no. 10, p. 1521-1527, October 2001.

[LI 08] LI X., GUNTURK B.K., ZHANG L. "Image demosaicing: a systematic survey", PEARLMAN W.A., WOODS J.W., LU L. (eds), *Proceedings of the SPIE Conference on Visual Communications and Image Processing (VCIP '08)*, vol. 6822, San Jose, California, USA, January 2008.

[LIA 05] LIAN N., CHANG L., TAN Y.-P., "Improved color filter array demosaicking by accurate luminance estimation", *Proceedings of the 12th International Conference on Image Processing (ICIP '05)*, vol. 1, Geneva, Italy, p. I-41-4, September 2005.

[LIA 07] LIAN N.-X., CHANG L., TAN Y.-P., ZAGORODNOV V., "Adaptive filtering for color filter array demosaicking", *IEEE Transactions on Image Processing*, vol. 16, no. 10, p. 2515-2525, October 2007.

[LIU 95] Liu Y.-C., Chan W.-H., Chen Y.-Q., "Automatic white balance for digital still camera", *IEEE Transactions on Consumer Electronics*, vol. 41, no. 3, p. 460-466, August 1995.

[LON 02] Longere P., Xuemei Z., Delahunt P.B., Brainar D.H., "Perceptual assessment of demosaicing algorithm performance", *Proceedings of the IEEE*, vol. 90, no. 1, p. 123-132, January 2002.

[LOS 10] Losson O., Macaire L., Yang Y., "Comparison of color demosaicing methods", *Advances in Imaging and Electron Physics*, vol. 162, p. 173-265, July 2010.

[LU 03] Lu W., Tan Y.-P., "Color filter array demosaicking: new method and performance measures", *IEEE Transactions on Image Processing*, vol. 12, no. 10, p. 1194-1210, October 2003.

[LU 10] Lu Y., Karzand M., Vetterli M., "Demosaicking by alternating projections: theory and fast one-step implementation", *IEEE Transactions on Image Processing*, vol. 19, no. 8, p. 2085-2098, August 2010.

[LUK 05] Lukac R., Plataniotis K.N., "Universal demosaicking for imaging pipelines with an RGB color filter array", *Pattern Recognition*, vol. 38, p. 2208-2212, April 2005.

[LUK 08] Lukac R., *Single-Sensor Imaging: Methods and Applications for Digital Cameras*, Image Processing Series, CRC Press, September 2008.

[MEN 06] Menon D., Andriani S., Calvagno G., "A novel technique for reducing demosaicing artifacts", *Proceedings of the XIVth European Signal Processing Conference (EUSIPCO '06)*, Florence, Italy, September 2006.

[MEN 09] Menon D., Calvagno G., "Regularization approaches to demosaicking", *IEEE Transactions on Image Processing*, vol. 18, no. 10, p. 2209-2220, October 2009.

[MOR 90] Morimura A., Uomori K., Kitamura Y., Fujioka A., Harada J., Iwamura S., Hirota M., "A digital video camera system", *IEEE Transactions on Consumer Electronics*, vol. 36, no. 4, p. 3866-3876, November 1990.

[MUK 01] Mukherjee J., Parthasarathi R., Goyal S., "Markov random field processing for color demosaicing", *Pattern Recognition Letters*, vol. 22, no. 3-4, p. 339-351, March 2001.

[RIB 08] Ribés A., Schmitt F., "Linear inverse problems in imaging", *IEEE Signal Processing Magazine*, vol. 25, no. 4, p. 84-99, July 2008.

[SOU 09] Soulez F., Thiébaut E., "Joint deconvolution and demosaicing", *Proceedings of the IEEE International Conference on Image Processing (ICIP '09)*, Cairo, Egypt, p. 145-148, November 2009.

[SPA 98] SPAULDING K.E., VOGEL R.M., SZCZEPANSKI J.R., Method and apparatus for color-correcting multi-channel signals of a digital camera, US patent 5,805,213, to Eastman Kodak Co., Patent and Trademark Office, Washington D.C., September 1998.

[TAU 00] TAUBMAN D.S., "Generalized Wiener reconstruction of images from colour sensor data using a scale invariant prior", *Proceedings of the 7th International Conference on Image Processing (ICIP 2000)*, vol. 3, Vancouver, BC, Canada, p. 801-804, September 2000.

[VAN 07] VANDEWALLE P., KRICHANE K., ALLEYSSON D., SÜSSTRUNK S., "Joint demosaicing and super-resolution imaging from a set of unregistered aliased images", *Proceedings of the 19th IST/SPIE Electronic Imaging Annual Symposium (SPIE '07)*, vol. 6502 of *Digital Photography III*, p. 65020A.1-65020A.12, San Jose, California, USA, January 2007.

[WU 04] WU X., ZHANG N., "Primary-consistent soft-decision color demosaicking for digital cameras", *IEEE Transactions on Image Processing*, vol. 13, no. 9, p. 1263-1274, September 2004.

[YAN 09] YANG Y., Contribution à l'évaluation objective de la qualité d'images couleur estimées par dématriçage, PhD thesis, University of Lille 1, Sciences et Technologies, October 2009.

[ZHA 97] ZHANG X., WANDELL B.A., "A spatial extension of CIELAB for digital color reproduction", *Journal of the Society for Information Display*, vol. 5, no. 1, p. 61-63, March 1997.

Chapter 7

Color and Image Compression

7.1. Introduction

The diversification of multimedia services, the movement toward all things digital, and the rapid development of new technologies require increasingly efficient algorithms and architectures for image, video and audio processing. With the advent of High Definition (HD) and 3D, this data becomes very large. An HD video for instance, without the audio, with a size of 1920×1080 pixels per frame, 25 frames per second, and 8 bits per pixel generates a rate of 51.4 Mbytes/sec. This bit rate is doubled when the color is considered (4:2:2 format), allowing the storage of only 43 seconds on a DVD of 4.5 Gbytes. To increase the storage and/or the transmission capacity of such data, compression is necessary.

Image compression is a process that aims to minimize the number of bits needed to represent that image while preserving its quality. The compression principle is to exploit the strong statistical redundancy of the signal. For an image, the redundancy is more spatial and is due to the correlation between neighboring pixels. For a video, in addition to the spatial redundancy inherent in each frame, the temporal redundancy

Chapter written by Abdelhakim SAADANE, Mohamed-Chaker LARABI and Christophe CHARRIER.

due to the correlation between adjacent frames is also used. Besides this redundancy, compression can also reduce the amount of information by keeping in the image only the relevant information from a visual point of view. Image compression can be lossless or lossy. In the lossless case where the process is reversible, the reduction of information is low, but the reconstructed image is numerically identical to the original image. Lossy compression, which is the subject of this chapter, can achieve a significant reduction. The quantization process that in this case allows the removal (irreversible loss) of the redundant information generates degradations in the reconstructed image. The challenge then is to find the best trade-off between the required compression ratio and the required quality of the reconstructed image.

The main compression methods are either prediction or transform-based methods. In predictive compression, the previously transmitted information is used to predict the current information. The difference between the prediction and the true value is then quantized and transmitted. For an image, the prediction is generally performed in the spatial domain. Transform-based compression projects the spatial original image into a space where the relevant information is better represented. A differential quantization of the thus obtained coefficients can then adjust the compression ratio to meet a specific quality.

In this chapter, the fundamentals of compression are recalled in section 7.2. The generic diagram of a lossy compression is first given (Figure 7.1). The predictive and transform-based compressions are then described with regard to this diagram by elaborating each of the blocks. The performance evaluation of compression algorithms is introduced through the distortion metrics in section 7.3. This briefly describes the main image and video compression standards and provides an overview of the use of the color by these standards. Section 7.4 deals with specific color compression methods.

7.2. Fundamentals of image compression

7.2.1. Introduction

The development of new image-based services is essentially related to the development of image compression algorithms. These algorithms enable the reduction of the number of bits needed to represent the image, allowing either its storage or its transmission with minimal resources in terms of bandwidth. The generic block diagram of a compression algorithm is given in Figure 7.1. The RGB components of the original color image are provided by the CCD sensors of the acquisition camera. A color transformation is used to project the image in the appropriate color space. To account for the difference in sensitivity of the human visual system (HVS) relative to the obtained color components, a sub-sampling is performed. The redundancy analysis is then considered through the analysis block to allow the next step to finely quantize only the relevant information. The entropy encoding can be incorporated before the generation of the final compressed stream.

Figure 7.1. *Generic block diagram of a compression algorithm*

7.2.2. *Color transformation*

Acquisition, restoration and display systems are often equipped with RGB input and/or output. Therefore, the RGB space constitutes the basic color space. However, it remains unsuitable for some applications of image processing. In compression, color transformations are necessary to avoid the strong correlation that exists between the different components R, G and B: of about 0.78 for B-R, 0.98 for R-G, and 0.94 for G-B [SAN 98]. The principle of these transformations is to project the original image onto a color space of Luminance-Chrominance type where the information (energy) is mainly concentrated in the luminance component. The standard color spaces commonly used in compression are YUV, YCbCr, CIEL*a*b* and CIEL*u*v*. In the YUV space, a color is represented by the combination of the luminance component Y and two color components U and V. The components Y, U and V are obtained from the R, G and B (after a gamma correction) by the following matrix transformation [LUK 07]:

$$\begin{bmatrix} Y \\ U \\ V \end{bmatrix} = \begin{bmatrix} 0.299 & 0.587 & 0.114 \\ -0.147 & -0.289 & 0.436 \\ 0.615 & -0.515 & -0.100 \end{bmatrix} \begin{bmatrix} R \\ G \\ B \end{bmatrix}$$

The YCbCr space is a variant of the YUV space and is also obtained by the following simple linear transformation [SAN 98]:

$$\begin{bmatrix} Y \\ Cb \\ Cr \end{bmatrix} = \begin{bmatrix} 0.299 & 0.587 & 0.114 \\ -0.168 & -0.332 & 0.5 \\ 0.5 & -0.418 & -0.082 \end{bmatrix} \begin{bmatrix} R \\ G \\ B \end{bmatrix}$$

Thus defined, the components Cr and Cb denote a weighted difference between the luminance component Y and respectively the red and blue component:

$$Cb = 0.564 \, (B - Y)$$

$$Cr = 0.713 \, (R - Y)$$

The recommendation [ITU 95] requires a luminance ranging between 16 and 235 and values ranging between 16 and 240 for the chrominance components. The last two spaces L*a*b* and L*u*v* are the standards of the CIE (International Commission on Illumination) and have the characteristic of being perceptually uniform. They are thus able to properly quantize the difference between two colors. In these spaces, a color is represented, as the HVS would perform, by the perceived brightness L* and a double antagonism red-green and yellow-blue (see [PLA 00] for more details on the calculation of the different components). These spaces are computed from the XYZ space of the CIE and assume the control of a white reference.

7.2.3. Color sampling formats

In addition to reducing the correlation between components induced by color transformations, the color spaces also exploit the low sensitivity of HVS to changes in color to sub-sample the color components. This sub-sampling allows a reduction in the amount of useful information and thus contributes to the performance of the compression algorithm. When the sub-sampling is of order 2 in the horizontal direction (one column over two), we will talk of format 4:2:2. This format indicates that for four samples of the luminance component, there are two samples for each of the two chrominance components. To further reduce the bit rate, the 4:1:1 format uses a sub-sample of order 4 of the chrominance components in the horizontal direction (one column over four). Depending on the applications, the 4:2:0 format is also used. For this format, the sub-sampling is of the order of two in each of the horizontal and vertical directions (one line over two and one column over two by interlacing). The 4:4:4 format is used by applications that require an image signal of high quality.

7.2.4. Redundancy analysis

The analysis block aims to analyze the input image signal to better describe, and therefore better exploit, the redundancy that characterizes it. Compression algorithms differ in the way they describe this redundancy. Two approaches are generally used. The first, that of prediction-based algorithms, uses the spatial redundancy between neighboring pixels of an image. The second, that of the transform-based algorithms, exploits the ability that some orthogonal transforms have, to focus relevant information in a limited number of coefficients. These two approaches are briefly described here.

7.2.4.1. Predictive compression

Predictive compression plays an important role in the coding standards of still images (JPEG in lossless mode) and video (MPEG-1, MPEG-2, H.264 for intra-frame encoding). The basic principle states that a current pixel can be predicted, given the correlation, from previous neighboring pixels with a prediction error of entropy lower than that of the original image. The spatial prediction exploits the DPCM (Differential Pulse Code Modulation) algorithm. The encoder in this case starts by calculating the prediction of the current pixel. This prediction uses a combination, that can be linear or not, weighted or not, of all or some of the previous neighboring pixels that have already been encoded. The prediction error, which results from the difference between the amplitude of the current pixel and that of the predicted pixel, is then quantized and conveyed. This is the only error that affects the reconstructed image. The predictor locally used by the encoder is identical to that used by the decoder. So it uses the same combination as that of the encoder to predict the value of the current pixel from the adjacent pixels that have already been rebuilt. The current pixel is reconstructed by summing the predicted value and the received prediction error. The order of the predictor is given by the number of reconstructed pixels used by the prediction. The neighboring pixels of the current pixel belonging to the previous line of the image can also be used by the prediction. The DPCM efficiency can be improved by adapting the quantization and/or the prediction depending on the local statistics of the image to be compressed. The predictive compression remains easy to implement and the achieved compression ratios are interesting for signals with low or medium spatial and/or time variations.

7.2.4.2. Transform based compression

The principle of the transform-based approach is to project the original image data into a space where the relevant information is found concentrated in a limited number of coefficients with high values. A rough quantization of the other coefficients will then allow us to compress the image without affecting its quality. The choice of these often orthogonal and invertible transforms depends on their computational complexity. These transforms can be applied independently to the luminance component and to the two chrominance components. The transforms used by most coding standards tend to fall into two classes: block-based and image-based.

The first or the Karhunen-Loeve transform (KLT) and the DCT transform (Discrete Cosine Transform) considers the image as a set of blocks of N*N size, adjacent and independent. The transform is applied to each block and the obtained coefficients are independently quantized from coefficients of the other blocks. The quantization of independent blocks results in "block effects", which are undesirable, in the reconstructed images. These effects are the main drawback of these methods while their advantage lies in the low computational complexity induced by the use of blocks of small size.

The image-based transforms focus on the whole image. The discrete wavelet transform (DWT), for instance, which is part of these transforms, decomposes the image into different sub-bands and at different levels of resolution. The advantage of such decomposition is that the quantization process that follows will be adapted to the statistical and visual characteristics of each sub-band. The use of the entire image as the base unit requires a lot of resources during the implementation of these transforms. The gain in compression at low bit rates, as evidenced by the comparison of the standards JPEG (DCT-based) and JPEG2000 (DWT-based), remains interesting however.

7.2.5. *Quantization*

Quantization in the compression process is a significant step, since the compression efficiency depends on the accuracy of that step.

7.2.5.1. *Basics of quantization*

The scalar quantization (SQ) functions permit the conversion of the values of a physical quantity into a finite set of representatives (such as the one that can be performed when a real value is converted into an integer value). The principle is then to divide the dynamic range of the physical quantity into a finite number of intervals, then to assign to all the values of the same interval a unique value. Mathematically, a scalar quantizer can be represented by the relation $y = Q(x)$ where $Q(.)$ denotes the quantization function. Consequently, any k-levels scalar quantizer is specified by k+1 decision thresholds $(q_0, q_1..., q_k)$ and k output levels $(y_1, y_2..., y_k)$. Thus, any sample of a physical quantity having a value ranging between the bounds q_{i-1} and q_i will be assigned a quantization value y_i. The quantization function can then be formulated as follows:

$$Q(u) = y_i \quad \forall q_{i-1} \le u < q_i, \quad i \in [1, 2, ..., k]$$

In the case of the use of uniform quantization functions, the quantization thresholds are evenly spaced, and the quantization values q_i are generally in the middle of the quantization intervals. This type of uniform quantization is optimal if the random variable to be quantized is distributed uniformly in each quantization interval $\left[q_{i-1}, q_i\right]$, $\forall i \in [1, 2, ..., k]$. In this case, the quantization error in the L1 $E[(Q(x) - x)]$ or L2 $E\left[(Q(x) - x)^2\right]$ norm is minimal. If the $L2$ norm is used, this is then called the Mean Squared Error Quantizer (MSQE). However, when images are quantized, whether they are color or not, the uniform distribution condition is seldom met and as a result a uniform quantization can only be optimal in the sense of quantization error in the $L1$ or $L2$ norm. In this case, it is then necessary to define a non-uniform quantization function, so as to have an optimal quantization in the end.

7.2.5.2. *The optimal quantization*

The search for an optimal quantizer was pioneered by Lloyd [LLO 82] in the mid-50s, although the results were published only in 1982. However, the first optimization results of the quantizer have been published in 1960 by Max [MAX 60]. Therefore, to avoid any kind of controversy about the authorship of the first optimization scheme of the quantizer, we talk of the Lloyd-Max quantization technique.

The optimal quantizer is the one that minimizes, for a set of values of a given physical quantity X and under the condition of a fixed maximum entropy, the average of the reconstruction error induced by quantization noises. The reconstruction levels are then distributed according to the probability density of the variable to quantize, and no longer uniformly.

The encoding part of the quantizer (the partition) should therefore be optimal according to the decoding part (the best representatives) and vice versa. The necessary condition that meets the first constraint is called the nearest neighbor condition and the second condition is commonly known as the centroid condition (which leads to the centroid in case of the measurement of the quantization error in the L2 norm).

These two conditions, used by the Lloyd-Max algorithm, are necessary but not sufficient, except in the case of a Gaussian variable. The quantizer adapts to the source (stationary and ergodic) by altering the quantization levels and the decision thresholds iteratively until convergence of the estimated quantization error. In fact, the Lloyd-Max algorithm leads to the best scalar quantizer that can be built for a fixed flow rate and a given distribution assuming that the achieved distortion is a global minimum, which is reached when the distribution is a concave log function [GER 78]. The optimization for a probability distribution known in advance can be replaced by an optimization from a statistical database.

Gersho *et al.* [GER 92] have shown that a non-uniform quantizer is equivalent to a uniform scalar quantizer preceded by a nonlinear transformation. Therefore, it is possible to perform a color transformation of the data in a perceptual color space (of CIE Lab, YCbCr, etc. type) and then apply a uniform quantization based on a color distance metric such as $\Delta E94$ or $\Delta E2000$ type. This will allow us to include the sensitivity of the human visual system to color degradations.

7.2.5.3. *The vector quantization*

The quantization step is to allocate a fixed number of representatives in a space of arbitrary dimension. This number depends mainly on the flow rate allocated to the quantizer. The efficiency of the quantizer is then measured using a quantization error that should be as low as possible to ensure a reconstruction of the original signal as accurately as possible. The vector quantization (VQ) is an extension of the scalar quantization to the multidimensional case. The sample x_i is no longer scalar (1-D), but vector (n-D). The VQ can be regarded as the result of two operations: encoding and decoding, as described in Figure 7.2. The encoder allows us to switch from a representative X of a space of dimension k R^k to a value i associated with a representative y_i of a finite subset of R^k which will be called C. This denotes the dictionary of the VQ. This subset C contains a finite number of vectors of dimension k and these vectors are called code vectors. Once all the representatives of the space R^k are processed by the encoder, an index list L is issued. The decoder in turn associates with each value i of L a representative of C. After the processing of all the data contained in L, the approximated signal is reconstructed. The key element of the success of a vector quantization undoubtedly passes through the construction quality of the dictionary C. In the case of SQ, it was shown that the optimal quantizer was obtained by the Lloyd-Max algorithm. Its vector counterpart is the K-means algorithm, also known as the Linde, Buzo and Gray (LBG) algorithm or the generalized Lloyd-Max algorithm [LIN 80].

Therefore, at the microscopic level for the interpretation of data, the case of the color may be seen as an extension of the scalar case

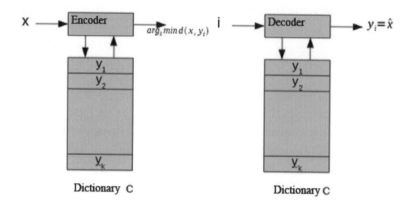

Figure 7.2. *Diagram of the encoder and decoder for the VQ*

(gray level) to the vector case since a color can be interpreted as a vector data. A second level of interpretation may be located at the macroscopic level. A given color will be seen as indivisible atomic data, and indeed the vector interpretation will be performed at the level of color data clustering. However, the problem related to the use of a color distance metric arises, depending on the analysis level that is considered.

7.2.6. *Distortion metric*

As discussed previously, the notion of a distortion metric is intrinsic to quantization techniques, whether they are of scalar or vector type. In fact, the distortion metric ultimately allows us to calculate the quality of the quantizer. The problem is that a unique distortion metric does not exist; everything depends on the data that is handled and the sought distortion type.

Whereas the use of an L_1 (known as Manhattan distance) L_2 (also referred to as Euclidean distance) or L_∞ (known as max distance) norm-based distortion metric is simple to implement in the case of scalar quantization, in the case of vector quantization, this concept of a distortion metric reaches a high degree of complexity.

In fact, in this case, the scalars are no longer compared but the vectors, that is, sets of scalar data are compared. Each of these sets can be considered a class. Therefore, applying a distortion metric in the case of scalar quantization amounts to measuring the distance between the elements of two classes. Thus we find the following metrics:

– of the nearest neighbor;

– of the maximum diameter;

– of the average distance;

– of the distance between the centers of gravity;

– of the Ward distance;

– etc.

However, it should be noted that the distortion metric based on the nearest neighbor is most commonly used for quantization. From this metric, the value of the PSNR (Peak Signal-to-Noise Ratio) is calculated, which provides an interpretation of the image quality obtained after compression. In fact, an image with a PSNR value greater than 30 dB is usually considered an image of good visual quality. This metric, however, is criticized by the scientific community. For more information on the concept of image quality, the reader may refer to Chapter 9. As part of the color and the scalar quantization, it is necessary to use a color-based distortion metric, such as the one defined by the $\Delta E94$ or $\Delta E2000$ metric (defined in Chapter 9). During the application of the vector quantization to color data, it becomes more complicated. In this case, it is necessary to define a distance metric between sets of color data. One solution is to extend one of the similarity metrics defined above to colorimetry. Therefore, the complexity of vector quantization algorithms applied to color is increased.

7.2.7. *Conclusion*

The fundamentals of image compression are presented in this section. The pre-processing associated with color imaging includes a color transformation and a sub-sampling. The color transformation is to project the input image from the RGB space in which it is usually represented, into a space where the components are supposed to be completely uncorrelated. The sub-sampling that follows aims to exploit the low sensitivity of HVS to changes in color by representing the color components in an appropriate format. The main color spaces and the main sampling formats used by this pre-processing are given. The principle and the basic operation of predictive compression and transform-based compression, which represent the two main approaches of image compression, are described briefly to focus more on quantization. In fact, quantization represents the most crucial step since the quality of the compression scheme depends on the quality of this step. The most common metrics for the measurement of the distortion generated by the quantization process are also given for both grayscale and color images.

7.3. Compression standards and color

7.3.1. *Introduction*

Different study groups belonging to both the ISO (International Organization for Standardization) and ITU (International Telecommunication Union) are responsible for the development and standardization of compression algorithms and the revision of adopted standards. JPEG [ISO 92] and JPEG2000 [ISO 00] are the two standards for monochrome and color still image compression derived from JPEG (Joint Photographic Experts Group). MPEG-1 [ISO 93] and MPEG-2 [ISO 95] are the standards for audio and video encoding used for the communication and storage of digital videos. These standards were developed by MPEG (Moving Picture Experts Group), which is a working group from ISO. VCEG (Video Coding Experts Group) is a working group from ITU, which has adopted the H.261 [ITU 93a] and H.263 [ITU 98] standards widely used in video telephony. JVT (Joint Video Team) is the collaboration framework between VCEG and MPEG that enabled the finalization and adoption of the latest video compression standard i.e. H.264/MPEG-4 Part 10 [ISO 03]. The purpose of this section is to briefly cover these standards. The processing of the color, which remains marginal for these standards, but which constitutes the guiding principle of this book, will also be addressed.

7.3.2. *Still image compression standards*

7.3.2.1. *JPEG*

The JPEG compression standard also addresses the typical compression scheme presented in the previous section. Thus, a transformation step of the image is firstly applied, followed by a quantization step. In the case of a color image, the three color planes are assumed to be independent. Each plane is processed independently from the other two according to the scheme applied to grayscale images. To obtain better results, a transformation of RGB pixels can be performed in advance so that a luminance plane and two chromatic planes are obtained.

In this standard, the images are divided into blocks of size 8×8 pixels, on which the transformation is applied, followed by the quantization step of the transformed coefficients.

Transformation

The transformation step is based on the (DCT) transform, which is similar to that by Fourier, except that the decomposition base uses only cosines. If $f(u, v, k)$ denotes the value of the transformed coefficient of block k at the coordinates (u, v) then:

$$f(u, v, k) = \frac{1}{4} C(u) C(v) \sum_{i=0}^{7} \sum_{j=0}^{7} \cos\left(\frac{(2i+1)\,u\pi}{16}\right)$$

$$\cos\left(\frac{(2j+1)\,v\pi}{16}\right) x(i, j, k)$$

with:

$$\begin{cases} C(x) = \frac{1}{\sqrt{2}} & \text{for } x = 0 \\ C(x) = 1 & \text{for } x \in [1, 7] \end{cases}$$

where $x(i, j, k)$ denotes the level of block k of the original image at the coordinates i and j. In the case of a block of size 8×8, the obtained 64 basis functions are shown in Figure 7.3. The low frequencies are located in the upper-left corner. The more one moves toward the lower-right corner, the more the frequencies increase.

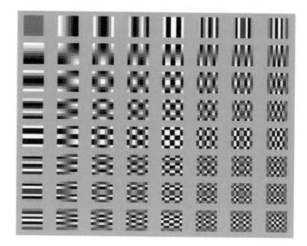

Figure 7.3. *The 64 basis vectors of the DCT*

Quantization

Once the 64 coefficients $f(u, v)$ are obtained, a scalar quantization should be performed. The aim is then to retain only the coefficients that are relevant according to predefined criteria. This is called a quantization matrix. It contains the 64 quantization steps used according to the sensitivity of the HVS to the frequencies, since it is commonly admitted that it acts as a low-pass filter. In addition, the definition of these coefficients depends on several parameters such as the type of image, the image content, and the nature of the color primaries. The user is often asked to define his own matrices according to experimental procedures, and mainly according to the objective. The quantized DCT coefficients are given by the following equation:

$$\hat{f}(u, v, k) = round\ (f\ (u, v, k)\ /q\ (u, v))$$

where round() denotes a quantization to the nearest integer and $q(u, v)$, the coefficient of the quantization matrix at the index (u, v). The quantization error is then given by:

$$e\ (u, v, k) = f\ (u, v, k) - \hat{f}\ (u, v, k)\ .q\ (u, v)$$

7.3.2.2. JPEG2000

The call for proposals for the novel compression format of the third millennium was launched in March 1997. Part 1, known as the JPEG2000 kernel, was published as an international standard at the NewOrleans meeting in December 2000. This new standard aims to offer new features allowing us to meet a growing demand, namely:

– obtain compression performance higher than its predecessor JPEG, especially for very low bit rates;

– organize the compressed file in several ways, especially according to the required resolution or the reconstruction quality;

– have an efficient lossless compression mode;

– provide the ability to encode regions of an image with better quality than others.

Several interesting papers have been published to describe the new JPEG2000 standard. The reader could refer to that of Rabbani and Joshi [RAB 01] or to the book of Taubman and Marcellin [TAU 01].

Encoding and decoding chain JPEG2000

The encoding and decoding of an image in JPEG2000 format take place in five steps (see Figure 7.4): the three classical steps in image compression (Transformations, Quantization and Entropy coding), a color transform step allowing us to improve the encoding efficiency and a final step of rate allocation.

Figure 7.4. *Diagram of the encoding chain of JPEG2000 algorithm*

Image preprocessing

In the JPEG2000 standard, each image is divided into a set of tiles (rectangular blocks) without overlapping. The purpose of this operation is to reduce the complexity of the algorithm for images of very large sizes, but also to facilitate navigation within such images. These square tiles are in size (64×64) or (128×128), for instance. As with the JPEG algorithm that differentially encodes the DC coefficient (first coefficient) of each block (encoding of the difference between the DC of the current block and that of the previous block), the algorithm removes the mean value of the image prior to transformation. The low-frequency coefficients can thus be encoded on a smaller number of bits. This step also includes a transformation of the RGB color space into the YCbCr space. This transformation is justified because the chromatic degradations have a smaller effect on the image than the achromatic degradations and then a sub-sampling of higher order is for chromatic components.

Discrete wavelet transform

The discrete wavelet transform (DWT) comes from the multi resolution analysis that was developed by Mallat and Meyer. The purpose of this theory is to decompose a signal by using different resolutions leading to a decorrelation of the information that it contains. The calculation of an image at a lower resolution is done by convolution with 2D separable filters. The low-pass $h(k)$ and high-pass $g(k)$ filters are applied independently on the rows and on the columns. The output of these filters can be written as follows:

$$x_i^L(n) = \sum_k h(2n - k) x_{i-1}(k)$$

$$x_i^H(n) = \sum_k g(2n - k) x_{i-1}(k)$$

where $x_i^L(n)$ and $x_i^H(n)$ denote, respectively, the low and high frequency components at the resolution i. The low resolutions denote the rough shape of the signal while the high resolution encodes the details of the signal. For 2D signals such as images, topological properties (directions, layout of the content) are therefore preserved after the transformation.

JPEG2000 performs a discrete wavelet decomposition on several levels, specified up to five. This transform can be configured to be lossy (filter 9/7 with non-integer or of Daubechies coefficients) or lossless (filter 5/3 with integer coefficients). The input pixels have a maximum dynamic of 12 bits for lossless compression and 10 bits otherwise.

Sub-band quantization

Figure 7.5 shows a decomposition into sub-bands using the DWT. The sub-bands of higher resolutions have a relatively low content while the sub-bands of low frequencies are much richer. JPEG2000 adopts a linear quantization for each sub-band. The used quantization step is however much lower for the low frequency sub-bands.

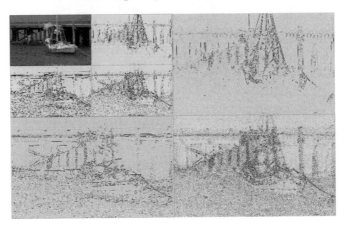

Figure 7.5. *Wavelet decomposition (3 levels)*

Sub-band encoding

The encoding algorithm of each sub-band encodes the quantization indices per plane and not per symbol. This algorithm therefore generates bit planes and provides a progressive flow both in resolution and quality. The important information (which is the most significant bit) is encoded first while the encoding of details (which are the least significant bits) comes after.

Encoding per regions of interest

The JPEG2000 algorithm also allows us to encode different regions of the image with different qualities. This feature is implemented by increasing the number of the most significant bits of the coefficients belonging to a region of interest. Due to the orientation of the coding, these coefficients will be primarily encoded. There are two different ways to encode a region of interest (Figure 7.6):

Figure 7.6. *Encoding of region of interest (ROI) of an image*

– through the insertion of a shape mask in the compressed file;

– through the doubling of the number of bits belonging to regions of interest.

Extension of JPEG2000 to digital cinema

Digital cinema has captured the attention of most researchers and industrialists. It describes the packaging, distribution, and projection of animated sequences in a digital format (Figure 7.7). The DCI (Digital Cinema Initiatives) has produced specifications for the range of digital cinema to ensure the quality, safety, and interoperability.

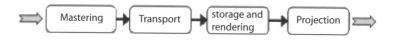

Figure 7.7. *Digital cinema system*

One of the major decisions of the DCI was the selection of JPEG2000 as the reference encoder of digital cinema. This is justified because a movie is an artistic work that should not be subjected to the prediction laws of standard video encoders. Of course, some changes were performed to suit the nature of the media and meet the requirements of both film fans and producers. Some of the key points of the cinema profile of JPEG2000 are as follows:

– the decoding of each color component in 12 bits/pixel and without spatial sub-sampling;

– the use of the irreversible wavelet transform 9/7 and the implementation of the inverse wavelet transform with at least 16 bits of precision;

– the tiles are not allowed. In other words, the entire image should be encoded as a single tile;

– the maximum number of levels of wavelet decomposition is 5 for a 2K content and 6 for a 4K content. 2K and 4K are the standard resolutions for digital cinema equal to 2048×1080 and 4096×2160, respectively. In addition, the number of decomposition is at least 1 for a 4K content so that the 2K image can be extracted using the scalability of JPEG2000;

– the color components of an image should have the same number of wavelet decomposition levels;

– the maximum bit rate is set to 250 Mbit/s irrespective of the content: 2K, 4K, stereoscopic.

In terms of color, the great novelty of digital cinema is the use of the space X'Y'Z' throughout the entire chain to ensure an optimal rendering and to be able to perform adjustments relative to the reference projector (Figure 7.8). The main difference between XYZ (CIE tristimulus values) and X'Y'Z' (values of the encoded Distribution Master "DCDM") comes from the normalization of the values of the latter over 12-bit (0-4095) on which a nonlinear transfer function (Gamma) of 1/2.6 is applied.

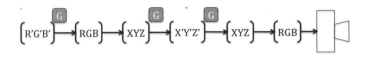

Figure 7.8. *Encoding of the color in digital cinema. The G reflects the application of a gamma correction of 2.6*

7.3.3. *Video compression standards*

The first video compression algorithms were developed in the 1950s. The first application dates back to 1960, when a digital videophone was developed. It is from the 1970s that the development of videoconferencing fully began. At the same time, users became interested in higher quality videos. Given the flood of computer solutions related to video compression, standardization activities emerged in the early 1980's. These activities were initiated by the CCITT (Consultative Committee for International Telegraph and Telephone), whose successor is the *International Telecommunication Union Telecommunication Standardization Sector* (ITU-T). Then followed the formation of the CCIR (Consultative Committee for International Radio), which later became ITU-R, ISO (International Organization for Standardization), and IEC (International Electrotechnical Commission). All these agencies coordinate the standardization works of compression standards. In what follows, only the major standards are described in the chronological order of their commissioning.

7.3.3.1. *H.210*

In the 1980s, a first codec (*enCOder/DECoder*) was developed by the COST (Pan-European Cooperation in Science and Technology) under the name Project 211 and published by the CCITT in 1984 under the H.210 standard. This standard was based on the DPCM (Differential Pulse Code Modulation) technique. The bit rate that can reach the codec is 2 Mbit/s. However, the resulting video quality was not satisfactory and only the grayscale images were considered. Nevertheless, this standard is the origin of the standards that appeared later, in particular its direct successor the H.261.

7.3.3.2. *H.261*

The ITU H.261 [ITU 93a] standard was specifically developed for video conferencing. It combines the use of DCT and inter-frame motion compensation. It was designed to operate with bit rates of multiples of 64 Kbit/s. That is why this standard is also referred to as the codec p. 64 Kbit/s (with p varying from 1 to 30). Finally, the bit rate is optimal for ISDN (Integrated Service Digital Networks) networks, for which this video codec was originally designed.

The encoder operates on non-interlaced images at a rate of 30 frames/s. Color images are first converted to an opponent color space (Y, Cb, Cr). The resulting components are then processed independently and sub-sampled to the 4:2:2 format. The standard was ratified in 1989. It was notably popularized by the game console Sony Playstation, which fully integrated it into its data decompression engine.

7.3.3.3. *MPEG-1*

MPEG-1 is a lossy compression standard for video and audio signals. It was designed to achieve a compression of digital video in VHS quality as well as audio CDs to achieve a bit rate of 1.5 Mbit/s without excessive quality loss. This bit rate is used for video CDs as well as for videos broadcasting by cable or satellite. Nowadays, MPEG-1 has become the audio/video compression format around the world, and is actually used in many products and technologies. The most famous part of the MPEG-1 standard is the MP3 audio format.

Like the H.261 format, the color image undergoes a color transformation toward the YCbCr space before being sampled to the 4:2:0 format (see section 7.2.3). Each of the three obtained plans is processed independently.

7.3.3.4. *MPEG-2*

MPEG-2 is the second generation standard (1994), from the Moving Picture Experts Group, that follows MPEG-1. MPEG-2 defines the compression aspects of both the image and the audio as well as their transport through the networks for digital television. MPEG-2 allows us to encode the video at bit rates ranging from 4 to 9 Mbit/s. This video standard is used for DVD and SVCD with different image resolutions. This has also been used in digital television broadcasting by satellite, cable, telecommunication or terrestrial network (DTT) since the late 1990s. MPEG-2 allows the use of color images sampled according to the format 4:4:4, 4:2:2, and 4:1:1 in addition to 4:2:0 of the MPEG-1. Moreover, the use of CIF and QCIF image formats is allowed. This compression standard is already used to broadcast programs for current channels through the DTT in France.

7.3.3.5. *H.263*

The H.263 [ITU 93b] standard was defined in the second half of 1990 to meet the requirements of video transmission on very low bit rates networks, such as applications of video telephony via the switched telephone network (H.324 video teleconferencing). It was then incorporated into the protocols of videoconferencing over IP (H.323).

The encoding algorithms are similar to those used by its predecessors (H.261, MPEG-1, and MPEG-2). This codec formed the basis for the MPEG-4 video codec.

The H.263+ [ITU 98] standard is version 2 of the H.263 standard. It was introduced in February 1998 to expand the application areas by being more flexible and improving the encoding efficiency, while remaining compatible with version 1 (the H.263 standard). This standard includes 12 new features such as scalability (temporal, spatial, quality) dynamic change of resolution, etc. The H.263++ [ITU 00] standard was standardized in the late 2000s and is considered as version 3 of the H.263 standard. It includes four new features.

Like its predecessors, color images are encoded as one luminance component and two color difference components (Y, Cb, and Cr). The Cb and Cr components are then subsampled [ITU 93b].

7.3.3.6. *MPEG-4*

The MPEG-4 [ISO 98] standard consists of a set of audio and video encoders allowing us to achieve bit rates ranging from 4800 bits/s to about 4 Mbits/s. This standard uses many features of its predecessors (MPEG-1 and MPEG-2) while incorporating new features such as the extended VRML (*Virtual Reality Modeling Language*), which is a language for describing virtual worlds in 3D, media for 3D presentations, object-oriented composite files (including audio, video, and VRML objects), media for Digital Rights Management and various types of interactivity.

This is thus well recognized as the standard dedicated to new media applications such as downloading and streaming on the Internet, mobile multimedia, digital radio, video games, television, and high definition media. The MPEG-4 video codec accepts only videos of QCIF (176×144 pixels) or CIF (352×288 pixels) format and the sampling format 4:2:0.

7.3.3.7. *H.264*

The H.264 standard was jointly developed by VCEG (Video Coding Experts Group) and MPEG to obtain an encoder dedicated to high-definition video. This is also known as H.264/AVC (Advanced Video Coding), which refers to Part 10 of the MPEG-4 standard. The H.264 codec achieves significant compression performance for a quality identical to that provided by the MPEG-4 or H.263 [SUL 01].

One of the fundamental concepts of the H.264 standard is the separation of the design into two distinct layers, namely the video encoding and the network adaptation. The first layer is dedicated to the representation of the video content and to its encoding in an efficient way, while the second layer manages the packaging of data appropriately encoded for its transmission over the network [ITU 01].

Following the first version of the standard, some extensions have been developed and are known as *Fidelity Range Extensions* (FREXt). They allow us to support an increased quantization accuracy (addition of 10-bit and 12-bit encoding) and have a better definition of the chrominance (4:2:2 and 4:4:4 sampling formats).

7.3.4. *New trends in compression*

Recently, the compression and image coding community found itself facing a serious problem: the difficulty of defining a new compression scheme that is both less complex and that provides a significant improvement in quality compared to current standards. Despite the quality of its results, JPEG2000 did not spread as the JPEG (ISO) committee hoped because of the complexity of its structure. Also, the abundance of physical memory at very low economic cost has reinforced the trend since there is no longer a need to strongly compress images on a camera equipped with a sensor of several million pixels.

To address the concerns of image industrials, the JPEG committee has launched a group called AIC (*Advanced Image Coding*). The AIC aims at the creation of the next-decade encoder that can adapt to new methods of acquisition such as the HDR (*High Dynamic Range*), the stereoscopic and the multi-view. The AIC group also seeks to define a reliable evaluation methodology ensuring technology choices. Thus, recommendations are being prepared within the JPEG committee for quality assessment and the performance metric. During calls for technologies, the committee noted a strong trend toward application-oriented coding. Among the targeted applications, we find the medical application opens itself slowly to lossy compression even if the aim is long-term storage and not diagnosis. Digital photography presents new problems such as the support of images derived from the sensor (CFA - *Color Filter Array*). This requires the deportation of demosaicing procedures at the user level instead of performing it on the mobile device. Security applications (video surveillance, border surveillance, and criminal evidence) are also waiting for an encoder that takes into account their specificities such as the maximization of DRI criteria (Detection, Recognition, Identification). Nowadays, among future directions, we can mention the approaches based on new x-lets transforms such as the quaternionic wavelets [SOU 10] or the use of bio-inspired models [MAS 08, BEN 10].

7.3.5. *Conclusion*

Compression standards have been presented in this section. Standards dedicated to still images have been briefly described. Those dedicated to video have been presented in chronological order of their commissioning, specifying the applications for which they have been developed. Color processing, which remains marginal for these standards, has been specified each time. This processing is usually limited to a color transformation and a spatial sub-sampling of the color components in a format that varies from one standard to another. The new trends in compression presage the development of more application-oriented encoding and the integration of quality metrics for performance assessment. In this perspective, color, through perceptual models, would stimulate the development of innovative approaches.

7.4. Color image compression

7.4.1. *Introduction*

The development of color image compression has for long relied on that of the compression of grayscale images since the methods proposed in the latter case were simply applied to each component of the color image. The so-called color approaches have for a long time been limited, on the one hand, to the use of luminance and chrominance representation to decorrelate the input R, G, B components and, on the other hand, to the sub-sampling that was performed to account for the low sensitivity of the HVS to chrominance components. The search for more efficient methods for color image compression, coupled with the rapid development of effective vision models having a reduced complexity, has led to various proposals. A rough classification of these methods enables us to distinguish two classes: those that seek to exploit the color inter-components correlation both in the spatial and in a transformed domain (which will be qualified as statistical methods) and those that seek to integrate models and/or certain features of the HVS both in the analysis process and in that of the quantization (which will be qualified as perceptual methods). This section presents some interesting contributions in both these classes.

7.4.2. *Statistical compression*

The use of the statistical characteristics of signals for their compression has obviously been the subject of several studies and leads to different encoders: EZW (*Embedded Zerotree Wavelet*) [SHA 93] and SPIHT (*Set Partitioning in Hierarchical Trees*) [SAI 96]. The extension of these algorithms to color, Color-EZW [SHE 97] and Color-SPIHT [KAS 03], was done by exploiting the correlation between color components. In general, statistical color compression is performed according to two orientations. The first one employs a decorrelation-based approach while the second, instead of decorrelating, exploits the existing correlation between the color primaries. The first orientation, adopted by the coding standards for still images such as JPEG and JPEG2000, seeks to convert the RGB representation to a representation where the components would be, in the ideal case, totally uncorrelated in order to independently encode them. Studies conducted in this context focus essentially on the choice of color transformation to apply. This is the case of [NAD 99] where three color spaces are compared in the context of a JPEG2000 encoder. For each of these spaces, the contrast sensitivity function is measured and integrated to the encoder. Another example is given in [GER 07b] where a distortion rate model is used to determine the optimal color components for compression. The encoder that combines the obtained color components and an adaptive quantization that is defined, is compared to the JPEG encoder. Besides an improvement in subjective visual quality of the reconstructed images, the proposed encoder exhibits on average a higher PSNR of 1.24 dB.

The use of the correlation between color components, which represents the second orientation, is an interesting way for encoding color images. In the wavelet domain, for instance, this correlation is widely discussed in [SAN 06]. The objectives are to specify the kind of correlation, to clarify its importance, and to define a context for the encoding of the chrominance components. Five test images are used. The RGB components first undergo JPEG2000 color transformation. The Luminance-Chrominance resulting components are then projected into the wavelet domain through the Daubechies 9/7 filters. The analysis is finally performed on the basis of the conditional probability of emergence of significant chrominance coefficients at different points compared to the significant luminance coefficients. It follows from this analysis that the corresponding 3×3 neighborhood of the luminance coefficients can be used for the encoding of the chrominance components. The use of this correlation between color components allows an average reduction of bit rate ranging between 5% and 15% and a PSNR higher than that displayed by the JPEG2000 encoder. The correlation between the input RGB components is used in [GOF 02, KOT 90, YAM 84] to interpolate two colors from a base component color (usually the green). This approach is also implemented in [ROT 07] with the particularity of using only the coefficients of the interpolation to encode the color information. The target is to exploit both the correlation between color components and a representation of the image in contour/texture. Then, the interesting proposed approach is to generate one luminance component from the RGB components. This will only serve as the region segmentation of the image. The advantage of this segmentation is to use, in addition to the inter-component correlation, the localized spatial correlation between pixels of the same region. The pixels belonging to the borders of the region and representing the contours are encoded separately (the differences in the directions of the contours are encoded by a Huffman coding table). The texture information is represented by the pixels located inside the regions. For each of these regions, the base color is modeled by a two-dimensional polynomial function and the "subordinate" colors are determined by a polynomial expansion of the base color:

$$R = r_1 + r_2 G \quad \text{and} \quad B = b_1 + b_2 G$$

The coefficients of the polynomial function and the polynomial expansion of each region are finally quantized and transmitted. This new algorithm allows us to display performances (compression ratio and PSNR) higher than those of the JPEG.

An interesting variant of the Roterman and Porat algorithm [ROT 07] is given in [GER 07a]. In this algorithm, the RGB components eventually undergo (the step is optional) a color transformation. A block DCT transformation is applied to each component. The correlation between the components is exploited throughout the calculation of the subordinate components by means, again, of a polynomial expansion of the color for each DCT sub-band. The coefficients of this expansion (2 coefficients per subordinate color), determined by minimizing the mean square error, are quantized and integrated into the compressed data. The rate-distortion theory is then used to optimize the bit allocation algorithm for each sub-band and to determine, where appropriate, the optimal color transform to be applied before encoding. The optimization uses the approximation errors that represent the difference between the true value color and the interpolated value of that color. These approximation errors are linearly quantized and also transmitted. The final step includes an entropy encoding similar to that used by JPEG. The two versions of this correlation-based algorithm, integrating a Laplacian probability model for the DCT coefficients (for a lower computational complexity and a better rate distortion ratio) and a subsampling of the two subordinated colors, yield better performance when they are compared to the decorrelation-based approach of JPEG: PSNR and PSPNR gains

(Peak Signal to Perceptible Noise Ratio) of 2 and 3 dB, respectively. The same approach is also included and compared with JPEG2000. The processing of the base color component in the case of JPEG2000 is identical to that of the luminance while the correlation is exploited for the subordinate colors. Again, the correlation-based approach shows greater performance than that of JPEG2000 and also generates fewer color artifacts at low rates.

7.4.3. Perception-based compression

The perceptual approach, like the statistical approach described above, initially focused on grayscale images. The developed algorithms were then applied to the chrominance signals by means of adaptations that were often arbitrary and, in any case, altered the encoding efficiency. The specific color perceptual approach provides a better estimate of the color perceptual redundancy and leads to more significant compression ratios. Many perceptual models exist in the literature and are used in color image compression [BEE 02, HÖN 00, CHA 05]. These models typically include two steps: one for retinal processing and the second for cortical processing.

Retinal processing first carries out a separation of the luminance and chrominance components. Then, it performs a contrast enhancement on the luminance and a low-pass filtering on the chrominance [HOP 10]. Cortical processing decomposes the visual information of the retina into bands of oriented spatial frequencies and integrates the masking phenomena that exist between the different bands.

The research conducted on perception-based color compression focuses on the modeling of these aspects and how to integrate these models in an encoding scheme. Retinal processing is often modeled by the contrast sensitivity function (CSF). While many models are available for the luminance component, data is scarce for the chromatic CSF. One of the first studies carried out in this context focused on the red-green and blue-yellow chrominance grids [MUL 85]. Since then, various CSF curves have been proposed for the chromatic components of color spaces such as YCbCr and La*b* [NAD 99, RAJ 92].

The use of only CSF in color image lossy compression is relatively uncommon. This is due to the detection methods used to measure this CSF. These methods are valid only at the detection threshold level while the degradations caused by the quantization process in a lossy compression may be located well beyond that threshold. An interesting study among those that have integrated, through various adaptations, the sensitivity function in a wavelet transform-based encoder is that conducted by Nadenau *et al.* [NAD 03]. From this study, four different approaches are considered for the implementation of the CSF. The first two approaches are conventional weighting approaches: each frequency sub-band is weighted by a multiplicative factor. This is invariant in one case, and it changes during the encoding phase in the other. The last two approaches are filtering approaches and seek to exploit the accuracy of the CSF in order to better adapt to local properties of the signal. The basic idea of the first filtering method, called ACM (Adaptive Modification Coefficient) is to weight the envelope of the quantization noise of each sub-band by a visual filter corresponding to a portion of the CSF and that meets the constraints of a wavelet-based encoder. The second filtering method, called AMD (Adaptive Modification of the Distortion function), is similar to the ACM but uses a visual filter less dependent on the characteristics of the quantization noise. These last two approaches, implemented in a JPEG2000 encoder, have significantly improved the compression ratio (around 30%) for the same visual quality of reconstructed images.

In the compression of color images, the work is more oriented toward the exploitation of the attributes of the cortical processing such as frequency bands and/or masking [SAA 97]. The general approach in this case consists of first seeking models for these attributes and then using them to determine the visibility threshold of the color differences. Once identified, these thresholds are used to minimize the perceptual distortion involved in the rate-distortion control. Thus, in [VAN 94] the average detection threshold of the luminance component and chrominance components, red-green and blue-yellow are measured empirically. The obtained thresholds are used as perceptual weights to optimize the bit allocation of a vector quantization-based encoder. In [YAN 03] the JND (Just Noticeable Difference) profiles of components Y, Cb and Cr are estimated from an analysis of local properties of the image signal and from a perceptual model that incorporates the masking effects and the sensitivity of the HVS to different frequency bands. These JND profiles per sub-band and per component are used to specify the relevant perceptual signals that should be finely quantized. The study conducted in [CHO 08] also tackles the color JND (JNCD) determination for color image compression. The basic idea of this study, which is actually an extension of the work presented in [CHO 05], is to limit the distortion induced by the encoding in the perceptual redundancy. The perceptual redundancy of a pixel is defined by the range of colors that are perceptually indistinguishable from the color of the pixel. To measure this redundancy, the colors are projected into a uniform color space where the Euclidean metric is applied to evaluate the perceptual differences between colors. The resulting indistinguishable colors are re-projected in the original color space. The triplet of values obtained for these colors along the three color axes represents the perceptual redundancy sought. This perceptual redundancy model expressed in terms of triple thresholds JND is validated through two coders: JPEG-LS for the spatial domain and JPEG2000 for the frequency domain. In the first case, the criterion for determining the encoding mode is altered by the inclusion of new thresholds according to:

$$encoding-mode = \begin{cases} entropy-encoding & if \quad |x - c| \le JND_z(x) \\ predictive-encoding & otherwise \end{cases}$$

where $JND_z(x)$ denotes, for the considered color component Z, the JND associated with the value of pixel x to be encoded. c is the reconstructed value of the previous pixel located on the left of pixel x. To ensure that the quantization error is not perceptible in the predictive encoding mode, the prediction error is quantized with an adaptive quantization step:

$$Q_z(x) = 2.JND_z(x) + 1$$

In the second case, the perceptual redundancy is, after its adaptation to the wavelet domain, used to minimize the perceived distortion in the rate control process of the JPEG2000 encoder. The contribution of this approach is evaluated in terms of E (mean square error in the CIE-Lab space), S-E (S-CIELAB metric), PE (perceptible mean square error in the CIE-Lab space) and the perceived quality. The measurement and integration of the color JND allow a gain in rate of about 11% compared to a color image encoded by JPEG-LS for the same visual quality (same PE and same perceived quality). The gain is even more striking (about 20%) in the case of JPEG2000.

The use of a perceptual distortion metric in JPEG2000 instead of the mean squared error (MSE) is also the subject of studies conducted by Tan *et al.* [TAN 10, TAN 04]. The described metric is a metric originally proposed for monochrome images and then extended to the YCbCr color space. This metric includes both retinal processing (through one CSF per resolution level) and cortical processing (through the sensitivity to frequency bands and both the spatial and frequency masking). Once defined, this metric is used to characterize perceptual errors perceived during the optimization of the rate-distortion criterion. The comparison between this optimized JPEG2000 encoder and the JPEG2000 encoder is subjective and shows that at low and medium rates (between 0.125 bpp and 0.5 bpp), the perceived quality is judged to be much better by a panel of 30 observers.

The use of the masking effect between the color components and the luminance component is taken into account in color image compression in [MEN 05]. In the proposed scheme, the input RGB color image is converted into the YCbCr space. This projection is followed by a sub-sampling 4:1:1 and a dyadic wavelet transformation (the scale is sampled on a dyadic series $\{2^j\}, j \in Z$) applied to each component. The wavelet coefficients of Cb and Cr components undergo a linear quantization and an entropy encoding. To include the masking of chromatic components on the luminance component, the Cb and Cr components are dequantized and used to calculate the threshold elevation factor induced by masking. Once this elevation factor, noted $w_{cm}\,(b,i,j)$, is defined for each sub-band b and each coefficient (i, j), the sub-bands of the luminance component are quantized level by level according to:

$$v_q\,(b,i,j) = \left[\frac{v\,(b,i,j)}{\Delta w_{CM}\,(b,i,j)} \right]$$

Δ denotes a uniform quantization step applied to each sub-band of the luminance component. The step is weighted by a threshold elevation factor that varies with the sub-band and the coefficient to be quantized allows the encoder to adjust the quantization step to the content of the image. This generates reconstructed images of better subjective quality. The performances of this approach, as for the previous approach, are also judged through subjective assessments. The results show, among other things, that at medium rates (around 0.75 bpp), taking into account the masking induced by the chromatic components on the luminance component reduces the rate by 0.1 bpp while maintaining the same perceived quality. An adaptive quantization exploiting the HVS properties is also proposed in [SRE 10]. The difference of this study, which is also its strength, compared to the study described above, is the integration of the visual model in the chrominance components. The proposed approach represents the input image in the YCbCr space and applies a wavelet transformation to each of the obtained components. The visually irrelevant information is discarded by comparing the obtained wavelet coefficients to contrast thresholds specific to each sub-band. Only the coefficients above the threshold are kept. The contrast thresholds for the luminance component are those defined by Chandler *et al.* [CHA 05]. The contrast thresholds of chromatic components are measured through psycho-visual experiments that were conducted. The followed methodology is described in [RAM 01]. For a lossy compression, the selected coefficients are partitioned into different groups through the use of the K-means algorithm. The number of groups is chosen such that the quantization error per sub-band remains below the threshold of the sub-band. The number of bits allocated to each sub-band is then decremented gradually until the error induced by quantization reaches the value of perceptual RMS determined for each sub-band.

The algorithm provides a flexibility to achieve the fixed bit rate by changing the scale factor of the contrast thresholds for both the luminance component and the chromatic components. It should also be noted that the thresholds obtained for the Cr and Cb components and the associated model can be used in any wavelet-based encoder for a visually lossless color image compression. The implementation of this algorithm leads to a significant improvement in visual quality of reconstructed images compared to that of images encoded by JPEG2000 at the same rates. The visual quality is measured in this study both subjectively, through the MOS (Mean Opinion Score) and objectively, through known perceptual metrics such as the SSIM (Structural Similarity Index), the VIF (Visual Information Fidelity) and the VSNR (Visual Signal-to-Noise Ratio). The adaptive nature of the quantization and the perceptual models that the algorithm uses for both the luminance and the chrominance allow it, for achieving very low target rates, to further reduce the number of bits allocated to the chromatic components without altering the colors of the encoded-decoded image.

7.4.4. *Conclusion*

Summaries gathering the specific techniques used in color image compression are very rare or even non-existent. The reason for this is probably related to the sub-sampling generally carried out on the chromatic components, which suggested that the performances, in terms of compression ratio and reconstructed image quality, were mainly determined by the luminance component. The studies described above show that the gain in performance is significant when the color is taken into account appropriately. A rough classification of compression methods that take into account the specificity of color images enables us to specify two classes. The first is that of statistical methods that exploit the correlation between the color components to interpolate two colors from a base color. Only the interpolation coefficients are then encoded. The second class is that of perceptual approaches that seek to include perception models in the quantization and/or bit allocation processes. The perceptual models used generally include both the retinal and cortical processing.

7.5. General conclusion

Color images, because of the redundancy that exists between their different components, exhibit a high correlation that enables them, in the case of encoding, to reach lower compression rates. Paradoxically, color compression has for long immediately sought to decorrelate the components and then treat them independently. This is especially the case with different standards of image and video compression that use a color transformation to switch from the RGB space to a perceptually uniform color space modeling the antagonist behavior of the HVS in response to the color. The chromatic components of these spaces are then sub-sampled before being subjected to exactly the same processing as the luminance component. For these standards, the compression of the color is therefore limited to this sub-sampling that is supposed to integrate the low sensitivity of HVS to color changes. Their performances essentially depend on the chosen approach, predictive or transform based, and on the quantization design.

The search for more efficient methods and the development of new multimedia services for which one seeks to ensure the quality of use have led to the development of color-specific compression. To allow the reader to understand color compression, the first section, dedicated to the fundamentals of compression, provides an overview of common color spaces, sampling formats, predictive compression, transform-based compression as well as both scalar and vector quantization. The second section uses these fundamentals to describe the main standards of image and video compression. It specifies, in particular, how color is processed by each standard. A summary of color-specific compression methods is discussed according to a classification that distinguishes between statistical methods and perceptual methods. This summary is, to our knowledge, unique and needs to be completed. From this summary, it can be shown that statistical methods follow two orientations. The first, used by the standard, seeks to decorrelate the three components of a color image. The focus is then on the selection and/or the definition of color spaces that optimize the rate distortion criterion. The second orientation aims, on the contrary, to exploit the inter-components correlation and eventually the local spatial correlation. The idea is to try to interpolate two subordinate colors from a base color. The focus is then on the search for interpolation models in which the encoding of coefficients should also meet the rate distortion criteria.

The second class of color compression methods is that associated with the use of perceptual models. Numerous studies conducted in this context reflect the interest generated by this approach. The required efforts are numerous and include both the definition of the models and their integration into a compression scheme. The perceptual models include two types of processing: retinal processing and cortical processing. Retinal processing is, essentially, modeled by the CSF. The integration of the latter is usually done by a conventional weighting approach. The various studies conducted and the various proposals made in this context focus on the measurement of the chromatic CSF and on their adaptation to the local properties of the signal to be encoded. Cortical processing incorporates the spatial-frequency selectivity and both the intra-component and inter-component masking. If for the spatial-frequency selectivity, the authors agree on the characteristics of the video channels, opinions are widely shared and highly disparate about the masking effects. Many studies, however, deal with these effects but the models remain rare and often difficult to adapt. This area of research remains as open as the way to implement these models. Nowadays, the integration of these models is done, for many, at the bit allocation block level and consists of defining a threshold of noticeable differences allowing us to contain the degradations induced by the quantization process.

7.6. Bibliography

[BEE 02] BEEGAN A.P., IYER L.R., BELL A.E., "Design and evaluation of perceptual masks for wavelet image compression", *10th IEEE Digital Signal Processing Workshop*, Pine Mountain, Georgia, USA, p. 88-93, 2002.

[BEN 10] BENSALMA R., LARABI M.C., "Using binocular energy modeling for stereoscopic color image coding", *18th European Signal Processing Conference*, Aalborg, Denmark, August 23-27, p. 120-124, 2010.

[CHA 05] CHANDLER D.M., HEMAMI S.S., "Dynamic contrast based quantization for lossy wavelet image compression", *IEEE Transactions Image Processing*, vol. 14, no. 4, p. 397-410, 2005.

[CHO 05] CHOU C.H., LIU K.C., LEI C.M., "Color image compression exploiting visual information", *IEEE International Symposium Signal Processing and its Applications*, Sydney, Australia, p. 231-234, 2005.

[CHO 08] CHOU C.H., LIU K.C., "Color image compression based on the measure of just noticeable colour difference", *IET Image Processing*, vol. 2, no. 6, p. 304-322, 2008.

[GER 07a] GERSHIKOV E., LAVI-BURLAK E., PORAT M., "Correlation-based approach to color image compression", *Signal Processing: Image Communication*, vol. 22, p. 719-733, 2007.

[GER 07b] GERSHIKOV E., PORAT M., "On color transforms and bit allocation for optimal subband image compression", *Signal Processing: Image Communication*, vol. 22, p. 1-18, 2007.

[GER 78] GERSHO A., "Principles of quantization", *IEEE Transactions Circuits Systems*, vol. 25, no. 7, p. 427-436, 1978.

[GER 92] GERSHO A., GRAY R.M., *Vector Quantization and Signal Compression*, Kluwer Academic, Boston, USA, 1992.

[GOF 02] GOFFMAN L., PORAT M., "Color image compression using intercolor correlation", *IEEE International Conference on Image Processing*, vol. 2, Rochester, NY, USA, p. 353-356, 2002.

[HÖN 00] HÖNTSCH I., KARAM L., "Locally adaptive perceptual image coding", *IEEE Transactions Image Process*, vol. 9, p. 1472-1483, 2000.

[HOP 10] HO PHUOC T., Développement et mise en oeuvre de modèles d'attention visuelle, Doctoral thesis, University of Grenoble, May 2010.

[ISO 92] ISO/IEC 10918-1 / ITU-T Recommendation T.81, Digital compression and coding of continuous-tone still images, (JPEG), 1992.

[ISO 93] ISO/IEC 11172, Information technology: coding of moving pictures and associated audio for digital storage media at up to about 1.5Mbit/s, (MPEG-1), 1993.

[ISO 95] ISO/IEC 13818, Information technology: generic coding of moving pictures and associated audio information, (MPEG-2), 1995.

[ISO 98] ISO/IEC JTC1/SC29/WG11 information technology: generic coding of audio-visual objects, Part 2: Visual. Draft ISO/IEC 14496-2 (MPEG-4), version 1, ISO/IEC, 1998.

[ISO 00] ISO/IEC 15444, Information technology, JPEG2000 image coding system, 2000.

[ISO 03] ISO/IEC 14496-10 and ITU-T Rec. H.264, advanced video coding, 2003.

[ITU 93a] ITU-T Recommendation H.261, video CODEC for audiovisual services at px64 kbit/s, 1993.

[ITU 93b] ITU-T Recommendation H.263, video coding for low bit rate communication, 1993.

[ITU 95] ITU-R BT.601-5, Paramètres de codage en studio de la télévision numérique pour des formats standards image 4:3 (normalisé) et 16 :9 (écran panoramique), 1995.

[ITU 98] ITU-T/SG16/Q15, Video coding for low bitrate communication, ITU-T Recommendation H.263, Version 2 (H.263+), ITU-T, Geneva, 1998.

[ITU 00] ITU-T/SG16/Q15, Draft for H.263++ annexes U, V, and W to recommendation H.263, Draft, ITU-T, Geneva, 2000.

[ITU 01] ITU-T/SG 16/VCEG(formerly Q.15 now Q.6), H.26L test model long term number 7 (TML-7), Doc. VCEG-M81, April 2001.

[KAS 03] KASSIM A.A., LEE W.S., "Embedded color image coding using SPIHT with partially linked spatial orientation trees", *IEEE Transactions on Circuits and Systems for Video Technology*, vol. 13, p. 203-206, 2003.

[KOT 90] KOTERA H., KANAMORI K., "A novel coding algorithm for representing full color images by a single color image", *Journal of Imaging Technology*, vol. 16, p. 146-152, 1990.

[LIN 80] LINDE Y., BUZO A., GRAY R., "An algorithm for vector quantizer design", *IEEE Transactions on Information Theory*, vol. 28, no. 1, p. 84-85, 1980.

[LLO 82] LLOYD S.P., "Least squares quantization in PCM", *IEEE Transactions on Information Theory*, vol. IT-28, no. 2, p. 129-137, 1982.

[LUK 07] LUKAC R., PLATANIOTIS K.N., *Color Image Processing, Methods and Applications*, CRC Press, Boca Raton, FL, USA, 2007.

[MAS 08] MASMOUDI K., ANTONINI M., KORNPROBST P., Analysis and compression of static images using bio-inspired schemas, GDR-PRC ISIS - Thème D, December 2008.

[MAX 60] MAX J., "Quantizing for minimum distortion", *IEEE Transactions on Information Theory*, vol. IT-26, no. 1, p. 7-12, 1960.

[MEN 05] MENG Y., GUO L., "Color image coding by utilizing the crossed masking", *Proceedings of ICASSP*, 2005, p. 389-392.

[MUL 85] MULLEN K.T., "The contrast sensitivity of Human colour vision to red-green and blue-yellow chromatic gratings", *Journal of Physiol.*, vol. 359, 1885, p. 381-400.

[NAD 99] NADENAU M.J., REICHEL J., "Opponent color, human vision and wavelets for image compression", *Proceeding of the 7th Color Imaging Conference*, Scottsdale, AZ, USA, November, p. 237-242, 1999.

[NAD 03] NADENAU M.J., REICHEL J., KUNT M., "Wavelet-based color image compression: Exploiting the contrast sensitivity function", *IEEE Transactions Image Process*, vol. 12, no. 1, p. 58-70, 2003.

[PLA 00] PLATANIOTIS K.N., VENETSANOPOULOS A.N., *Color Image Processing and Applications*, Springer, Berlin, Germany, 2000.

[RAB 01] RABBANI M., JOSHI R., "An overview of the JPEG2000 still image compression standard", *Signal Processing: Image Communication*, vol. 17, no. 1, 2001.

[RAJ 92] RAJALA S.A., TRUSSELL H.J., KRISHNAKUMAR B., "Visual sensitivity to color-varying stimuli", *Proceeding of the SPIE Human Vision, Visual Processing and Digital Display III*, vol. 1666, p. 375-386, 1992.

[RAM 01] RAMOS M.G., HEMAMI S.S., "Suprathreshold wavelet coefficient quantization in complex stimuli: Psychophysical evaluation and analysis", *Journal of the Optical Society of America*, vol. A 18, p. 2385-2397, 2001.

[ROT 07] ROTERMAN Y., PORAT M., "Color image coding using regional correlation of primary colors", *Image and Vision Computing*, vol. 25, p. 637-651, 2007.

[SAA 97] SAADANE A., BEDAT L., BARBA D., "Masking effects of achromatic gratings on chromatic components of a psychovisual color space", *Picture Coding Symposium*, 10-12 September 1997.

[SAI 96] SAID A., PEARLMAN W.A., "A new fast and efficient image codec based on set partitioning in hierarchical trees", *IEEE Transactions on Circuits and Systems for Video Technology*, vol. 6, p. 243-250, 1996.

[SAN 98] SANGWINE S.J., N.HORNE R.E., *The Colour Image Processing Handbook*, Chapman & Hall, London, UK, 1998.

[SAN 06] SAN X., CAI H., LI J., "Color image coding by using inter-color correlation", *Proceeding IEEE International Conference on Image processing*, 2006.

[SHA 93] SHAPIRO J.M., "Embedded image coding using zerotrees of wavelets coefficients", *IEEE Transactions on Signal Processing*, vol. 41, p. 3445-3462, 1993.

[SHE 97] SHEN K., DELP E.J., "Color image compression using an embedded rate scalable approach", *Proceedings of IEEE International Conference on Image Processing*, Santa Barbara, USA, 1997.

[SOU 10] SOULARD R., CARRÉ P., "Quaternionic wavelets for image coding", *Proceedings of EUSIPCO*, Aalborg, Danmark, 2010.

[SRE 10] SREELEKHA G., SATHIDEVI P., "An HVS based adaptive quantization scheme for the compression of color images", *Digital Signal Processing*, vol. 20, p. 1129-1149, 2010.

[SUL 01] SULLIVAN G.J., WIEGAND T., STOCKHAMMER T., "Draft H.26L video coding standard for mobile applications", *Proceedings of IEEE International Conference on Image Processing*, p. 573-576, 2001.

[TAN 04] TAN D.M., WU H.R., YU Z., "Perceptual coding of digital monochrome images", *IEEE Signal Processing Letters*, vol. 11, no. 2, p. 239-242, 2004.

[TAN 10] TAN D.M., TAN C.S., WU H.R., "Perceptual color image coding with JPEG2000", *IEEE Transactions Image Processing*, vol. 19, no. 2, p. 374-383, 2010.

[TAU 01] TAUBMAN D., MARCELLIN P., *JPEG2000: Image Compression Fundamentals, Practice and Standards*, Kluwer Academic Publisher, Norwell, USA, 2001.

[VAN 94] VAN DYCK R.E., RAJALA S.A., "Subband/VQ coding of color images with perceptually optimal bit allocation", *IEEE Transactions Circuits System Video Technology*, vol. 4, no. 1, p. 68-82, 1994.

[YAM 84] YAMAGUCHI H., "Efficient encoding of colored pictures in R,G,B components", *IEEE Transactions on Communication*, vol. 32, p. 1201-1209, 1984.

[YAN 03] YANG X.K., LIN W.S., "Just-noticeable distortion profile with nonlinear additivity model for perceptual masking in color images", *Proceedings IEEE International Conference Acoustics, Speech, and Signal Processing*, vol. 3, p. 609-612, 2003.

Chapter 8

Protection of Color Images

8.1. Introduction

In this chapter, we show how watermarking and encryption algorithms secure the content of color images. Over the last decade, more and more digital visual data, such as images, videos and 3D objects, has been transferred through computer networks and digitally archived. No particular system has currently been proposed for the transfer and secure archiving of digital visual data. The work presented in this chapter show the recent progress in this field. Protection of color images consists of the protection of either the entire image or only the color information, partially or selectively. The watermarking of a color image can also be used to cover up another digital message within the color image itself.

Protection should be ensured for the transmission of color images, but also for the archiving of this digital data. The problem is also to make this protection robust against processing such as the change of format, compression or any other manipulation that does not change the visual appearance of the original color image. In fact, the amount of information (entropy) to be transmitted increases sharply between the original image

Chapter written by William PUECH, Alain TRÉMEAU and Philippe CARRÉ.

and the encrypted image. In the particular case of some types of images, large homogeneous regions may occur and can disrupt the efficiency of encryption and watermarking algorithms of images.

Networks are complex and attacks are numerous. This therefore raises a real concern about security when transmitting data. The best suited protection for digital communication systems lies in a completely closed system based on full encryption techniques. Since ancient times, humans have always tried to encode secret messages to prevent malicious attacks. In the first sketches of this science of secrecy, security was perceived by the confidentiality of the algorithm that provided the encryption and decryption. It is over time that the concept of a key gradually emerged. Nowadays, security systems are based on algorithms made available to all and it is the key, specific secret code, which is confidential and that enables the owner to extract the secret message [KER 83].

In section 8.2, we present the different types of protection and security for color images as well as standard encryption algorithms. We then show in section 8.3 how it is possible to insert data into images in a hidden way while maintaining high data quality and then we show, in section 8.4, how to apply encryption algorithms to color images. Finally, we conclude in section 8.5.

8.2. Protection and security of digital data

In this section, before detailing some encryption algorithms, we present different levels and types of protection.

8.2.1. *Secure transmission and archiving*

There are four main objectives for the protection of digital data, used for different purposes, namely confidentiality, integrity, authentication, and non-repudiation:

– confidentiality: confidentiality or data masking is the most commonly used characteristic in data protection. It aims to make the secret message, known as cipher-text, unintelligible to those who do not possess the key;

– integrity: the integrity of the received message should be able to ensure to the receiver that the content perfectly corresponds to the sent message. In fact, the concept of integrity allows us to verify that the message has not been deliberately tampered with during transmission;

– authentification: authentication allows the sender to sign the message. Thus, the receiver will have no doubt about the identity of the sender;

– non-repudiation: non-repudiation is the guarantee that neither of the two individuals who have completed a transaction can deny having sent or received the messages.

8.2.2. *Different types of protection*

Depending on the application, different types of protection are to be implemented, namely fragile, robust or safe protection and partial protection:

– fragile, robust or safe protection: data protection can be fragile, robust and/or safe, depending on the required application. For integrity check, for instance, the insertion of a hidden message in a message should be fragile to detect any changes that might occur on the image during transmission. On the contrary, in copyright protection, the marking should be robust so that no one can erase the identification of the owner, or even over-mark the image with another identification;

– partial protection: partial protection allows us to protect only a portion of the transmitted data. The notion of partial protection can therefore protect only a portion of the data or only a certain quality level. In imaging, the concept of ROI (Region of Interest) allows us to locate specific regions of the image. These ROI are often the most sensitive regions or with a market value requiring some protection. By securing some quality levels, partial protection allows us, for instance, to protect the high-resolution of a color image and to keep a clear, low-resolution version of the image accessible to everyone.

It is however interesting to note that the compatibility of protection systems through encryption or watermarking is not yet fully resolved. In fact, the integration of these protection systems should be completely transparent in compression standards such as JPEG for images or H.264 for video.

Researchers and industrialists are concerned by many applications, especially with the dramatic increase in video transmission. For example, the *fingerprint* should be able to track a person who illegally distributes a video on the Internet. Furthermore, more and more visual data is freely available on the Internet. It is very easy to copy multimedia data and appropriate it. It is therefore urgent to protect the copyright of the data submitted in open access. In this case, the protection should be transparent to the users. The watermarking of multimedia data seems to be an elegant solution to this problem.

8.2.3. *Encryption algorithms*

In this section, after presenting a classification of encryption algorithms, we detail the AES and RSA algorithms, and then conclude this section by presenting the different types of encryption.

8.2.3.1. *Classification of encryption algorithms*

As detailed in section 8.2.1, there are four objectives for the protection of digital data, used for different purposes, namely confidentiality, integrity, authentication, and non-repudiation. The most important characteristic in color imaging is the first, namely the confidentiality. But the integrity characteristic, which can be perceived as visual integrity, as well as the other two, also important for the protection of images.

Encryption algorithms can be separated according to several characteristics: secret key systems (symmetric systems) illustrated in Figure 8.1 and public-private key systems (asymmetric systems) illustrated in Figure 8.2 [DIF 76, STI 96]. The secret key systems are those that can encrypt and decrypt with the same key. The sender and receiver should have previously shared a secret key by another different secure means of communication.

Public key or asymmetric systems allow us to overcome this inconvenience by using a key to encrypt and another key to decrypt. Each

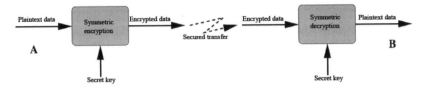

Figure 8.1. *Principle of symmetric encryption*

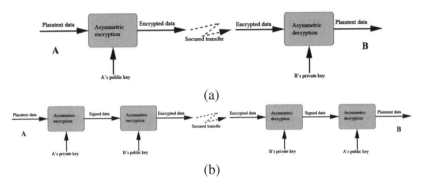

(a)

(b)

Figure 8.2. *a) Principle of asymmetric encryption, b) Double asymmetric encryption to ensure confidentiality and authenticity*

individual X will possess a pair of keys, where one will be confidential (private key) and the other known to all (public key). To write to X, just encrypt the message with the public key of X which everyone knows. Upon receipt, only X can decrypt with his private key. In this section we present the two most common data encryption systems, namely the AES algorithm, which is a secret key system and the RSA algorithm, which is an asymmetric system.

8.2.3.2. AES encryption algorithm

The AES (Advanced Encryption Standard) encryption algorithm replaced the DES (Data Encryption Standard), which is part of the standard symmetric encryption systems illustrated in Figure 8.1. In 1974, the DES algorithm became the first standard of modern cryptography [SCH 97]. Today, even if the algorithm is still robust, its key is limited to 64 bits. In fact, the current performance of machines in terms of computation speed made the DES breakable. The attack, known as brutal, which is to try all the 2^{64} potential keys, is now feasible through large computers. A solution was found to increase the security, and it is called the triple-DES. The triple-DES is to encrypt the input block three times with different keys K_1, K_2 and K_3. It exists in several variants, but generally the first and third operations are encryption operations, while the second is a decryption operation.

The AES (Advanced Encryption Standard) encryption algorithm is the current standard system of symmetric encryption. In January 1997, the NIST (National Institute of Standards and Technology, U.S.) made a call for entries of a new block symmetric encryption method. The AES aims to replace the DES (Data Encryption Standard), which becomes vulnerable. Among five finalists (MARS, RC6, Rijndael, Serpent and Twofish), Rijndael, submitted by Joan Daemen and Vincent Rijmen, was declared the winner in October 2000. The Rijndael algorithm is preferred over others because of its efficiency and low memory cost as it relies on the use of simple binary operations.

The AES algorithm is a set of steps repeated a number of times (rounds). The number of rounds depends on the size of the key and the size of the data blocks. For example, the number of rounds is 9 if the blocks and the key are of length 128 bits. To encrypt a block of data with AES (see Figure 8.3), one must first perform a step named AddRoundKey, which is to apply an exclusive OR between a sub key and the block. The incoming data and the key are thus added together in the first step AddRoundKey. Then, the algorithm enters into the operation of a round. Each regular operation of round involves four steps. The first step is called "SubByte", where each byte of the block is replaced by another value derived from an S-box. The second step is the step named "ShiftRow" where the rows are cyclically shifted with different *offsets*. In the third step, named "MixColumn", each column is processed as a polynomial, multiplied over GF(2^8) (*Galois Field*) by a matrix. The last step of a round is again the step named "AddRoundKey", which is a simple exclusive OR between the current data and the sub-key of the current round. The AES algorithm performs an additional final routine that consists of the SubByte, ShiftRow and AddRoundKey steps before producing the final encryption.

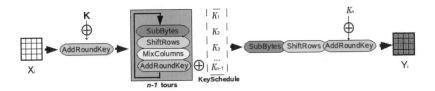

Figure 8.3. *The general scheme of AES*

The process applied to the plaintext data is independent from that applied to the secret key. The result on the secret key is called the Key Schedule. It consists of two components: the Key Expansion and the Round Key Selection [AES 01, DAE 02].

8.2.3.3. *The RSA encryption algorithm*

In this section, we present the RSA algorithm, which is currently the most used asymmetric system. The RSA algorithm is secure because it is physically too slow to factor in very large numbers of products of prime factors [RIV 78, SCH 97].

Let p and q be two distinct large prime numbers[1], and n be a large number, which is the product of p and q. $\phi(n)$ denotes the Euler function in n, which is the number of natural numbers less than n and coprime with n, with $\phi(n) = (p - 1)(q - 1)$.

The public key/private key pair will reside in two numbers d and e associated with n. e is first calculated randomly between 2 and $\phi(n)$ and should be coprime with $\phi(n)$. This is the pair (n, e), which is the public key. Then d is calculated so that $d = e^{-1}mod(n)$. The extended Euclidean algorithm allows us to calculate this inverse instantly, even with very large numbers. The pair (n, d) is the private key. The use of keys for encryption and decryption is as follows. If m is the plaintext message (less than n; otherwise, it is divided per block), it is then encrypted with the private key (n, e) by raising it to the power e, modulo n. The encrypted message is then obtained: $m' = m^{e}mod(n)$. For decryption, the second key (n, d)

---

1 Two numbers are coprime if and only if their greatest common divisor is 1.

should be available. By raising the encrypted message to the power d modulo n, and because d and e are inverse modulo n, we obtain:

$$(m')^d mod(n) = (m^e mod(n))^d mod(n) = m^{ed} mod(n) = m$$

For example, if Bob wants to send a message to Alice, he converts his message into a number and divides the message into blocks of smaller size than n. For each block m_i, by using the Alice's public key, Bob computes and encrypts the block as follows:

$$c_i = m_i^e mod\ n \qquad [8.1]$$

where i is the block position in the text, $i \in [1, N]$, if N is the number of blocks.

Alice, with her private key can then decrypt the message as follows:

$$m_i = c_i^d\ mod\ n \qquad [8.2]$$

Thus, the RSA algorithm differs from symmetric encryption systems by using two different keys for encryption and decryption (Figure 8.2a). One of these two keys, the public key, is supposed to be known by all, and the other, the private key, known by a single individual.

For some protocols of secure data exchange, the RSA algorithm allows us to encrypt with a public key, in which case only the recipient can decrypt the message with his private key or encrypt with his own private key (signature). In this case, anyone can read the message using the public key, but the sender has been able to sign the message as he is potentially the only one who could encrypt with his private key. A double encryption public key–private key allows us to combine signature and confidentiality as shown in Figure 8.2b.

Unfortunately, RSA is a very slow algorithm, much slower than any symmetrical system, and especially when the used numbers are large. In addition, this is nowadays easily breakable, even for numbers of 512 bits[2]. It is currently recommended to use key of length 1,024 bits[3],

---

2 An RSA with a key of 768 bits was broken in late 2009.
3 The RSA Laboratory offers \$1,00,000 to the one who will break a RSA with a key of 1,024 bits.

or even 2,048 bits. In fact, the 1,024-bit RSA keys, which form the basis of encryption of e-commerce, are still regarded as inviolable and use numbers of 308 digits. Experts estimate that they will no longer be safe in the next 5 years. Since RSA is slow, it is better to encrypt a message with AES for example and to encrypt the secret key with RSA in order to securely send the secret key to the receiver.

8.2.3.4. *Stream cipher encryption modes*

The stream cipher encryption algorithms can be defined as block cipher algorithms, where each block is of unit dimension (1 bit, 1 byte, etc.) or relatively small. Their main advantages are their great speed and their ability to change at each symbol of plaintext message. With a stream cipher encryption algorithm, it is possible to separately encrypt each character of the plaintext message one by one, by using an encryption function that varies each time. Therefore, the stream cipher encryption algorithms need memories. Generally, stream ciphers encryption algorithms are composed of two steps: the generation of a dynamic key and the output encryption function depending on the dynamic key.

The AES algorithm presented in section 8.2.3.2 is an algorithm, which by default, encrypts the data block by block by using the ECB mode (*Electronic Codebook*). In fact, the ECB mode is the mode of the standard AES algorithm, which is described in the documentation 197 of the standard FIPS (*Federal Information Processing Standards*). From a binary sequence $X_1, ..., X_n$ of plaintext blocks, each X_i is encrypted with the same secret key k to produce the encrypted blocks $Y_1, ..., Y_n$. However, the AES algorithm can support other encryption modes, such as CBC (*Cipher Block Chaining*), OFB (*Output FeedBack*), CFB (*Cipher FeedBack*), and CTR (*Counter*). The OFB, CFB and CTR modes operate as stream cipher encryption algorithms. These methods require no special action concerning the length of the messages that are not the size of a multiple of one block since they all operate by performing an exclusive OR between the plaintext message and the output of the block cipher encryption. Each described mode has different advantages and disadvantages. In the ECB and OFB modes, for instance, any change in the block of the plaintext message X_i causes a modification in the corresponding encrypted block Y_i but the other encrypted blocks are not affected. On the other hand, if a plaintext message of the block X_i is changed in the CBC and CFB modes, then Y_i and all the following encrypted blocks will be affected. These properties mean that the CBC and CFB modes are useful for authentication problems and the ECB and OFB modes separately process each block. Therefore, we can note that the OFB mode does not spread the noise, while the CFB mode spreads it.

The CBC (Cipher Block Chaining) mode supplements the cipher block encryption with a feedback mechanism. Each encrypted block Y_i is supplemented with an exclusive OR with the input plaintext block X_{i+1} before being encrypted with the key k. An initialization vector (VI) is used for the first iteration. In fact, all modes (except ECB) require a VI. In the CFB (*Cipher FeedBack*) mode $VI = Y_0$. The dynamic key Z_i is generated by $Z_i = E_k(Y_{i-1}), i \geqslant 1$ and the encrypted block is produced by $Y_i = X_i \oplus Z_i$. In the OFB (*Output FeedBack*) mode, as in CFB, $Y_i = X_i \oplus Z_i$ but $VI = Z_0$ and $Z_i = E_k(Z_{i-1}), i \geqslant 1$. The input data is encrypted by an exclusive OR with the output Z_i. The CTR (Counter) mode has very similar characteristics to the OFB mode, but it also allows a random access property for decryption. It generates the following dynamic key by successive value encryption of a counter. This counter can be a simple function that generates a pseudo-random sequence. In this mode, the output of the counter is the input of the AES encryption.

When the dynamic key is generated independently of the plaintext and encrypted message, the stream cipher encryption algorithm is said to be synchronous. With a stream cipher encryption, the sender and receiver should be synchronized by using the same key and by using it at the same position. The synchronous stream cipher encryptions are commonly used in environments where errors are numerous because they have the advantage of not propagating the errors [GUI 02]. With regard to active attacks, such as the insertion, deletion and copying of the encrypted message digits by an active opponent, they immediately produce a loss of synchronization. The encryption process of a synchronous stream cipher encryption is described in Figure 8.4a, where $f()$ denotes the function that determines the next state, $g()$ the function generating the dynamic key and $h()$ the encryption output function:

$$\begin{cases} s_{i+1} &= f(K, s_i) \\ z_i &= g(K, s_i) \\ c_i &= h(z_i, m_i) \end{cases} \qquad [8.3]$$

where K is the key, s_i, m_i, c_i and z_i are respectively the ith state, the plaintext message, the encrypted message, and the dynamic key. The decryption process is shown in Figure 8.4b.

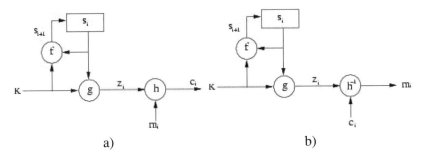

a)   b)

Figure 8.4. *Synchronous stream cipher encryption principle:*
a) encryption, b) decryption

When the dynamic key is generated from the key and a number of digits previously encrypted, the stream cipher encryption algorithm is said to be asynchronous, also called self-synchronizing stream cipher encryption. The propagation of errors is limited to the size of the memory. If the digits of the encrypted message are deleted or inserted, the receiver, through the memory, is able to resynchronize with the sender. Regarding active attacks, if an active opponent alters a portion of the encrypted message digits, the receiver is able to detect it. The process of asynchronous stream cipher encryption is described in Figure 8.5a, where $g()$ denotes the function generating the dynamic key and $h()$ the encryption output function:

$$\begin{cases} z_i &= g(K, c_{i-t}, c_{i-t+1}, \ldots, c_{i-2}, c_{i-1}) \\ c_i &= h(z_i, m_i) \end{cases} \qquad [8.4]$$

where K is the key, m_i, c_i and z_i are the ith plaintext message, encrypted message, and the dynamic key respectively. We can note in equation [8.4], that the dynamic key depends on the t previous encrypted message digits. To be robust against many statistical attacks, the function generating the dynamic key $g()$ should generate a sequence of a large period with good statistical properties that can be called pseudo-random binary sequences. The decryption process is shown in Figure 8.5b.

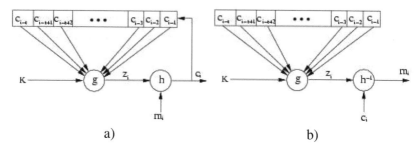

a)   b)

Figure 8.5. *Asynchronous stream cipher encryption principle:*
a) encryption, b) decryption

We will now describe an additional operation, namely the watermarking of images. We will see that in this case a new constraint will appear: the concept of invisibility.

8.3. Color image watermarking

In this section, after presenting the principles of image watermarking, we present the problem of selection of insertion spaces as well as the fidelity metrics to complete the study of the protection of color image palettes.

8.3.1. Watermarking principle of color image

The general watermarking principle is to insert data into a host image by presenting imperceptible changes to the human eye but whose data is easily recoverable by a computer program. The locations of the inserted data in the image are determined by a secret key so that attackers cannot have direct access to them as shown in Figure 8.6. The watermarking algorithms are used in emission control domains, in the identification of the owner, for proof of ownership, of transaction tracking, content authentication, copy control as well as device controls [COX 02]. According to the applications, watermarking systems should be robust to various attacks such as the deletion or duplication of trademarks, unauthorized detection or the print-and-scan processes. The watermarking systems should also be robust to signal processing algorithms such as the compression, the encoding transformations, the contrast and color enhancement, the distributions, the resampling and the geometric transformations such as the rotations, translations, cutting or scaling.

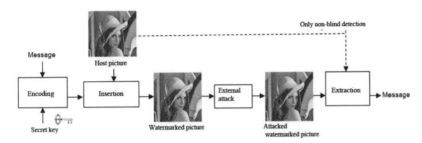

Figure 8.6. *Overview of an image watermarking scheme (for a color version of this figure, see www.iste.co.uk/fernandez/digicolor.zip)*

In particular, *print-and-scan* attacks, as shown in Figure 8.7, are a real challenge for most watermarking systems. In fact, with the advent of the Internet and multimedia, the protection of intellectual property after printing and rescanning is a key problem. In addition to being invulnerable to attacks, a watermarking system should transport a large amount of data and be invisible to the human visual system.

Although many methods have been proposed to watermark grayscale images, few methods have been applied to color images. The first reason for this is the difficulty for color image watermarking to resist the color–grayscale conversion. During the last decade, color image watermarking algorithms were based on additive or multiplicative processes [LUK 07]. Most of these methods insert data independently in each of the three color components. Therefore, they can be considered as scalar approaches. However, color cannot be regarded as a vector of independent components. We will see in this section that the correlation between these components is nevertheless considered by some color image watermarking approaches.

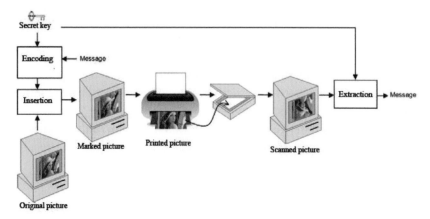

Figure 8.7. *Print-and-scan attacks after a watermarking image process (for a color version of this figure, see www.iste.co.uk/fernandez/digicolor.zip)*

The fact that the human visual system (HVS) is more sensitive to some variations in the spatial domain and frequency domain has always been used in watermarking. But recently, there is a trend toward watermarking techniques that take into account the sensitivity of the HVS. Therefore, we will discuss the solutions and arguments supporting this idea and will demonstrate that these methods provide more robustness than others.

Most watermarking methods insert either in the spatial domain or in the frequency domain. By working in the spatial domain, the pixel values of the image are directly altered to insert the message. On the other hand, the schemes that operate in the frequency domain have to transform the image by using transformations such as the DCT (Discrete Cosine Transform) [ALT 00, BRI 05, HER 00, LIN 00], the DFT (Discrete Fourier Transform) [DER 00, GAN 05, KAN 03, PIV 98, SOL 01], the DWT (Discrete Wavelet Transform) [AGR 07, BAR 01, FAN 04, WAN 08, XIA 98, ZHU 06], etc. The frequency coefficients are then modified to insert the message and finally an inverse transformation is applied to obtain the watermarked image. These schemes thus require more computation time than the schemes that insert data in the spatial domain. However, as they work in the frequency domain, these schemes are more robust to rotation, scaling, and translation. More recently, new schemes have been proposed based on a color image quantization process.

8.3.2. *Choice of insertion color spaces*

The overall goal of watermarking is thus to hide data in an image or a video. While some approaches proposed to hide data in images encoded with a palette of 256 colors (8 bits) or in so-called true color images [CHA 05, LIN 02, YU 07], most earlier watermarking techniques (24 bits) were mainly carried on grayscale images [CHA 06a, CHA 07b].

Method	Class	Marking	Color space
Battiato *et al.* (2000) [BAT 00]	3D-vector	Color index table	A BY RG (color opponency space)
Tsai *et al.* (2004) [TSA 04]	3D-vector	Color index table	RGB
Roy *et al.* (2002) [ROY 04]	2D-vector	Color components (CrCb)	YCrCb
Piva *et al.* (1999) [PIV 99]	Embedding: 3 × 1D-scalar Detection: 3D-vector	Color components (R, G, B)	RGB
Chou *et al.* (2003) [CHO 03]	3 × 1D-scalar	Color components (L*, a*, b*)	L*a*b*
Pei *et al.* (2006) [PEI 06]	3 × 1D-scalar	Color components (a*, b*) Lightness component (L*)	L*a*b*
Lo-varco *et al.* (2005) [LOV 05]	3 × 1D-scalar	Color components (Y, Cr, Cb)	YCrCb
Fu *et al.* (2007) [FU 07]	3 × 1D-scalar	Color components (R, G, B)	RGB
Chen (2007) [CHE 07]	3 × 1D-scalar	Color components (R, G, B)	RGB
Barni *et al.* (2002) [BAR 02]	3 × 1D-scalar or 1D-scalar	Principal components	RGB
Kuo *et al.* (2005) [KUO 05]	1D-scalar/edges detection 1D-scalar/color quantization	First principal component	RGB
Hsieh *et al.* (2006) 23	1D-scalar	Lightness component (Y)	YUV
Kutter *et al.* (1997) [KUT 97] Yu *et al.* (2001) [YU 01] Tsai *et al.* (2007) [TSA 07]	1D-scalar	Blue component (B)	RGB
Fleet *et al.* (1997) [FLE 97]	1D-scalar	Yellow-blue component (YB)	BW RG YB (color opponency space)
Tsui *et al.* (2006) [TSU 06]	1D-scalar	Yellow-blue component (b*)	L*a*b*
Kim *et al.* (2001) [KIM 01]	1D-scalar	Saturation component (magnitude of CrCb)	YCrCb
Huang *et al.* (2005) [HUA 05]	1D-scalar	Saturation component (S)	IHS

Table 8.1. *Summary of color watermarking methods with their representations of colors*

Table 8.1 summarizes the characteristics of the main methods of color image watermarking. This table shows that most methods of color watermarking can be considered as scalar methods because the color is considered as three independent components of grayscale type. However, the correlation between color components cannot be ignored. In fact, it is well known that the RGB color components are highly correlated, while the YCbCr components are less correlated [GIL 02]. To solve this problem of cross-correlation between color components, the Karhunen Loeve transformation (KLT) has been used in many studies [BAR 02]. This transformation is based on principal component analysis (PCA) which aims to transform a color space that consists of correlated components into a new space in which the three components are uncorrelated, and where the first principal component is the largest eigenvalue. The advantage of a KLT is that, after the transformation, the color components can be inserted separately using a scalar scheme [BAR 02]. Figure 8.8 shows the different color image watermarking strategies. It shows that, in a color image, a message can be inserted either as a vector in three dimensions (3D in Figure 8.8) or as three independent scalars (3 × 1D in Figure 8.8). In most cases, the message is independently inserted into the color components. This can be inserted either in a weakly correlated color space (3 × 1D in Figure 8.8) as YCbCr, where Y denotes the achromatic component and Cb and Cr the chromatic components, or in the de-correlated color components (3 × 1D independent in Figure 8.8) resulting from a KLT transformation. In all cases, the message can be inserted into one (1D), two (2 × 1D), or three (3 × 1D, 1D + 2 × 1D, 3D) components. However, in the end, few methods exploit the cross-correlation between the color components in the insertion process. For instance, Piva *et al.* proposed a DCT-based watermarking scheme where the mark is inserted separately in each color component without any use of correlations among the three components [PIV 99].

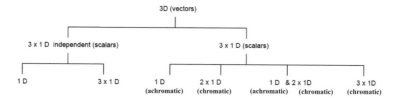

Figure 8.8. *A classification of color watermarking methods*

Ultimately, this scheme takes into account the redundancy between color components only to extract the message. The cross-correlation is exploited to improve the detection process but not for insertion. In this scheme, the strength of the mark is 10 times greater for the blue component than for the green component, and five times greater for the blue component than for the red component. This choice of weights can be explained by the differences in sensitivity of the HVS to variations in the blue or the green.

One problem of this scheme is that it is difficult to develop a theoretical model describing the probability density function of DCT coefficients for different color components. Vidal *et al.* have encountered the same problem [VID 02]. Barni *et al.* proposed to solve this problem by inserting different marks in uncorrelated bands along with an additive or multiplicative insertion [BAR 02]. To maintain high reliability of detection, Barni *et al.* proposed to insert the message only in one band. More recently, Kuo *et al.* proposed a watermarking method based on the fusion of two processes, on the one hand, the detection of color segments, on the other hand, the color quantization [KUO 05]. The segments are detected using a specific approach based on a PCA in a 3D color space. Similarly, the authors proposed a partitioning strategy based on a PCA to quantize the image. The problem of a PCA or KLT-based watermarking is that the projection in the new space depends on the content of the image. Therefore, since an attack of the image can change the content, the transformation before and after an attack can be different and the watermarking may not be detected.

8.3.3. *Fidelity of color image watermarking methods*

Although *benchmarks* have been proposed, such as Stirmark or Checkmark, the question of evaluation and comparison of watermarking methods is still open. One of the major weaknesses of most of these benchmarks is that they are limited to grayscale images. In fact, to evaluate the differences between an original image and a watermarked image, color images are converted to grayscale images by considering only the intensity component of the HSI (hue-saturation-intensity) color space. A second weakness of these *benchmarks* is that they use a black box approach to evaluate the performance of a scheme.

In fact, traditional assessments consist of the computation of the weighted average of different metric results and then the total score is produced. It would be more interesting to evaluate each metric independently. Xenos *et al.* have proposed a model based on four criteria that are hierarchically organized into three levels [XEN 05]. The purpose of this model is to evaluate the fidelity of watermarking schemes. The four main considered factors are the properties (such as the type of image), the color (such as color depth), the characteristics (such as brightness, saturation and shade) and the regions (such as the contrast, position, size, and color). The proposed model seems very promising for the evaluation of the fidelity of watermarking. However, this model is more effective when it is applied to algorithms operating in the spatial domain than in the frequency domain. According to Xenos *et al.* further work is needed for an analysis of methods operating in the frequency domain, because the model tends to find the most noticeable damage for the observers. The fidelity evaluation can be assessed by observers or by a perceptual distance metric. This should be analyzed through the variation in robustness with a constant capacity. Similarly, the capacity should be analyzed through the variation of the fidelity with a constant robustness. For each watermarking scheme, the aim is to assess the relative impact of the variation of a property to find a space defined by the fidelity, the robustness, and the capacity. Fidelity evaluation through metrics is a difficult problem because of the sensitivity to the HVS. Many articles offer an evaluation based on the mean square error (MSE) between the original image and the marked image. It is strongly recommended to calculate this metric directly in the L*a*b* color space [CHA 07a] rather than computing the MSE on each color component. When the CIE L*a*b*ΔE difference is used to evaluate the fidelity, it is accepted that a difference is visible to the HVS if ΔE is greater than three [CHA 07a]. However, such a threshold depends on the content of the image. The PSNR (peak signal-to-noise ratio) is also often used to assess the fidelity.

Let us consider, for example, the parrots and lighthouse images shown in Figures 8.9 and 8.10. The lighthouse image shows higher frequencies than the parrot image. We can note that for the insertion of seven bits per pixel in each image, we obtain a $\Delta E = 2.07$ and a PSNR = 37.34 dB for the parrot image and a $\Delta E = 1.70$ and a PSNR = 37.91 dB for the lighthouse image. The difference between the original image and the watermarked image is thus greater for the parrot's image than for the lighthouse image while an observer would say the opposite because

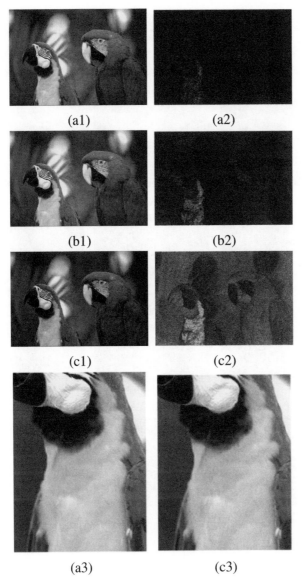

(a1)

(a2)

(b1)

(b2)

(c1)

(c2)

(a3)

(c3)

Figure 8.9. *The parrot image marked respectively with: a1) 1 bpp, $\Delta E = 0.23$ and PSNR = 53.95 dB, b1) 4 bpp, $\Delta E = 0.56$ and PSNR = 49.55 dB, c1) 7 bpp, $\Delta E = 2.07$ and PSNR = 37.34 dB. a2), b2), c2) Image of the differences between the original image and the marked images (a1), (b1) and (c1), respectively. The color differences between the original image and the watermarked image are computed pixel by pixel and displayed with a logarithmic scale. a3) and c3) Zooms on the watermarked images with 1 and 7 bpp (for a color version of this figure, see www.iste.co.uk/fernandez/digicolor.zip)*

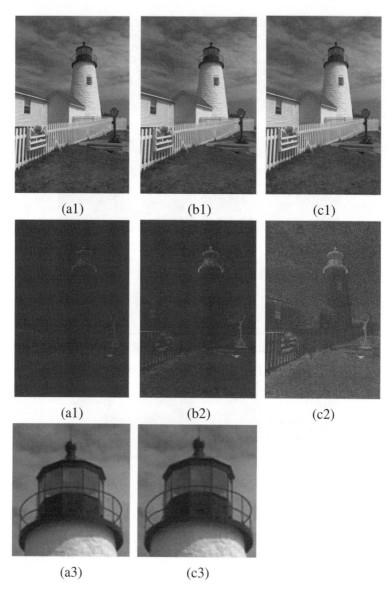

Figure 8.10. *Lighthouse image marked respectively with: a1) 1 bpp, ΔE = 0.20 and PSNR = 54.60 dB, b1) 4 bpp, ΔE = 0.48 and PSNR = 50.10 dB, c1) 7 bpp, ΔE =1.70 and PSNR=37.91 dB. a2), b2), c2) Image of the differences between the original image and the marked images (a1), (b1) and (c1), respectively. The color differences between the original image and the watermarked image are computed pixel by pixel and displayed with a logarithmic scale. a3) and c3) Zooms on the watermarked images with 1 and 7 bpp (for a color version of this figure, see www.iste.co.uk/fernandez/digicolor.zip)*

the watermarked beacon image appears more blurred than the original. The standard distortion metrics such as the MSE and PSNR are simple and not dependent on subjective assessments. Their main disadvantage is that they are not correlated with human perception of fidelity [CHA 07a, XEN 05]. In addition, the MSE does not consider the spatial frequencies or the color analysis for the evaluation of colors while the HVS does it. The fidelity evaluation through HVS-based metrics currently remains an open problem. These metrics should incorporate both human sensitivity to color and spatial frequencies, as proposed by the S-CIELAB space and the iCAM color space [FAI 04].

Even if the CIE L*a*b* ΔE metric can be considered a color Euclidean metric, the S-CIELAB space has the advantage of taking into account the sensitivity of the HVS in the spatial domain. Current research has focused on the use of color appearance models (CAM) and saliency maps to develop new watermarking schemes. This is a very open research topic. Similarly, it would be interesting to undertake new research into color image watermarking based on high-level color descriptors such as those used in MPEG-7 for instance. Most watermarking schemes propose to take into account the sensitivity of the HVS either only as a function of the frequency content, or only as a function of color. We consider that to increase the fidelity and robustness of these schemes, hybrid watermarking schemes should be defined by combining the spatial, frequency and color characteristics.

8.3.4. *Protection of color palettes*

Other work proposes to protect the colors of an image by concealing the information of the color palette in the image, by combining color image processing and data protection. In fact, these methods propose to hide the color information by using the decomposition of a color image into an image index and a color palette. Therefore, the insertion can be done in the image index [FRI 99] or in the palette color [TZE 04, WU 03]. In [TZE 04, WU 03], the color palettes are used to watermark and authenticate images. In particular, Wu *et al.* proposed to construct a new palette to insert a binary message into each palette color [WU 03]. Other work, such as [CAM 02, QUE 06, ZHA 04], is based on a DWT and use substitutions as sub-bands to insert the color information into a grayscale image. Their main objectives relate to compression, image authentication [CAM 02, ZHA 04] and image printing [QUE 06]. Although [QUE 06] inserts the color information into a grayscale image, their method is used to retrieve the color information from color documents but printed with a black and white printer or transmitted with a conventional fax in black and white. None of these methods aims to protect color information by hiding the color palette in the index image.

On the other hand, some work proposes to rearrange the colors of the palette to improve compression of images that are based on indexed colors [MEM 96, PIN 04, BAT 07]. These approaches show that the rearrangement of the color palette can be very important but really depends on the application. Other work proposes to protect the color information by hiding the color palette in the index image [CHA 06b]. In fact, in [CHA 06b], the approach shows a rearrangement of the colors of the palette to get an index image that is closest to the luminance image and with closer consecutive colors in the palette. In other work, improvements of this approach have been presented [CHA 08].

We will finally discuss a particular strategy, namely the protection of color images according to an encryption that adapts to the content.

8.4. Protection of color images by selective encryption (SE)

In this section, we review a set of methods allowing us to selectively encrypt color images or videos, and then present a method for combining SE and JPEG compression of color images.

8.4.1. *SE of color images*

SE is an approach allowing us to reduce the processing time while maintaining a certain level of confidentiality by encrypting only part of the data stream [LOO 04]. The SE, as well as the partial encryption (PE), are applied only to certain parts of the bitstream. During the decoding step, the encrypted and unencrypted data should be properly identified to be displayed [CHE 00, MAR 05, ROD 06b]. For instance, in the context of video surveillance cameras, the protection of individual privacy should be ensured. The idea is thus to encrypt only the faces of people and leave all the rest unencrypted to allow an operator to remotely monitor an area. The technical challenges for such systems are very high and many approaches have not completely succeeded in solving this problem [LIN 05].

In [TAN 96] a technique called "zigzag permutation" is proposed. This is applicable to images and videos compressed by DCT-based approaches. The proposed method shows a certain level of confidentiality, and it increases the total size of the protected data. The combination of a PE and an image or video compression using a set of hierarchical tree partitions was proposed by [CHE 00]. The problem is that this approach requires a large computational complexity. A method that requires no additional computation time and that operates directly in the bit planes of the image was proposed by [LUK 05]. The video SE that can be integrated into the standard H.264 format has been studied in numerous articles, including [WEN 02]. An approach based on entropy coding for encryption using statistical models has been proposed by [WU 05]. In [DRO 02], a technique that encrypts a number of AC frequency coefficients is presented. The DC coefficients are not encrypted as they carry significant visual information and are easily predictable. Even if the flow rate is maintained and the method remains consistent with the bit stream, this approach generates codes that are not hierarchical (in terms of protection). In addition, the compression and the encryption process are separated and, consequently, the computation time increases sharply. Fisch *et al.* [FIS 04] proposed a method where the data is organized in a hierarchical stream. Data streams are constructed with the DC coefficients and with a few AC coefficients for each block. They are arranged in layers according to their visual importance. The SE process is then applied to these layers. Other encryption methods are based on the DC coefficients derived from image sequence [CHE 00, WEN 02, ZEN 99].

The AES [DAE 02] standard described in section 8.2.3.2 is applied on a discrete wavelet transform on compressed images [OU 06]. The color image encryption in the wavelet domain was proposed by [MAR 05]. In this approach, the encryption is applied to the encoded wavelet coefficients. In [ROD 06a] an SE was proposed on color images compressed with JPEG by selectively encrypting only the luminance component Y. The JPEG 2000 data stream encryption was presented in [IMA 06, LIU 06]. An SE using a function map was developed in [LIU 06].

Figure 8.11. *Original image of Lena (for a color version of this figure, see www.iste.co.uk/fernandez/digicolor.zip)*

[SAI 05] studied the robustness against attacks of a partially encrypted image by exploiting the information of unencrypted bits. The protection of the rights and privacy of individuals in the context of a video surveillance system by using a viewer that generates a mask and AES was proposed by [YAB 05]. In the remainder of this section, we present the results of a color image protection approach by simultaneously applying an SE based on a Huffman coding of high frequencies of DC coefficients in the ROI and a JPEG compression.

8.4.2. *Analysis of an encryption jointly with a JPEG compression*

In this section, we present the results of an approach that simultaneously applies an SE and a JPEG compression on various images [ROD 06a]. At first, we show the results obtained when the SE is applied to the entire image compressed by JPEG. The original image of Lena, 512×512 pixels, is shown in Figure 8.11. The compressed image of Lena with a quality factor (QF) of 100% is shown in Figure 8.12a and the compressed image with a QF of 10% is shown Figure 8.12d.

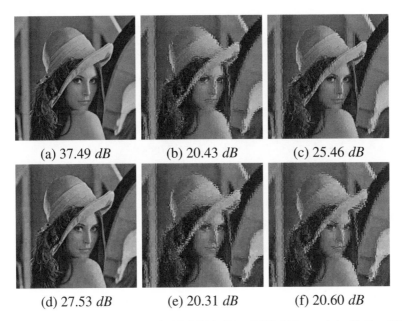

(a) 37.49 *dB*   (b) 20.43 *dB*   (c) 25.46 *dB*

(d) 27.53 *dB*   (e) 20.31 *dB*   (f) 20.60 *dB*

Figure 8.12. *a) Image compressed with JPEG, QF = 100%, b) Image (a) with C = 128 bits/block, c) Image (a) with C = 8 bits/block, d) Image compressed with JPEG, QF=10%, e) Image (d) with C = 128 bits/block, f) Image (d) with C = 8 bits/block (for a color version of this figure, see www.iste.co.uk/fernandez/digicolor.zip)*

Initially, we analyzed the available space for the encryption in the images compressed by JPEG. In Table 8.2, we indicate the number of bits available for the SE of Lena, 512 × 512 pixels, corresponding to different quality factors (QF) of JPEG compression. In the same table, for each QF, we specify the distortion in terms of PSNR as well as the number of encrypted bits per block in the quantized DCT coefficients. We can observe that when the QF decreases, and therefore when the compression ratio increases, we are able to encrypt fewer bits of the compressed image. This is because the JPEG compression produces flat regions in the blocks resulting in a significant number of blocks containing many AC coefficients equal to zero. Therefore, the Huffman coding creates blocks for such regions that this method cannot encrypt. It should be noted that the available bits, shown in the third column of Table 8.2 are not automatically all encrypted because of the constraint imposed by C. To optimize the computation time, C should be smaller than the ratio of the average number of bits to the blocks size.

QF	PSNR (dB)	Number of available bits		
		Total Y component	Percentage for Y component	Average Bits/block
100	37.49	5,37,936	25.65	131
90	34.77	1,53,806	7.33	38
80	33.61	90,708	4.33	22
70	32.91	65,916	3.14	16
60	32.41	50,818	2.42	12
50	32.02	42,521	2.03	10
40	31.54	34,397	1.64	8
30	30.91	26,570	1.27	6
20	29.83	17,889	0.85	4
10	27.53	8,459	0.40	2

Table 8.2. *Results for different JPEG quality factors*

In Figure 8.13, we show a graphical representation of the last column of Table 8.2, by showing the variance of the ratio between the number of bits available for the SE and the total number of bits per block. We can observe that the variance decreases with the QF because the number of flat regions increases in the compressed image.

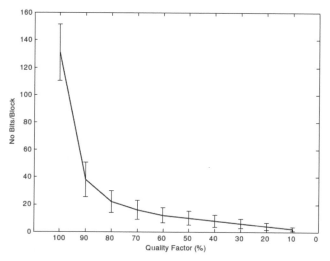

Figure 8.13. *Ratio between the average number of bits per available block for SE to the block size*

In Figure 8.14, we show the evaluation of PSNR between the crypto-compressed image of Lena and the original image, for different QP and different values of C. In the same figure, we also show the PSNR between the compressed image with different QF and the original image. From this figure we can observe that for a large value of C we encrypt a large number of bits and therefore, the image is more distorted from the original. We can observe that when $C \in \{32, 64, 128\}$, the difference in terms of PSNR is similar and varies slowly when the QF decreases. Since the reasoning is performed in terms of amount of information we have, for simplicity purposes, used the PSNR to evaluate the information degradation. However, it is well known that this does not fully reflect the visual degradations.

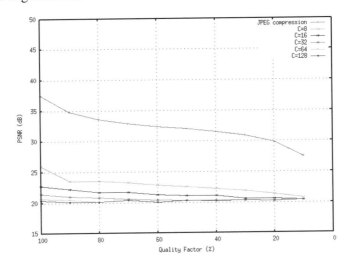

Figure 8.14. *PSNR of the crypto-compressed image of Lena for different quality factors and constraints (for a color version of this figure, see www.iste.co.uk/fernandez/digicolor.zip)*

In Figure 8.12b we show the original image of Lena, image encrypted using a constraint $C = 128$ bits/block, while in Figure 8.12c the same image is encrypted using a constraint $C = 8$ bits/block. In Figure 8.12e we show the image of Lena with a QF of 10%, encrypted using a constraint $C = 128$ bits/block, while in Figure 8.12f the same image is encrypted with the constraint $C = 8$ bits/block. We can see that the degradation introduced by the encryption in the image with QF = 100% (see Figure 8.12b) is greater than the degradation in the image from Figure 8.12c because we encrypt fewer bits per block for the latter. When we combine a high JPEG compression (QF = 10%) with an SE, as shown in the images of Figures 8.12e and 8.12f, we observe a large visual degradation compared to images of Figures 8.12b and 8.12c, respectively. The greatest distortion is due to the increase in artifacts in the blocks. This distortion is highly noticeable when we observe image characteristics such as the eyes.

8.4.3. *SE of regions of interest in color images*

In this section, we applied the previously presented method on the color image shown in Figure 8.15a and on a sequence of color images

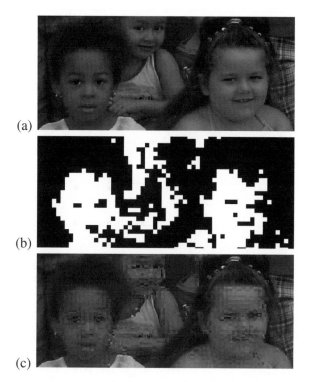

Figure 8.15. *SE of the skin: a) original image 416 × 200 pixels, b) detection of regions of interest, c) protected image (for a color version of this figure, see www.iste.co.uk/fernandez/digicolor.zip)*

shown in Figure 8.16a. We used the DC components of the chrominance planes to select regions of interest (ROI) corresponding to skin colors. From several experiments, for the original color image displayed in the RGB space (see Figure 8.15a) we considered the following values as thresholds: $T = 15$, $C_{r_s} = 140$ and $C_{b_s} = 100$. The detected ROI are shown in 8.15b. We can observe that all skin regions are detected. Each selected DC coefficient corresponds to a block of pixels marked in white in Figure 8.15b. Only those blocks are selectively encrypted. We have encrypted 3,597 blocks for a total of 11,136 blocks in the full image size $1,024 \times 696$ pixels, resulting in an encryption of only 7.32% of the image. The result of the SE of these ROI is shown in Figure 8.15c.

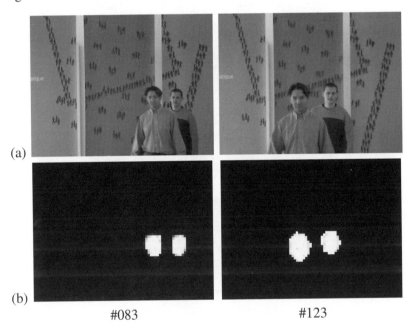

(a)

(b)

#083   #123

Figure 8.16. *a) Sequence of original images, b) detection of regions of interest representing the skin (for a color version of this figure, see www.iste.co.uk/fernandez/digicolor.zip)*

For the video sequence, we extracted two images of a color image sequence of 186 images, illustrated in Figure 8.16a. Each of these images is in JPEG format with a QF of 100%. For the encryption, we used an AES encryption in CFB mode with a key of 128 bits as described in section 8.2.3.4. Each original RGB image (of size 640 × 480 pixels) of the sequence was converted in YC_bC_r, as shown in Figure 8.17 for image #83. For the detection of the skin, we used the DC components of the chrominance planes C_b and C_r. After morphological processing [SER 88] we obtained the binary image shown in Figure 8.16b. Skin detection mainly corresponds to faces represented by white pixels. We have mapped this bitmap that consists of blocks of 8 × 8 pixels of the original image. Finally, we have applied the same method as above on the selected blocks.

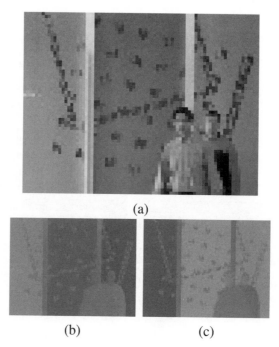

(a)

(b)   (c)

Figure 8.17. *DC coefficients of the image #083 for the three components YC_bC_r:*
a) Y component, b) and c) C_r and C_b components after resampling

After an analysis, we can infer that the amount of encrypted bits is very small compared to the size of the full image. This approach can thus be used for systems with low capacity such as video-protection systems. Figures 8.18 and 8.19 show the final results.

#083   #123

Figure 8.18. *Sequence of selectively encrypted images (for a color version of this figure, see www.iste.co.uk/fernandez/digicolor.zip)*

(a)   (b)

Figure 8.19. *Region of size* 216 × 152 *pixels of the image #123: a) original image, b) protected image (for a color version of this figure, see www.iste.co.uk/fernandez/digicolor.zip)*

8.5. Conclusion

In this chapter, we showed different approaches to protect color images. Initially, we defined the different concepts related to the protection for the transmission and storage of color images. We then reviewed a set of methods for concealing data in images in an invisible way. Some of these methods are not amenable to changes, while others allow you to insert a relatively large amount of data. The use of color is not yet sufficiently exploited to improve the invisibility, capacity, and robustness criteria. Moreover, the fidelity metrics are based more on the luminance than on the color. We have completed this chapter by presenting methods allowing us to protect only a portion of the color images, either high resolution or regions of interest. The main challenge is to combine these protection methods with a compression step while maintaining an interesting compression rate and respecting the standard formats. We conclude, either in the watermarking domain or in the SE domain that the research on quality metrics (including the color dimension) is not yet fully integrated into the work on security.

8.6. Bibliography

[AES 01] AES, "Announcing the advanced encryption standard", *Federal Information Processing Standards Publication*, 2001.

[AGR 07] AGRESTE S., ANDALORO G., PRESTIPINO D., PUCCIO L., "An image adaptive, wavelet-based watermarking of digital images", *Journal of Computational and Applied Mathematics*, vol. 210, no. 1-2, p. 13-21, 2007.

[ALT 00] ALTURKI F., MERSEREAU R., "An oblivious robust digital watermark technique for still images using DCT phase modulation", *Proceedings of the Acoustics, Speech, and Signal Processing, 2000 on IEEE International Conference*, vol. 4, p. 1975-1978, Istanbul, Turkey, 2000.

[BAR 01] BARNI M., BARTOLINI F., PIVA A., "Improved wavelet based watermarking through pixel-wise masking", *IEEE Transactions on Image Processing*, vol. 10, p. 783-791, 2001.

[BAR 02] BARNI M., BARTOLINI F., ROSA A.D., PIVA A., "Color image watermarking in the KLT domains", *Journal of Electronic Imaging*, vol. 11, no. 1, p. 87-95, 2002.

[BAT 00] BATTIATO S., CATALANO D., GALLO G., GENNARO R., "Robust watermarking for images based on color manipulation", *Lecture Notes in Computer Science*, vol. 1768, p. 302-317, 2000.

[BAT 07] BATTIATO S., RUNDO F., STANCO F., "Self organizing motor maps for color-mapped image re-indexing", *IEEE Transactions on Image Processing*, vol. 16, no. 12, p. 2905-2915, December 2007.

[BRI 05] BRIASSOULI A., TSAKALIDES P., STOURAITIS A., "Hidden messages in heavy-tails: DCT-domain watermark detection using alpha-stable models", *IEEE Transactions on Multimedia*, vol. 7, no. 4, 2005.

[CAM 02] CAMPISI P., KUNDUR D., HATZINAKOS D., NERI A., "Compressive data hiding: an unconventional approach for improved color image coding", *EURASIP Journal on Applied Signal Processing*, vol. 2002, no. 2, p. 152-163, 2002.

[CHA 05] CHAN C.S., CHANG C.C., HU Y.C., "Color image hiding scheme using image differencing", *Optical Engineering*, vol. 44, no. 1, 2005.

[CHA 06a] CHAUMONT M., PUECH W., "A color image hidden in a grey-level image", IS&T, *Conference on Colour in Graphics, Imaging and Vision*, p. 226-231, 2006.

[CHA 06b] CHAUMONT M., PUECH W., "A color image hidden in a grey-level image", *CGIV '06*, Leeds, UK, 2006.

[CHA 07a] CHAREYRON G., TRÉMEAU A., "Image watermarking based on a color quantization process", *The International Society for Optical Engineering*, vol. 6506, p. 603-01-603-12, 2007.

[CHA 07b] CHAUMONT M., PUECH W., "A fast and efficient method to protect color images", *The International Society for Optical Engineering*, Visual Communications and Image Processing, vol. 65089, 2007.

[CHA 08] CHAUMONT M., PUECH W., "A 8-bit-grey-level image embedding its 512 color palette", *European Signal Processing Conference*, Lausanne, Switzerland, 2008.

[CHE 07] CHEN W.Y., "Color image steganography scheme using set partitioning in hierarchical trees coding, digital Fourier transform and adaptive phase modulation", *Applied Mathematics and Computation*, vol. 185, no. 432, 2007.

[CHE 00] CHENG H., LI X., "Partial encryption of compressed images and videos", *IEEE Transactions on Signal Processing*, vol. 48, no. 8, p. 2439-2445, August 2000.

[CHO 03] CHOU C., WU T., "Embedding color watermarks in color images", *EURASIP Journal on Applied Signal Processing*, vol. 1, p. 32-40, 2003.

[COX 02] COX I., MILLER M., BLOOM J., *Digital Watermarking*, Morgan Kaufmann Publishers, 2002.

[DAE 02] DAEMEN J., RIJMEN V., AES Proposal: The Rijndael Block Cipher, Report, Proton World Int.l, Katholieke Universiteit Leuven, ESAT-COSIC, Belgium, 2002.

[DER 00] DE ROSA A., BARNI M., BARTOLINI F., CAPPELLINI V., PIVA A., "Optimum decoding of non-additive full frame DFT watermarks", *Information Hiding*, p. 159-171, 2000.

[DIF 76] DIFFIE W., HELLMAN M.E., "New directions in cryptography", *IEEE Transactions on Information Theory*, vol. 26, no. 6, p. 644-654, 1976.

[DRO 02] DROOGENBROECK M.V., BENEDETT R., "Techniques for a selective encryption of uncompressed and compressed images", *Proceedings of Advanced Concepts for Intelligent Vision Systems (ACIVS)*, Ghent, Belgium, p. 90-97, September 2002.

[FAI 04] FAIRCHILD M., JOHNSON G., "The iCAM framework for image appearance image difference and image quality", *Journal of Electronic Imaging*, vol. 13, p. 126-138, 2004.

[FAN 04] FAN Z., HONGBIN Z., "Wavelet domain watermarking capacity analysis", *EUSIPCO Conference*, Vienna, Austria, 2004.

[FIS 04] FISCH M.M., STGNER H., UHL A., "Layered Encryption Techniques for DCT-Coded Visual Data", *Proceedings of European Signal Processing Conference (EUSIPCO)*, p. 821-824, Vienna, Austria, September, 2004.

[FLE 97] FLEET D., HEEGER D., "Embedding invisible information in color images", *IEEE International Conference on Image Processing*, vol. 1, p. 532-535, 1997.

[FRI 99] FRIDRICH J., "A new steganographic method for palette images", *IS&T PICS*, Savannah, Georgia, USA, p. 285-289, April 1999.

[FU 07] FU Y., SHEN R., "Color image watermarking scheme based on linear discriminant analysis", *Computer Standards and Interfaces*, 2007.

[GAN 05] GANIC E., DEXTER S.D., ESKICIOGLU A.M., "Embedding multiple watermarks in the DFT, domain using low and high frequency bands", *Proceedings of SPIE: Security, Steganography, and Watermarking of Multimedia Contents VII*, p. 175-184, San Jose, CA, USA, 2005.

[GIL 02] GILANI S., KOSTOPOULOS I., SKODRAS A., "Colour image-adaptive watermarking", *International Conference on Digital Signal Processing*, vol. 2, Santorin, Greece, p. 721-724, 2002.

[GUI 02] GUILLEM-LESSARD S., www.uqtr.ca/~delisle/Crypto, 2002.

[HER 00] HERNNDEZ J.R., AMADO M., PREZ-GONZLEZ F., "DCT-domain watermarking techniques for still images: detector performance analysis and a new structure", *IEEE Transactions on Image Processing*, vol. 9, no. 1, p. 55-68, 2000.

[HUA 05] HUANG P., CHIANG C., "Novel and robust saturation watermarking in wavelet domains for color images", *Optical Engineering*, vol. 44, no. 11, p. 117002.1-117002.15, 2005.

[IMA 06] IMAIZUMI S., WATANABE O., FUJIYOSHI M., KIYA H., "Generalized hierarchical encryption of JPEG2000 codestreams for access control", *Proceedings of IEEE International Conference on Image Processing*, Atlanta, USA, p. 1094-1097, October 2006.

[KAN 03] KANG X., HUANG J., SHI Y., LIN Y., "A DWT-DFT composite watermarking scheme robust to both affine transform and JPEG compression", *IEEE Transactions on Circuits and Systems for Video Technology*, vol. 13, no. 8, p. 776-786, 2003.

[KER 83] KERCKHOFFS A., "La cryptographie militaire", *Journal des sciences militaires*, vol. 9, p. 5-38, 1883.

[KIM 01] KIM H., LEE H., LEE H., HA Y., "Digital watermarking based on color differences", *The International Society for Optical Engineering, Security and Watermarking of Multimedia Contents III*, vol. 4314, p. 10-17, 2001.

[KUO 05] KUO C., CHENG S., "Fusion of color edge detection and color quantization for color image watermarking using principal axis analysis", *IEEE International Conference on Image Processing*, vol. 1, p. 233-236, 2005.

[KUT 97] KUTTER M., "Digital signature of color images using amplitude modulation", *The International Society for Optical Engineering, Storage and Retrieval for Image and Video Databases*, vol. 3022, p. 518-526, 1997.

[LIN 00] LIN S., CHIN C., "A robust DCT-based watermarking for copyright protection", *IEEE Transactions Consumer Electronics*, no. 46, p. 415-421, 2000.

[LIN 02] LIN M.H., HU Y.C., CHANG C.C., "Both color and grayscale secret images hiding in a color image", *International Journal of Pattern Recognition and Artificial Intelligence*, vol. 6, p. 673-713, 2002.

[LIN 05] LIN E., ESKICIOGLU A., LAGENDIJK R., DELP E., "Advances in digital video content protection", *Proceedings of the IEEE*, vol. 93, no. 1, p. 171-183, 2005.

[LIU 06] LIU J., "Efficient selective encryption for JPEG 2000 images using private initial table", *Pattern Recognition*, vol. 39, no. 8, p. 1509-1517, August 2006.

[LOO 04] LOOKABAUGH T., SICKER D., "Selective encryption for consumer applications", *IEEE Communications Magazine*, vol. 42, no. 5, p. 124-129, May 2004.

[LOV 05] LO-VARCO G., PUECH W., DUMAS M., "Content based watermarking for securing color images", *Journal of Imaging Science and Technology (JIST)*, vol. 49, no. 5, p. 450-459, 2005.

[LUK 05] LUKAC R., PLATANIOTIS K., "Bit-level based secret sharing for image encryption", *Pattern Recognition*, vol. 38, no. 5, p. 767-772, May 2005.

[LUK 07] LUKAC R., PLATANIOTIS K.N., *Color Image Processing: Methods and Applications, Secure Color Imaging*, CRC Press, New York, USA, 2007.

[MAR 05] MARTIN K., LUKAC R., PLATANIOTIS K., "Efficient encryption of wavelet-based coded color images", *Pattern Recognition*, vol. 38, no. 7, p. 1111-1115, July 2005.

[MEM 96] MEMON N., VENKATESWARAN A., "On ordering color maps for lossless predictive coding", *IEEE Transactions on Image Processing*, vol. 5, no. 11, p. 1522-1527, November 1996.

[OU 06] OU S., CHUNG H., SUNG W., "Improving the compression and encryption of images using FPGA-based cryptosystems", *Multimedia Tools and Applications*, vol. 28, no. 1, p. 5-22, January 2006.

[PEI 06] PEI S., CHEN J., "Color image watermarking by Fibonacci lattice index modulation", *Conference on Colour in Graphics, Imaging, and Vision*, p. 211-215, 2006.

[PIN 04] PINHO A., NEVES A., "A survey on palette reordering methods for improving the compression of color-indexed images", *IEEE Transactions on Image Processing*, vol. 13, no. 11, p. 1411-1418, November 2004.

[PIV 98] PIVA A., BARNI M., BARTOLINI F., "Copyright protection of digital images by means of frequency doMayn watermarking", *Mathematics of Data/Image Coding, Compression, and Encryption*, SCHMALZ M.S. (ed.), *Proceedings of SPIE*, vol. 3456, p. 25-35, July 1998.

[PIV 99] PIVA A., BARNI M., BARTOLINI F., CAPPELLINI V., "Exploiting the cross correlation of RGB-channels for robust watermarking of color images", *IEEE International Conference on Image Processing*, vol. 1, p. 306-310, 1999.

[QUE 06] DE QUEIROZ R., BRAUN K., "Color to gray and back: color embedding into textured gray images", *IEEE Transactions on Image Processing*, vol. 15, no. 6, p. 1464-1470, 2006.

[RIV 78] RIVEST R.L., SHAMIR A., ADLEMAN L., "A method for obtaining digital signatures and public-key cryptosystems", *Communications of the ACM*, vol. 21, no. 2, p. 120-126, 1978.

[ROD 06a] RODRIGUES J.-M., PUECH W., BORS A., "A selective encryption for heterogenous color JPEG images based on VLC and AES stream cipher", *Proceedings of European Conference on Colour in Graphics, Imaging and Vision (CGIV '06)*, p. 34-39, Leeds, UK, June 2006.

[ROD 06b] RODRIGUES J.-M., PUECH W., BORS A., "Selective encryption of human skin in JPEG images", *Proceedings of IEEE International Conference on Image Processing*, p. 1981-1984, Atlanta, USA, October 2006.

[ROY 04] ROY S., CHANG E., "Watermarking color histograms", *IEEE International Conference on Image Processing*, vol. 1, p. 2191-2194, 2004.

[SAI 05] SAID A., "Measuring the strength of partial encryption scheme", *Proceedings of IEEE International Conference on Image Processing*, vol. 2, p. 1126-1129, Genova, Italy, 2005.

[SCH 97] SCHNEIER B., *Cryptographie appliquée : protocoles, algorithmes et codes sources en C*, Wiley, 1997.

[SER 88] SERRA J., *Image Analysis and Mathematical Morphology*, Academic Press, London 1988.

[SOL 01] SOLACHIDIS V., PITAS L., "Circularly symmetric watermark embedding in 2-D DFT doMayn", *IEEE Transactions on Image Processing*, vol. 10, no. 11, p. 1741-1753, 2001.

[STI 96] STINSON D., *Cryptographie - Théorie et et pratique*, Thompson Publishing, 1996.

[TAN 96] TANG L., "Methods for encrypting and decrypting MPEG video data efficiently", *Proceedings of ACM Multimedia*, vol. 3, p. 219-229, 1996.

[TSA 04] TSAI P., HU Y., CHANG C., "A color image watermarking scheme based on color quantization", *Signal Processing*, vol. 84, no. 1, p. 95-106, 2004.

[TSA 07] TSAI H., SUM D., "Color image watermark extraction based on support vector machines", *Information Sciences*, vol. 177, p. 550-569, 2007.

[TSU 06] TSUI T., ZHANG X., ANDROUTSOS D., "Color image watermarking using the spatio-chromatic fourier transform", *IEEE International Conference on Acoustics, Speech and Signal Processing*, vol. 2, p. 305-308, 2006.

[TZE 04] TZENG C., YANG Z., TSAI W., "Adaptative data hiding in palette images by color ordering and mapping with security protection", *IEEE Transactions on Communications*, vol. 52, no. 5, p. 791-800, 2004.

[VID 02] VIDAL J., MADUENO M., SAYROL E., "Color image watermarking using channel-state knowledge", *The International Society for Optical Engineering, Security and Watermarking of Multimedia Contents IV*, vol. 4675, p. 214-221, San Jose, CA, USA, 2002.

[WAN 08] WANG J., LIU G., DAI Y., SUN J., WANG Z., LIAN S., "Locally optimum detection for Barni's multiplicative watermarking in DWT doMayn", *Signal Processing*, vol. 88, no. 1, p. 117-130, 2008.

[WEN 02] WEN J., SEVERA M., ZENG W., LUTTRELL M., JIN W., "A format-compliant configurable encryption framework for access control of video", *IEEE Transactions on Circuits and Systems for Video Technology*, vol. 12, no. 6, p. 545-557, June 2002.

[WU 03] WU M.-Y., HO Y.-K., LEE J.-H., "An iterative method of palette-based image steganography", *Pattern Recognition Letters*, vol. 25, p. 301-309, 2003.

[WU 05] WU C., KUO C., "Design of integrated multimedia compression and encryption systems", *IEEE Transactions on Multimedia*, vol. 7, no. 5, p. 828-839, October 2005.

[XEN 05] XENOS M., HANTZARA K., MITSOU E., KOSTOPOULOS I., "A model for the assessment of watermark quality with regards to fidelity", *Journal of Visual Communication and Image Representation*, vol. 16, no. 6, p. 621-642, 2005.

[XIA 98] XIA X., BONCELET C., ARCE G., "Wavelet transform based watermark for digital images", *Optics Express*, vol. 3, no. 12, p. 497-511, 1998.

[YAB 05] YABUTA K., KITAZAWA H., TANAKA T., "A new concept of security camera monitoring with privacy protection by masking moving objects", *Proceedings of Advances in Multimedia Information Processing*, vol. 1, p. 831-842, 2005.

[YU 01] YU P., TSAI H., LIN J., "Digital watermarking based on neural networks for color images", *Signal Processing*, vol. 81, no. 3, p. 663-671, 2001.

[YU 07] YU Y.U., CHANG C.C., LIN I.C., "A new steganographic method for color and grayscale image hiding", *Computer Vision and Image Understanding*, vol. 107, no. 3, p. 193-194, 2007.

[ZEN 99] ZENG W., LEI S., "Efficient frequency domain video scrambling for content access control", *Proceedings of ACM Multimedia*, p. 285-293, Orlando, FL, USA, November 1999.

[ZHA 04] ZHAO Y., CAMPISI P., KUNDUR D., "Dual domain for authentication and compression of cultural heritage images", *IEEE Transactions on Image Processing*, vol. 13, no. 3, p. 430-448, 2004.

[ZHU 06] ZHUANCHENG Z., DIANFU Z., XIAOPING Y., "A robust image blind watermarking algorithm based on adaptive quantization step in DWT", *Journal of Image and Graphics*, vol. 11, no. 6, p. 840-847, 2006.

Chapter 9

Quality Assessment Approaches

9.1. Introduction

9.1.1. *What is quality?*

At first glance of an object (in the semantic sense of the term), a human being is able to tell if the sight of it is pleasant to him or not. He then performs nothing more than a classification of the perception of that object based on the feeling provided and experienced in, for instance, two categories, "I like" or "I don't like". Even if it is logical to think that several criteria may influence the final decision, such an ability to classify visual sensations should undoubtedly be linked with the consciousness inherent to every human being. Consciousness is related to what Freud calls "the perception-consciousness system" [FRE 38]. This is a peripheral function of the psychic apparatus, which receives information from the outside world and from memories and internal sensations of pleasure or displeasure. The urgent nature of this perceptual function leads to a consciousness inability to keep a permanent record of this information. It communicates it to

Chapter written by Mohamed-Chaker LARABI, Abdelhakim SAADANE and Christophe CHARRIER.

the preconscious as a first memory. Consciousness perceives and transmits sensory qualities. Freud uses phrases such as "perception, quality, reality index" to describe the content of the operations of the perception-consciousness system.

Thus the perception of an object by a human observer is considered as one of the various scales internal to a process leading to an overall assessment of the quality of an object or, in this case, of an image.

At this point, it should be interesting to differentiate between two expressions used interchangeably to refer to this notion of quality: "image quality" and "image fidelity". In fact, it should be noted that by abuse of language, these two concepts are often confused. The notion of quality could to the artist be what the notion of fidelity is to the forger. The artist usually works using concepts, impressions related to his social and/or professional environment, and places himself in an existing art movement (student-teacher relationship) or a new movement that he has created from scratch. The artwork performed is thus considered as original, and experts talk about the quality of the artwork. Behind this approach, we realize that the notion of originality is associated with the term quality. Who has never found himself facing a work of art that puzzled him while his neighbor was amazed by it? One just has to stroll through museums to see this phenomenon. Thus, the quality of a work of art is described according to the person's consciousness and personal sensitivity pre-defined by economic and social environment.

The forger usually works from a model and tries to reproduce it as accurately as possible. In this case the forger has to provide a faultless work of art, and it is not uncommon for him to use the same techniques used by the author several centuries ago (combination of several pigments to produce the color, use of a canvas of that same time, etc.). The copy must be true to the original. Some might argue that, in some cases, the copy may outweigh the quality of the original. As an anecdote, one of the most famous scandals in the history of the art market began with a small mundane advertisement in an English newspaper: "False authentic copies (19th and 20th Centuries) for 150 pounds". John Myatt, art teacher in desperate straits had thus found a way to get rich. A great crook and a connoisseur of the art world, John Drewe, sniffed out the case of the century and immediately partnered with the advertiser. They continued their forgery for almost 10 years. Drewe and Myatt deceived the greatest experts, Sotheby's and Christie's auction houses, and renowned museums such as the Tate Gallery or the Victoria and Albert Museum. With masterly copies of Giacometti or Dubuffet and false certificates of authenticity, the system was perfect.

9.1.2. *Quality vs. fidelity*

Research on image processing is increasingly focusing on quality. The whole problem is to characterize the quality of an image, as human beings can do. Therefore, we should separate the following two types of metrics:

1) the fidelity metrics;

2) the quality metrics.

The fidelity metric, as the name suggests, refers to whether the image reproduction is true to the original or not. In this case, a metric that calculates the distance between the two images is implemented. This distance numerically represents the gap that may exist between the two reproductions of the image. The ultimate goal is to validate this measure of gap in the human visual system.

The quality measure should be related to what humans do naturally and instinctively in front of any new work of art; they give it a subjective appreciation based on their consciousness. Therefore, humans cannot be separated from the quality measure. Thus, the study of mechanisms allowing us to understand the internal scales used in the quality assessment by a human being has become an area of research in itself. In 1860, Gustav Theodor Fechner proposed to measure the physical events triggered intentionally by the experimenter, and the responses were obtained according to specified models.

9.1.3. *Strong link with the compression*

Image or video compression is one of the areas where quality assessment is essential. For a long time, researchers in these areas have used the PSNR (metric derived from the signal processing field) as the only single metric. Its extensive use during recent decades is partly because digital images were considered as 2D signals or an extension of a 1D signal. However, when working on digital images, it is clear that they cannot simply be purely 2D signals. In fact, unlike the 1D signal, the final recipient of the images is overwhelmingly still a human being. Therefore, it appears that this mathematical metric based on signal tools is often uncorrelated to human judgment because it does not include a model or information on how the human visual system (HVS) operates. In fact, for the latter, the quality is not measured pixel by pixel but globally through a process that is supposed to be multiscale and multiplexed.

Thus, for these recent years, standardization committees, whether JPEG or MPEG, have been highly aware of issues of quality assessment. Consequently, a new working group was created for the JPEG committee called AIC, which, stands for *Advanced Image Coding*. The latter aims not only to define the compression standards of the next decade but also to pre-define the guidelines allowing us to regulate the assessment procedure whether it is subjective or objective.

9.2. Color fidelity metric

The quality assessment, whether subjective or objective, often requires the measurement of the color fidelity between the original image and the degraded image. Thus, for natural images, Yendrikhovskij [YEN 98] showed that in the cognitive process, the image quality was going through a kind of fidelity measurement between the colors of the scene and the memory of colors such as sky, grass, etc. It is therefore very important to have metrics that relate as accurately as possible the color difference between two stimuli. This work is mostly conducted through the International Commission on Illumination (CIE).

9.2.1. ΔE94, ΔE2000

In 1994, the CIE recommended the use of a new equation for color difference based on the works by Berns *et al.* [ALM 89, BER 91]. This new equation is derived from subjective tests carried out with patches of acrylic paint. The formulation of this equation is similar to the CMC structure (l:c) with simplified weighting factors [BER 91]:

$$\Delta E_{94} = \sqrt{\left(\frac{\Delta L_{ab}^*}{K_L S_L}\right)^2 + \left(\frac{\Delta C_{ab}^*}{K_C S_C}\right)^2 + \left(\frac{\Delta H_{ab}^*}{K_H S_H}\right)^2} \qquad [9.1]$$

with: $S_L = 1$, $S_C = 1 + 0.045 \times C_{ab,1}^*$, $S_H = 1 + 0.015 \times C_{ab,1}^*$ and K_L, K_C, K_H are weighting factors dependent on experimental conditions. The CIE recommends that we set all weighting factors to 1, except for applications in the textile industry.

In 2000, the CIE proposed a final equation for computing the color difference based on the works by Luo *et al.* [LUO 00, GUA 99]. Compared to $\Delta E94$, $\Delta E2000$ formulation is more complex but yields better results. The formulation of this distance is as follows:

$$\Delta E_{2000} = \sqrt{\left(\frac{\Delta L'}{K_L S_L}\right)^2 + \left(\frac{\Delta C'}{K_C S_C}\right)^2 + \left(\frac{\Delta H'}{K_H S_H}\right)^2 + R_T \left(\frac{\Delta C'}{K_C S_C}\right)\left(\frac{\Delta H'}{K_H S_H}\right)}$$

$$[9.2]$$

The method is divided into four steps based on the CIE $L^* a^* b^*$ values:

1) calculation of the chromaticity using $C = \sqrt{a^{*2} + b^{*2}}$;

2) readjustment of a* levels for neutral hues and thus correction of the definitions of the chromaticity C and the hue h:

$$a' = (1 + G) \times a^*$$

$$C' = \sqrt{a'^2 + b^{*2}}$$

$$h' = arctan(\frac{b*}{a'})$$

with:

$$G = 0.5 \left(1 - \sqrt{\frac{\bar{C}^7}{\bar{C}^7 + (25)^7}}\right)$$

where $\bar{C}$ is the average of C values of the two colors to be compared;

3) determination of differences in luminance (ΔL), hue ($\Delta C'$) and chromaticity ($\Delta H'$).

9.2.2. s-CIELAB

As its name suggests, the s-CIELAB metric is an extension to the CIELAB ΔE [ZHA 97]. Its operation is fairly basic. The first step is to transform the original image and the degraded one into a representation in opposite colors. The data for each component is filtered by separable 2D spatial filters of the form:

$$f = k \sum_i \omega_i E_i \qquad [9.3]$$

where:

$$E_i = k_i e^{-\frac{x^2+y^2}{\sigma_i^2}} \qquad [9.4]$$

The scale factor k_i is chosen such that the sum of E_i is equal to 1. Similarly, the scaling factor k is chosen such that, for each component, the sum of its 2D filter f is equal to 1. The parameters (ω_i, σ_i) are given in degrees of visual angle depending on the used component. Figure 9.1 gives an example of perceptual error s-CIELAB (c) obtained between the original image (a) and the compressed one using JPEG 2000 (b).

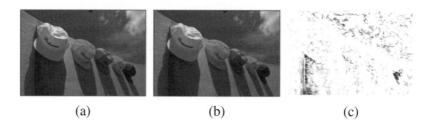

(a)   (b)   (c)

Figure 9.1. *Application example of the s-CIELAB color metric ($\Delta E = 3.34$) (for a color version of this figure, see www.iste.co.uk/fernandez/digicolor.zip)*

An extension of this metric called x-CIELAB has been proposed [ROS 08] introducing a filter using an anisotropic contrast sensitivity function (CSF) built by estimating the perception threshold. This filtering is performed in the frequency domain by matching the spatial frequencies in cycles per degrees. The $\Delta E2000$ distance was used in place of $\Delta E94$ to exploit the performances of the new distance. This extension has been proved to be effective in comparison to the s-CIELAB.

9.3. Subjective assessment of the quality

Despite significant research efforts, understanding the complex interaction between models of images and models of the HVS remains insufficient to quantify visual quality. Thus, psychophysical experiments remain the only viable means for assessing the performances of image processing tools, such as compression or watermarking.

Psychophysical experiments belong to the category of *human in the loop assessment*. They are characterized by the participation of human observers to exploit the abilities of the HVS to measure the quality of an object [CHA 98, LAR 02].

It can be experiments in which the observer is asked to make a choice between two images or ranking experiments of a series of images in order of decreasing quality. Human observers are indispensable in their ability to assess quality. Moreover, this judgment adapts to different situations where the notion of quality is totally different.

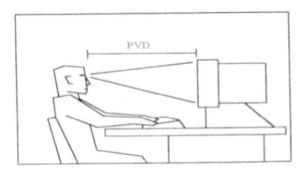

Figure 9.2. *Observation conditions*

During psychophysical experiments, it is essential to ensure that the human observer has on the one hand, a normal vision of colors and, on the other hand, a correct vision acuity. To do this, ophthalmologic tests exist such as the famous Ishihara test and that by Snellen are conducted. Other precautions should be taken regarding the devices used and the environment in which psychophysical tests are conducted. In fact, we cannot speak of quality assessment without being in a standard environment. This standardization consists of several criteria such as the distance between the display screen and the back of the room, the coatings reflection and the gamma monitors as well.

9.3.1. *Experimental plans*

To analyze a system, it is interesting to identify at first the different questions that we want to answer before making an inventory of existing information afterward. Once these two steps are performed, and if the literature provides no information on the system, an experimentation method should then be chosen [QUI 08]. The three essential characteristics of the experimental plan include:

– the experimentation method;

– the analysis of results;

– the gradual acquisition of the results.

These three steps will help us to answer the following questions:

– what are the most influential factors in the system?

– are there any interactions between these factors?

– can we linearize the process according to these factors? Is the resulting model predictive?

– how to minimize the number of measurement points while obtaining as much information as possible?

– is there any bias in the measurement results?

There are several types of experimental plans:

1) single-factorial plan: when only one independent variable is measured, two single-factorial plan methods are possible, nested single-factorial plan and cross single-factorial plan;

2) multifactorial plan: this is used when two or more independent variables are involved. Three types of plans are available: the full nested, full cross and mixed method;

3) repeated measurements plan: in the case of the mixed design or the full cross plan, one same group of subjects is used for all the cells of the

experiment. This has the advantage of being able to control the overall variability and remove the error term, related to differences between subjects. The error component is thus related to the differences between the modalities of one variable and not to the subjects.

9.3.2. *Measurement scales*

Different measurement scales can be used in an experimental design. They are the subject of debate within the various communities of specialists. For some, they are of paramount importance whereas, for others, they are insignificant. Nevertheless, it is useful to know their existence. There are four versions of these scales:

1) the nominal scales allow us to perform a classification by the sex and age of the subject or other categorical data;

2) the ordinal scales rank according to a *continuum*. If a score of 5 is better than a score of 4 and a score of 4 is better than a score of 3, the interpretation of the difference between 3-4 and 4-5 is not necessarily the same;

3) the interval scales follow the same logic as the ordinal scales with each interval denoting the same value. Thus, the difference in temperature between 23 and 24 or 18 and 19 is the same. On the contrary, on an ordinal scale, the feeling of comfort between 18 and 19 may not be the same as between 23 and 24;

4) ratio scales are those which have a true zero. These are the physical measurement scales: weight in kilograms, distance in meters, volume, etc.

Depending on the measurement scale used during an experimental design, it will not be possible to use the same method of analysis.

9.3.3. *Psychophysical experiments*

As described above, psychophysical experiments allow us to draw upon the sensitivity of the human being and specifically to measure this sensitivity. There are different types of psychophysical tests. Among them:

– comparative tests: allow us to make a comparison between two or more images;

– absolute measurement tests: we show a single image to the observer and he is asked to assign it a score representing its quality;

– flash presentations: images appear suddenly and disappear just as suddenly;

– progressive presentations: in this test, the image gradually appears on the screen.

9.3.4. *Subjective assessment methods*

The subjective assessment of the quality is the one and only way to assess the quality of the user experiment. Several methods, mostly defined for the video, are recommended by the ITU-T and ITU-R organizations (ITU: International Telecommunication Union).

9.3.4.1. *DSCQS (Double Stimulus Continuous Quality Scale)*

This method [ITU 02, ITU 05] requires the evaluation of two versions of each test image in which one is the original and the other can be degraded as shown in Figure 9.3. The original image is used as reference but observers do not have information on its position. The latter should be positioned pseudo-randomly.

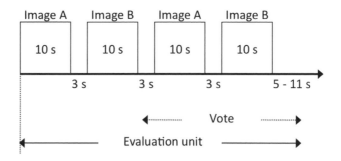

Figure 9.3. *DSCQS method*

In this test, observers are instructed to assess the overall quality of the image by giving a score on a vertical scale printed in pairs to evaluate the two images. The scale is continuous to avoid the problems of forced quantization. However, it is divided into five parts corresponding to the adjectives: bad, poor, fair, good, excellent. The evaluation scores are obtained by measuring the lengths of the segments and converting them to a value between 0 and 100 (see Figure 9.4). With the advances in technology, this evaluation is done nowadays with a graphical interface allowing us to reduce measurement errors.

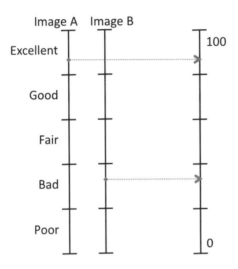

Figure 9.4. *DSCQS quality scale*

Finally, the quality is differentially expressed by exploiting the score of the degraded image and that of the original image as shown in the following equation:

$$SD_{DSCQS} = |S(Im_{deg}) - S(Im_{ori})| \qquad [9.5]$$

9.3.4.2. *DSIS (Double Stimulus Impairment Scale)*

This method [ITU 02, ITU 08] implies that the images are presented in pairs. As described in Figure 9.5, the first image is always the reference and the second corresponds to the degradations studied in the current test.

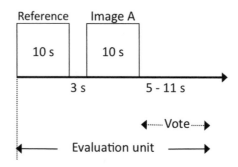

Figure 9.5. *DSIS method*

Each observer selects a category of quality among those proposed to assess the degradation (1: very annoying, 2: annoying, 3: slightly annoying, 4: perceptible but not annoying and 5: imperceptible). The quality is thus expressed with values ranging between 1 and 5.

9.3.4.3. *ACR5/ACR5-HR*

This method [ITU 02, ITU 08] is part of the categorical judgment group where the test sequences are presented one at a time (see Figure 9.6).

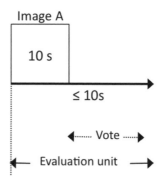

Figure 9.6. *ACR5/ACR11 methods*

Each observer selects one of the 5 categories of the discrete scale (1: poor, 2: bad, 3: fair 4: good, 5: excellent). The quality is thus expressed with values ranging between 1 and 5 for the ACR5 test.

The ACR5-HR test is a variant of ACR5 with a hidden reference (HR-Hidden Reference). The quality is differentially expressed as shown by the following equation:

$$SD_{ACR5} = S(Im_{deg}) - S(Im_{HR}) + 5 \qquad [9.6]$$

9.3.4.4. ACR11/ACR11-HR (Absolute Category Rating)

As for ACR5, this method [ITU 08] is part of the categorical judgment group where the test sequences are presented one at a time. Each observer selects a score on a discrete scale of 11 levels corresponding to the 5 categories of ACR5. The quality is thus expressed with values ranging between 0 and 10 for the ACR11 test.

The ACR11-HR test is a variant of ACR11 with a hidden reference (HR-Hidden Reference). The quality is differentially expressed as shown by the following equation:

$$SD_{ACR11} = S(Im_{deg}) - S(Im_{HR}) + 10 \qquad [9.7]$$

9.3.4.5. SAMVIQ/SAMVIQ-HR (Subjective Assessment Methodology for Video Quality)

In this method [ITU 07a, ITU 07b], the observer, through a graphical interface, has access to several variants of the sequence that can be selected randomly. When they have all been evaluated, he can move to the next sequence. The major differences of this type of test lie in the fact that the observer is able to stop or watch a sequence once more and return to the score he gave to one of the sequences. The evaluation is performed scene by scene with both an implicit reference and an explicit one.

The SAMVIQ method uses a continuous score scale between 0 and 100 annotated by the five qualifiers used in the DSCQS. The assigned score is the one selected on the continuous scale except in case of a hidden reference where the differential score is given by:

$$SD_{SAMVIQ} = S(Im_{deg}) - S(Im_{HR}) + 100 \qquad [9.8]$$

9.3.5. *Processing of the results*

Because of their variation with the area, it is not appropriate to interpret the judgments of most methods in absolute terms. For each parameter of the test, the mean and the confidence interval at 95% of the statistical distribution of the scores, should be calculated.

9.3.5.1. *MOS: mean opinion score*

The first step in analyzing the results is the calculation of the mean score, $\bar{u}_{jkr}$, or MOS (mean opinion score) for each of the presentations:

$$\bar{u}_{jkr} = \frac{1}{N} \sum_{i=1}^{N} u_{ijkr} \qquad [9.9]$$

where u_{ijkr} is the score of observer i for the degradation j of the image/sequence k and the repetition r, and N is the number of observers. In a similar way, we can calculate the global mean scores, $\bar{u}_k$ for each test condition (degradation) and $\bar{u}_j$ and each test sequence/image.

9.3.5.2. *Confidence interval*

To better assess the accuracy of results, it is advisable to associate a confidence interval with each mean (MOS). In general, it has been agreed to use the confidence interval at 95% given in the case of mean scores for each of the presentations, by the following equation:

$$\left[\bar{u}_{jkr} - \delta_{jkr}, \bar{u}_{jkr} + \delta_{jkr} \right] \qquad [9.10]$$

where:

$$\delta_{jkr} = 1.95 \frac{S_{jkr}}{\sqrt{N}} \qquad [9.11]$$

The standard deviation, for each presentation S_{jkr}, is given by:

$$S_{jkr} = \sqrt{\sum_{i=1}^{N} \frac{(\bar{u}_{jkr} - u_{jkr})^2}{(N-1)}} \qquad [9.12]$$

With a 95% probability, the absolute value of the difference between the experimental mean score and the "true" mean score (for a very large number of observers) is less than 95% of the confidence interval, with the condition that the distribution of individual scores meets certain rules.

9.3.5.3. *Rejection of inconsistent observations*

The verification of the observations is to reject from the study any observation that significantly deviates from the mean. This avoids bias, which may affect the results. The outlier rejection may be related to several factors; the most common are noted as follows:

– inadequate understanding of the test method by the participant, which would be the consequence of an incomplete explanation during the presentation phase of the test and the voting instructions;

– decline in attention due to fatigue, stress, nervousness or lassitude;

– influence of the content of the image/video.

Algorithm 9.1. Outlier rejection procedure

---

if $(2 \leq \beta_{2jkr} \leq 4)$ **then**
$\quad$ **if** $(u_{ijkr} \geq \bar{u}_{ijkr} + 2\sigma_{jkr})$ **then**
$\quad\quad | \quad P_i = P_i + 1;$
$\quad$ **end**
$\quad$ **if** $(u_{ijkr} \leq \bar{u}_{ijkr} - 2\sigma_{jkr})$ **then**
$\quad\quad | \quad Q_i = Q_i + 1;$
$\quad$ **end**
end
else
$\quad$ **if** $(u_{ijkr} \geq \bar{u}_{ijkr} + \sqrt{20}\sigma_{jkr})$ **then**
$\quad\quad | \quad P_i = P_i + 1;$
$\quad$ **end**
$\quad$ **if** $(u_{ijkr} \leq \bar{u}_{ijkr} - \sqrt{20}\sigma_{jkr})$ **then**
$\quad\quad | \quad Q_i = Q_i + 1;$
$\quad$ **end**
end
if $\left(\frac{P_i+Q_i}{J.K.R} > 0.05\right)$ *and* $\left(\left|\frac{P_i-Q_i}{P_i+Q_i}\right| < 0.3\right)$ **then**
$\quad |$ Rejection of the observer.
end

This step ensures the homogeneity of the results. The recommendations of the ITU advocate the use of the kurtosis test. The latter allows us to reject observations whose decisions are statistically inconsistent with that of others. Its role is to ensure that the distribution of responses of the observers follows a normal distribution. It is expressed as the ratio between the fourth moment and the square of the second moment:

$$\beta_{2jk} = \frac{\frac{1}{N}\sum_{i=1}^{N}(\bar{u}_{jk} - u_{ijk})^4}{\left(\frac{1}{N}\sum_{i=1}^{N}(\bar{u}_{jk} - u_{ijk})^2\right)^2} \tag{9.13}$$

Once calculated, the next step is to verify that the value of this coefficient is between 2 and 4. The following algorithm gives the procedure:

9.4. Objective evaluation of quality

9.4.1. *Full reference metrics*

9.4.1.1. *Mathematical metrics*

Simple mathematical metrics are often used to have a "first idea" of the quality of processed images. The most common simple metric remains the peak signal-to-noise ratio (PSNR) metric for the right balance it provides between its complexity and performances. Other simple metrics are also "error-based" metrics such as the mean square error (MSE) and its two variants: the norm L_p and the variance in difference of images (VDI) defined respectively by:

$$L_p(Im_{ori}, IM_{deg}) = \left[\frac{1}{MN}\sum_{i=1}^{N}\sum_{j=1}^{M}|Im_{ori}[i,j] - Im_{deg}[i,j]|^p\right]^{1/p} \quad for\, p \geq 1 \tag{9.14}$$

and:

$$VDI = \frac{1}{MN}\sum_{i=1}^{N}\sum_{j=1}^{M}\left[\begin{array}{c}(Im_{ori}[i,j] - Im_{deg}[i,j]) \\ -\frac{1}{MN}\sum_{i=1}^{N}\sum_{j=1}^{M}(Im_{ori}[i,j] - Im_{deg}[i,j])\end{array}\right]^2 \tag{9.15}$$

where N and M denote the number of rows and columns, and Im_{ori}, Im_{deg} denote the original image and the degraded image, respectively. These metrics generally exhibit limited performances because the used calculation of differences between pixels completely ignores the content of images.

For color images, the color fidelity metrics of section 9.2 can be used. As for the PSNR, it generally derives (although there is no consensus) from the mean of PSNR computed on each of the color planes.

9.4.1.2. *HVS balanced metrics*

These metrics generally use a single-channel modeling of the human visual system (HVS). In this context, the HVS is seen as a spatial filter whose characteristics are given by the contrast sensitivity function (CSF). The operation of the CSF is the basis of metrics weighted by the HVS. The first metric developed under this framework is that of Mannos and Sakrison [MAN 74]. The principle of this metric is to weight the spectrum of the error image between the original image and the degraded one, by a CSF obtained from psychophysical experiments based on the detection of sinusoidal gratings. The distortion measure of this metric is given by the energy calculation according to:

$$E = \int_f \int_\theta CSF(f).|Im_{ori}(f,\theta) - Im_{deg}(f,\theta)|^2 df\ d\theta \qquad [9.16]$$

where f and θ denote the spatial frequency and orientation. $Im_{ori}(f,\theta)$ and $Im_{deg}(f,\theta)$ are the spectra of the original image and the degraded image. The obtained results showed an interesting correlation with subjective measures and generated interest in the introduction of HVS models in image processing.

Based on the same principle, other metrics have been proposed for brightness images [HAN 94, KAR 93, KAR 94, XU 94], for color images [FAU 79] and video [LUK 82, TON 99]. For color images, a colorimetric transformation is usually necessary to switch from the starting RGB space to a colorimetric space composed of an achromatic component and two components of opposing colors reflecting the oppositions red-green and blue-yellow of the HVS. This decomposition is essential to be able to use the CSF that is built on the basis of the antagonisms of the HVS. Thus, the three represented error images are then weighted by appropriate CSFs for the calculation of the final distortion measure.

The metrics weighted by the HVS are still used for their simplicity and low computational complexity. The single-channel model that is used in these cases, describes quite well the evolution of the visibility thresholds of simple gratings. For complex signals, the detection techniques used so far are not enough to explain the behavior of the HVS. The implemented masking and adaptation techniques make use of the concept of channels, multiple, parallel and selective in spatial, radial and angular frequencies. The resulting multi-channel modeling is exploited by the perceptual metrics that are the subject of section.

9.4.1.3. Perceptual metrics

The perceptual metrics represent an interesting approach in the evaluation of image quality. A summary of various studies carried out in this context shows that these metrics are modeled on the operation of HVS and use the perceptual factors that are known to have a direct influence on the visibility of distortions [PAP 00]. A generic block diagram of these metrics is given in Figure 9.7.

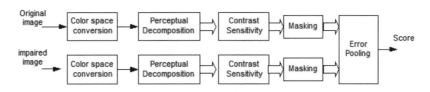

Figure 9.7. *Block diagram of perceptual metrics*

The reference image and the degraded image are subjected to the color space conversion discussed in the preceding section. At this point, an emphasis is usually placed on the luminance component because it is believed that the performance gain, generated by the consideration of color, is far from balancing the complexity induced by the processing of the chrominance components. The "multi-channel decomposition" block aims to account for the spatial-frequency sensitivity of the HVS. As mentioned earlier, the latter analyzes the input signals through a set of selective channels in radial and in orientation. Two questions arise for the implementation of this sensitivity. The first is about the choice of the decomposition. For the luminance component, several decompositions are proposed [PAR 05, TOL 05, SEN 01]. The most used decompositions are those of Daly [DAL 94], Lubin [LUB 93] and Watson [WAT 87]. Those of Watson and Daly are both characterized by a dyadic radial selectivity (five channels of bandwidth equal to the octave1[1]) and a constant angular selectivity. The difference lies in the size of the bandwidth that is set to 30 degrees for Daly against 45 degrees for Watson. The Lubin decomposition requires seven radial bands and four different orientations. Figure 9.8 shows examples of frequency decomposition by Lubin and Daly. The second question concerns the choice of the linear transform to be implemented. This transform should satisfy a number of properties among which are the radial and angular selectivity, the linear phase, the minimum recovery between adjacent channels, the invertibility, etc. The Cortex transform and the oriented Gabor filters are often used. The output of this block thus results in a set of luminance images. For each of these images, a local contrast is calculated at each point.

The "masking" block aims to exploit the masking abilities of the HVS. Along with the cumulation block, this predominantly determines the performances of perceptual metrics. Its role is to specify for each sub-band and for each point, the variation of the visibility threshold when the masking effect is taken into account. The knowledge of such values allows us to keep only the errors located above their threshold and thus contribute to the development of the final quality. This block has prompted a lot of studies and different results are available in the literature [BEK 04, BRA 96, DAL 93, LUB 95]. The variety of the proposed models depends on the type of the considered masking and thus the used stimuli [FOL 94, HEE 92, LEG 80, TEO 94].

---

1 The octave characterizes the width of a frequency band whose highest frequency is twice the lowest frequency.

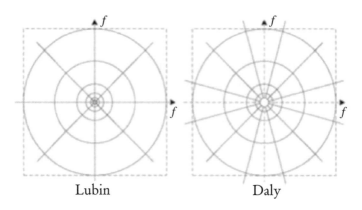

Figure 9.8. *Frequency decomposition by Lubin and Daly*

At the output of the masking block, only the visible errors remain because they directly contribute to the development of the quality (other errors are set to zero). The cumulation block is designed to reduce this dimensionality. Generally, cumulation is performed in two steps. The first where the error images spread across all frequency channels are combined into a single error image (the frequency cumulation). The second step is dedicated to spatial cumulation and is to combine the spatial errors in a final measure that represents the score given by the algorithm to the degraded image.

Perceptual metrics are generic metrics. They can be used for any type of degradation and are known to have a high rate of correlation with subjective scores. However, the use of increasingly developed models of the HVS tends to increase their computational complexity. The alternative would then lie in specific metrics [HAM 99, HOR 96, MAR 96, WAT 93] that have the advantage of exploiting a prior knowledge of the artifacts in question.

9.4.2. Reduced-reference metrics

The reduced reference metric is booming nowadays because it provides an additional answer to the metric with or without reference. On the one hand, it conveys a description, usually negligible, of the reference, which allows a consistent comparison. On the other hand, it allows a less complex measurement and gets rid of the pixels content of the reference image. In other words, the challenge in this family of metrics is to be able to extract the attributes of the original image (similar to the notion of signature for indexing) allowing us to quantify the difference between the images before and after degradation and in environments where the access to the original image is almost impossible. The key application for this type of metric is undeniably the image transmission where the presence of the original image on the user device is impossible. Figure 9.9 gives a simplified diagram of the reduced reference metrics. In the literature, several reduced reference metrics have been developed. They can be classified into two families, namely those based on the attributes representing the image content and those based on distortion attributes. The two are of course directly or indirectly related. We will thus find in the first family the metric proposed in [VOR 92] based on attributes describing the spectral content of the image. This metric is extended to the video through the use of time attributes and the use of the summation of the image attributes of all the *frames* to produce only one score at the end. Generalized Gaussian densities have been used by Wang *et al.* [WAN 05] to represent the wavelet coefficients of an image used as the reduced reference. The same procedure is used at the receiver side to calculate the attributes used to generate the final score. In [GHA 03], a reduced reference metric is proposed based on the robustness of the local harmonics (LHS). The latter represents the gain and loss of information extracted from an image, corresponding to the blurring and block effects generated by the compression. A quantization allows us to lead to an acceptable level of information as part of a transmission.

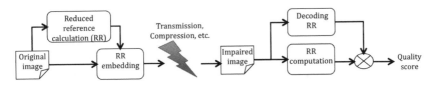

Figure 9.9. *Simplified block diagram of a reduced reference metric*

Also in the same register, Zepernick *et al.* [ZEP 03] proposed an RR metric based on hybrid wavelets and directional filter banks. This RR metric keeps from the reference image only a predefined threshold value in addition to coefficients extracted from the different subbands, to be compared with the values of the impaired image. In 2009, Maalouf *et al.* [MAA 09] proposed a metric exploiting grouplets that are based on the work of the psychophysics school of Gestalt about perceptual association fields. This property gives to grouplets a discriminating power significantly higher than other multiscale representations. To create a better correlation with the human judgment, a CSF filtering and masking effect is applied to the grouplet coefficients. This step also reduces the reference for a use on low rate flow channels.

The second family of reduced reference metrics consists of those that exploit attributes based on the distortions. Thus, in [KUS 03], the authors propose a quality index based on the importance of blurring effects by using the Marziliano method [MAR 04], of block effects by exploiting the Wang approach [WAN 00] as well as the Saha *aliasing* effects [SAH 00].

A weighted sum is used to achieve the final score of quality. This metric can also be seen as a metric without reference with the difference that the energy of the image is necessary for calculation and should therefore be transmitted. Several variants of this metric can be found in the literature. They are often based on the metrics described in the next section. Recently, Nauge *et al.* proposed a metric exploiting the lack of invariance of the interest points such as Harris, as well as the notion of salience of objects for quality measurement [NAU 10]. The reference extracted by this approach is of 24 bytes. The obtained results compete the major full reference metrics.

9.4.3. *No-reference metrics*

The metrics without reference are particularly suitable for quality assessment in real time and at any point in the processing chain. They may therefore contribute to the development of new services. The approach to the implementation of these metrics is totally different from that of fidelity metrics since it no longer exploits the comparison between the original image and degraded image, but is based on an analysis of the degradations that exhibits the image to be assessed. All the quality metrics without reference therefore assume a prior knowledge of the degradations involved. This section will mainly focus on the degradations induced by the two main image encoders that are

JPEG and JPEG 2000. These degradations, some of which are also associated with MPEG encoders, are first described to better present afterward the metrics associated with them.

– block effect:

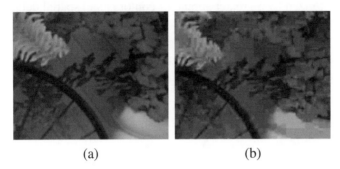

(a)   (b)

Figure 9.10. *Illustration of the block effect (b) obtained after compression of (a) (for a color version of this figure, see www.iste.co.uk/fernandez/digicolor.zip)*

The block effect (see Figure 9.10) is associated with the compression standard of still images JPEG. It occurs in the reconstructed image through spatial discontinuities at the edges of adjacent blocks. These discontinuities are caused by the independence of the blocks during the quantization of DCT coefficients. The perception of the block effect is dependent on the content of the blocks and their neighborhood. The block effects tend to be more visible in regions of the image slightly textured and of low to moderate luminance.

– blurring effect:

(a)   (b)

Figure 9.11. *Illustration of the blurring effect (b) obtained after compression of (a) (for a color version of this figure, see www.iste.co.uk/fernandez/digicolor.zip)*

The blurring effect (see Figure 9.11) considered by quality metrics is usually the one generated by the process of quantization of any low-rate compression system. It therefore results from the suppression of the high frequencies induced by a coarse quantization. It is a global distortion that is characterized by a greater spread of contours and spatial details.

– ringing effect:

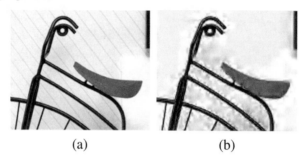

(a)   (b)

Figure 9.12. *Illustration of the ringing effect (b) obtained after compression of (a) (for a color version of this figure, see www.iste.co.uk/fernandez/digicolor.zip)*

The *ringing* effect (see Figure 9.12) is characterized by strong oscillations along strong edges of sparsely textured regions. For the chrominance components, it appears as color transitions between the chrominance of the contour and the content of the neighborhood including that contour. It is due to a differential quantization of the high frequencies. It generally occurs in encoding schemes, such as JPEG 2000, that use a quantization in the frequency domain.

– color bleeding:

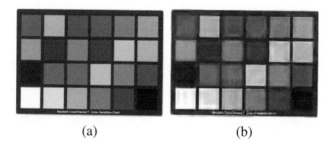

(a)   (b)

Figure 9.13. *Illustration of the color bleeding effect (b) obtained after compression of (a) (for a color version of this figure, see www.iste.co.uk/fernandez/digicolor.zip)*

Color bleeding (see Figure 9.13) is generated by the same process as the blurring described above but for the chromatic components: suppression of high frequencies from color components. It is characterized by a mixture of colors between regions of high chromatic difference, giving the impression to an observer of perceiving a loss of colors.

9.4.3.1. *Blocking metrics*

Many metrics have focused on block effects that represent the most annoying artifact of DCT-based compression algorithms. A classification of these metrics allows us to distinguish three categories. In the first category, the measures that quantify the block effect directly exploit the spatial domain [GAO 02, MUI 05, PAN 04a, WU 97, PAN 04b]. The majority of these metrics assume a fixed grid of blocks of size 8×8. Only the last two seek to get rid of the position of the grids. The metric by Wu *et al.* [WU 97], one of the first proposed metrics, estimates for instance the block effect by starting with calculating the horizontal and vertical differences between the rows and the columns located on both sides of the border between two neighboring blocks. Weightings are then introduced to account for masking effects. The resulting measure is finally weighted by the mean of the same measures calculated on the rows and columns that are not located on the border. The second category of blocking metrics is the one that uses the frequency domain to quantify the strength of the block structure [LIU 02, WAN 00]. The typical case of such a metric is the measure proposed by Wang *et al.* [WAN 00] where the image with block effect is modeled as an image without blocks noised by a blocks signal. The approach thus consists of detecting and measuring the strength of the blocks signal. For such a measure, a 1D FFT is first applied to the horizontal and vertical absolute differences. The periodical spectral peaks of blocks of size 8×8 are then identified by their position in the frequency domain. The power spectrum of the image without blocks is estimated from that of the image to be evaluated by applying a median filter. The overall measure of the block effect is given by the difference between the two spectra at the frequencies of the peaks. The third and final category of metrics, which will not be discussed here because it is mainly dedicated to video, is the one that estimates the block effect by combining the information from the spatial and frequency domains [VLA 00].

9.4.3.2. *Blur metrics*

As opposed to the blocking metrics, the blur metrics are much less numerous in the literature. This finding is particularly surprising that nowadays the majority of DCT-based decoder block integrates a post-filtering that reduces the block effects, but increases the blur. The metrics without reference are usually based on the measurement of contours spreading [CHU 04, MAR 04, ONG 03a, RAM 09]. The general architecture integrates the edge detection, the measure of the spreading at each point of the contours and finally the spatial cumulation of measured spreading. Thus in [MAR 04], the authors propose a measure based on the smoothing effect of blur on the edges. A detection of vertical edges by thresholding of the Sobel filter response is first applied to the luminance component. The positions of the start and end of contours are then searched and recorded. These start and end points are defined as local extrema near the considered contour. The local measure of the blurring effect is then defined as the distance between these two extrema. Finally, the overall measure of the blurring effect is calculated as the mean of local measures on the entire image. Another example of the operation of contours spreading is given in [CHU 04] where the authors evaluate the blur of an image by considering the loss of precision in its contours. For this, strong contours are detected and contour regions are defined (set of blocks). For each block, the local measurement of contour accuracy is estimated by the 2D kurtosis. The overall measure of contour accuracy is calculated by averaging the local measurements on all the blocks in question. Finally, let's note that in [RAM 09], in addition to a recent state of the art of the main metrics, the author proposes a new metric of the effects of the partial and full loss of details.

9.4.3.3. *JPEG-specific metrics*

In general, compression standards generate multiple artifacts simultaneously. For more performance, the metrics should therefore seek to quantify any degradation. This is what the metrics described in [BAB 05, BAR 07, SAZ 06, WAN 02] for JPEG compressed images do. The general approach of these metrics is based on a prior measurement of each of the degradations, followed by a cumulation whose model coefficients are optimized using a training set. In [WAN 02] for example, the authors use three measures of degradations related, on the one hand, to the block effect, and on the other hand, to the pixels activity. The three measures are then combined by a nonlinear relationship to produce a quality score of the compressed image. The extension to color of this model is performed in [SAZ 06]. From this perspective, the image is first projected into the YCbCr color space. The three previous measurements are then calculated for each of the three color components. The resulting terms are again combined here by a nonlinear relationship to generate the final quality score. In [BAR 07], the measures of the block and blur effects are normalized and then cumulated by a model that incorporates a cross term defining the potential interaction that exists between the two effects in addition to the individual contribution of each measure.

9.4.3.4. *JPEG 2000-specific metrics*

The blurring and ringing effects are the main artifacts caused by the JPEG 2000 compression in addition to color bleeding. The process of JPEG 2000-specific metrics thus propose prior measures for these two effects and then seek to combine these measures to obtain a quality score correlated with subjective scores. The various metrics proposed in this case [FER 06, ONG 03b, SHE 02], are often limited to the measurement of the blurring effect alone that relies primarily on the lightness information. [FER 06, ONG 03b] exploit the contours spreading while [SHE 02] uses a statistical model to quantify the quality loss due to the wavelet coefficients. In [BAR 06], measures of blur and ringing effects are proposed, normalized, and then cumulated by a linear model incorporating the potential interaction between the two effects. The color is mainly useful to quantify the degradations caused by colors bleeding, which can be measured by a ΔE distance of the CIE.

9.4.4. *Application to video*

In comparison with still images, the problem of defining such measures for video is complicated by the fact that, in addition to the necessary existing spatial distortions, temporal distortions are also to be integrated. This requires a better modeling of natural motions, through an efficient modeling of perceived motions and a better understanding of the psycho-cognitive bonds that exist with the human visual judgments. Most quality metrics available with or without reference either intentionally hide the temporal aspect or use simple models specialized for a specific type of application.

One of the reasons why the development of a quality metric without video reference is complex lies in the great variety of distortions that may be encountered. Although many studies have focused directly on the modeling of spatial distortions, very few studies have aimed at the modeling of the temporal distortion. Similarly, if the community agrees on the fact that motion is an important item of data to consider when attempting to quantify the quality of a video, this consensus is no more valid when attempting to take into account the influence of attributes related to the motion, such as the displacement speed, the size of the object, the movement of the camera, the motion direction, and the salience of the motion. Similarly, modeling the masking effects is very well controlled in the spatial domain, while it still poses many challenges in the temporal domain. Moreover, when we consider the case of video transmission through communication channels (cable TV, satellite reception, smart phones, etc.), the generated distortions are of spatial and temporal natures. The spatial distortions (such as the blurring) affect only the spatial appearance of *frames* of the video, while the temporal distortions (such as the *jittering* effects) may not be directly visible because they affect the movement of objects and, therefore, are visible only through a succession of *frames*. There is a third category of distortion that is of space-time nature, such as the *ghosting* effect, the Gibb effect (*mosquito noise*), the *smearing* effect, etc. The visual discomfort created by time and space-time distortions is linked to the processing of movement performed in the cortical areas of the brain. Therefore, improving the modeling of temporal distortions (including space-time distortions) passes through an improvement of models of motion processing in the human brain.

9.4.4.1. *Full reference metrics*

A classification of quality measurement algorithms can be implemented in two classes, which are not necessarily disjoint. The first class is mainly about techniques that use specific models of the human visual system, while the second class consists primarily of algorithms based on statistical models of natural scenes and motions.

9.4.4.1.1. HVS modeling for motion

Thus, [FRE 98, WEI 02] have, for example, modeled the processing of motion as well as of the temporal aspect of the HVS, paying particular attention to a post-retinal processing using simple linear filters. In this case, these are a low-pass filter and a bandpass filter applied on the time dimension of the video following a spatial processing of the video. Given that the motion can cause variations in luminance, a multi-band time filtering can be appropriate in the search for motion information. The time mechanisms were then modeled using the first and second derivatives of the impulse response. Thus the first derivative is a low-frequency response while the second derivative is interpreted as a band-pass response.

Moreover, the spatial decompositions allowing us to model the responses of cortical neurons were also widely used: cortex transform [WAT 87], steerable pyramids [SIM 95], Gabor filters [SRI 03], or even the discrete wavelet transforms [WIN 99]. A number of visual area models of the brain that are located outside of the primary cortex are also relevant to the development of video quality measure with reference to the near future. In particular, the striped visual area of the cortex MT/V5 plays an important role in motion perception, by integrating information about the local motion in the global precepts of motion, of eye motion, or even of stereoscopic calculations. Recently Seshadrinathan and Bovik [SES 09] have developed such a model of a video quality measure with reference. Another promising area of research concerns the study of the inferior temporal circumvolution, where the retinotopic map of the responses of area V1 is apparently used for the high-level processes such as object recognition [ADA 03]. While the models are largely absent for the calculations in this area of the brain, the development of such models would be extremely beneficial because the degradations present in the video affect the object recognition process.

9.4.4.1.2. Statistical modeling of natural scenes and motions

The general philosophy of this approach is based on the assumption that natural scenes belong to a specific subspace within which all the images evolve. Thus, the defenders of this argument believe that the characteristics associated with natural motion span a subspace of a more general space where these characteristics are derived. This approach bypasses the need to model the HVS, which is a complex task and requires an approximation of the subspace containing the natural scenes. The general idea is to observe, to isolate, and explain the statistical trends observed in the videos, and model the distortions.

Volumes of research have focused on the statistical modeling of natural scenes in still images as well as on the statistical modeling of motions in videos. For instance, Wang *et al.* [WAN 07] proposed a theoretical framework based on a modelization of the perception of the speed by the HVS developed by Stocker and Simoncelli [STO 06]. This model mainly aims to estimate the content of motion information as well as the perceptual uncertainty present in the video. This model incorporates space-time factors (weight) whose values increase in the presence of motion and decrease in the presence of uncertainty. This method is based on the calculation of the local content as well as on the uncertainty allowing us to generate a perceptual weighting function.

9.4.4.2. *No-reference metrics*

The general idea of no-reference video quality assessment is based on a feature extraction of the image followed by a learning step. Naturally, the efficiency of such methods is highly dependent on the features extracted from the video as well as the statistical learning method used. In particular, the perceptual relevance of attributes is intrinsic to the performance of such algorithms. Nevertheless, research in this area is still very recent and limited. Recently, Maalouf *et al.* [MAA 10] proposed a quality metric without reference for color video whose results are interesting. It is based on a wavelet decomposition, which considers the video as a 3D block (2D + t) thus allowing us to distribute the information according to different perceptual channels. Then a tensor is defined on the time axis and is weighted by the properties of the HVS. The metric is defined as a combination of the inter-frames coherence and the sharpness of the contours.

9.5. Performance evaluation of the metrics

9.5.1. *Test plans of the VQEG group*

The VQEG (Video Quality Experts Group) is a group that consists of experts from diverse backgrounds, academic and industrial, working on the theme of the evaluation of video quality. This group depends on the ITU (International Telecommunications Union) that produces usage recommendations according to the type of media to be assessed. The website of VQEG (http://www.its.bldrdoc.gov/vqeg/) is a reliable and scalable source of information on the procedures for quality measurement. It notably includes all the test plans defined over time. The purpose of a VQEG test plan is to give a procedure and rules of use for quality assessment in a specific context (TV, multimedia, HDTV, 3DTV) and on the rules of measurement of the performance of a given metric. In addition, these plans relate to the proposed metrics and their efficiency relative to the processed data.

9.5.2. *Data preparation*

Data preparation is highly dependent on the type of subjective test previously adopted. We will give in this section the procedure for an ACR test as an example. The reader may refer to the VQEG test plans for other procedures. As a general rule, for the performance measurement of metrics with full or reduced reference, the differential MOS (DMOS) is used. For metrics without reference, the MOS is used. Due to the nature of human judgments, subjective scores are often condensed either around the mean or on the ends. Therefore, it is not logical to force an objective metric to mimic this behavior defect that could bias the results. For this reason, a nonlinear *mapping* (or *fitting*) is applied before any performance measure. In the VQEG test plans, it is possible to find different ways to perform the adequacy of the data. It is almost impossible to find provable justification for these choices. In most cases, the empirical validation takes over. In the case of the ACR, the selected function is a polynomial of order 3:

$$DMOS_p = ax^3 + bx^2 + cx + d \qquad [9.17]$$

where $DMOS_p$ is the predicted DMOS and the coefficients a, b, c and d are obtained by the mapping procedure. The variable x denotes the DMOS.

9.5.3. Accuracy of the prediction

The accuracy of the prediction is defined as the ability of the metric to predict estimates of subjective scores with a minimum average error. It is determined by the Pearson linear correlation coefficient and by the mean square error. The normalized correlation coefficient CC and the mean square error RMSE, expressed as a function of the predicted scores $DMOS_p$ and the subjective measures predicted $DMOS$, are written as follows:

$$CC = \frac{\sum_{i=1}^{N}(DMOS_i - \bar{DMOS})(DMOS_{pi} - \bar{DMOS}_p)}{\sqrt{\sum_{i=1}^{N}(DMOS_i - \bar{DMOS})^2 \sum_{i=1}^{N}(DMOS_{pi} - \bar{DMOS}_p)^2}}$$

[9.18]

$$RMSE = \sqrt{\frac{1}{N}\sum_{i=1}^{N}(DMOS_i - \bar{DMOS})^2}$$

[9.19]

where N is the number of the test images. The value of the linear coefficient is always between -1 and 1. The more its absolute value tends to 1, the higher is the linear dependence between the predicted scores and the subjective scores. The more the RMSE error tends to 0, the smaller is the difference between the predicted scores and the subjective scores.

9.5.4. Monotonicity of the prediction

Monotonicity seeks to investigate whether the increase or decrease of the prediction is associated with an increase or decrease of the subjective measure. For N test images, the degree of monotonicity is estimated by the Spearman correlation coefficient SRCC that is defined by:

$$SRCC = 1 - \frac{6\sum_{i=1}^{N}d_i^2}{N(N^2 - 1)}$$

[9.20]

where d_i is the rank difference between the predicted score $DMOS_p$ and the subjective measure $DMOS$, for the ith image. An SRCC that tends toward 1 is desired because it would mean that the metric predicts scores by ranking the tested images from the worst to the best quality, just like a casual observer would proceed.

9.5.5. *Consistency of the prediction*

The consistency of the prediction of a metric is determined by the number of outliers. An outlier is a point at which the prediction error exceeds a given threshold. The consistency of the prediction is evaluated by the percentage of outliers in the data set. Algorithmically, for N test images, this percentage, denoted OR (Outlier Ratio), is given by:

$$OR = \frac{N_{OR}}{N} \qquad [9.21]$$

with:

$$N_{OR} = N_{OR} + 1 \ si \ |DMOS_i - DMOS_{pi}| > 2\sigma_i \qquad [9.22]$$

where σ_i denotes the standard deviation of the scores given by observers for image i.

The smaller the percentage of outliers, the better the prediction.

9.6. Conclusion

As mentioned in the introduction, a human oberver will not give a score to any object he looks at. Instead, he will prefer to use semantic classification to describe the sensation he felt when he contemplates the object in front of him. For example, "it's nice" or "I like it" could be one of the sensations that the observers might feel.

Thus, the [ITU 02] has adopted in its BT-R500.11 recommendation such a semantic classification. So, during the psychophysical tests to which human observers are subject, they have to select a quality class from "very poor quality" (associated with the numerical value 1) to "excellent quality" (associated with the numerical value 5). However, to simplify the requested task and thus avoid that the observer hesistates between two adjacent classes, the grading scale is extended by linear extrapolation between 0 and 100. Thus the observer can modulate his score with respect to its feeling.

Often the concept of quality measure (or fidelity, according to the context of study) is dealt with by using a classification-type approach. In fact, after all that was mentioned in the previous sections, when we attempt to assign a quality score, several factors are calculated on the candidate image and then combined linearly to yield a numeric value. Thus, we will consider these factors before combination so that a feature vector is built. This vector will serve as a reference when the classification approach through statistical learning is achieved.

For example, Gastaldo *et al.* [GAS 07] developed a CBP (*Continuous Back-Propagation*) neural network that can be used to measure the quality of MPEG2 video sequences. This neural network was trained so that the scoring of those sequences by a human observer can be predicted. A similar neural network was used to determine the quality of images produced by the application of an algorithm for image enhancement [CAR 01]. In this case, the neural network was trained so that the quality of the image is estimated into two classes: 1) inferior quality or 2) superior quality or equal to that of the original image. In [CHA 07], the authors used a statistical learning method based on SVM (*Support Vector Machine*) to achieve a five classes of image quality, such as the five classes recommended by the ITU. A decomposition method one-against-all was used, followed by a majority vote for the choice of the final class.

Whatever the learning methods used, the emphasis during the construction phase of the feature vector is essential. So, more features will be retained and the learning will be better. Therefore, a question arises: how to choose the factors to incorporate in the vector? This challenge is to be compared with the difficulty of designing a quality metric called classical (without the use of classification methods) since the success of one metric or the other is inherent to the choice of the defects that we seek to measure and the nature of the images on which the metric will be assumed to be applied.

However, at least two answers can be expressed: the first is to consider a custom work, which is to consider a strong *a priori* on the characteristics to be used. This will prove to be effective once we have a relatively accurate idea of the degradations that can be expected. For instance, if an image is compressed using the JPEG standard, we expect to observe the block effects, the colorimetric degradations, etc. This approach was used in [GAS 07, SAA 10], and yields very convincing results, since all the authors describe a correlation rate with MOS value of around 97%. Another undeniable advantage of using a statistical learning method is the ability to perform the selection of attributes, which is the second answer to the previous question. In fact, let us suppose that we have to blindly measure the quality of an image, meaning that we do not have access to the original image. In this case, many questions remain about the quality of the original image: is the candidate image an image obtained by applying a degradation scheme (such as compression, or other) or is it derived from a restoration process of *inpainting* type for example. Thus, depending on the addressed problem, the interpretation we have of the quality will not be the same, since in the first case the quality will be degraded according to known defects (block or blurring effect for still images, jittering, or ghosting effect for videos), while in the second case, the image has been restored and in this case the defects generated are much less identifiable. The results thus obtained highlight the strong generalization ability of the metric thus generated since, irrespective of the nature of the degradation of the image, the correlation with MOS is greater than 98%. However, this latter approach requires the construction of a vector of very high dimension. Therefore, one might be tempted to add a large number of features to ensure an exhaustive coverage as possible. Yet, even if this approach seems to be promising, it is a red line that should not be crossed to avoid the well known dimension malediction problem. This occurs when the number of features is close (or higher) to the number of available examples. This implies having either an effiicient feature selection process or an efficient dimension reduction technique.

However, the undeniable advantage of this approach lies in the possibility of defining a single quality metric that would be applicable whether a reference image is available or not. In this case, the appropriate attribute just has to be selected. Thus, by using statistical learning techniques, it is found that the design of a quality metric would be similar to what the human observer performs when he expresses his feelings by implementing different internal levels of his perception-consciousness system (as suggested by Freud) to make his verdict. The fact remains that the statistical learning-based approach is very promising and could be proved to be the missing link between the quality score and the semantic expression of the so-called quality.

Finally, color is under-exploited in the quality measure in general. The main reason is the complexity of the interpretation of the degradations on the chromatic components that carry rich information but are difficult to reach. Thus, most metrics focus on the lightness component that allows us to reach a more or less accurate approximation of quality depending on the targeted degradation. However, the use of color in the prediction of quality remains a very important issue to be explored to come as close as possible to human mechanisms of judgments of quality.

9.7. Bibliography

[ADA 03] ADAMS D., HORTON J., "A precise retinotopic map of primate striate cortex generated from the representation of angioscotomas", *Journal of Neuroscience*, vol. 23, no. 9, p. 3771-3789, 2003.

[ALM 89] ALMAN D., BERNS R., SNYDER G., LARSEN W., "Performance testing of color difference metrics using a color tolerance dataset", *Color Research and Application*, vol. 14, p. 139-151, 1989.

[BAB 05] BABU R., PERKIS A., "An HVS-based no-reference perceptual quality assessment of JPEG coded images using neural networks", *International Conference on Image Processing*, 2005.

[BAR 06] BARLAND R., SAADANE A., "Blind quality metric using a perceptual map for JPEG2000 compressed images", *Proceedings of IEEE, ICIP*, Atlanta, GA, USA, 2006.

[BAR 07] BARLAND R., Evaluation objective sans référence de la qualité perçue: applications aux images et vidéos compressées, PhD thesis, University of Nantes, 2007.

[BEK 04] BEKKAT N., SAADANE A., "Coded image quality assessment based on new contrast masking model", *Journal of Electronic Imaging*, vol. 13, no. 2, p. 341-348, 2004.

[BER 91] BERNS R., ALMAN D., RENI L., SNYDER G., BALONON-ROSEN M., "Visual determination of suprathreshold color difference tolerances using probit analysis", *Color Research and Application*, vol. 16, p. 297-316, 1991.

[BRA 96] DEN BRANDEN LAMBRECHT C.J.V., VERSCHEURE O., "Perceptual quality measure using a spatio-temporal model of the human visual system", *SPIE*, *Digital Video Compression Algorithms and Technologies*, vol. 2668, p. 450-461, 1996.

[CAR 01] CARRAI P., HEYNDERICH I., GASTALDO P., ZUNINO R., "Image quality metric assessment by using neural networks", *IEEE International Symposium on Circuits and Systems (ISCAS-2001)*, Sydney, p. 253-256, 2001.

[CHA 98] CHARRIER C., Vers l'optimisation statistique et perceptuelle de la qualité pour la compression des images couleur par quantification vectorielle, PhD thesis, University Jean Monnet Saint-Etienne, 1998.

[CHA 07] CHARRIER C., LEBRUN G., LEZORAY O., "Selection of features by a machine learning expert to design a color image quality metric", *Third International Workshop on Video Processing and Quality Metrics for Consumer Electronics*, Scottsdale, Arizona, USA, p. 25-26, 2007.

[CHU 04] CHUNG Y.-C., WANG J.-M., BAILEY R., CHEN S.-W., CHANG S.-L., "A non-parametric blur measure based on edge analysis for image processing applications", *IEEE Conference on Cybernetics and Intelligent Systems*, 2004.

[DAL 93] DALY S., "The visible differences predictor: an algorithm for the assessment of image fidelity", *Digital Images and Human Vision*, p. 197-206, MIT press, 1993.

[DAL 94] DALY S., "A visual model for optimizing the design of image processing algorithms", *International Conference on Image Processing*, p. 16-20, 1994.

[FAU 79] FAUGERAS O.D., "Digital color image processing within the framework of a human visual model", *IEEE Transaction Acoustic Speech Signal Processing*, vol. 27, no. 4, p. 380-393, 1979.

[FER 06] FERZLI R., KARAM L., "A human visual system-based no-reference objective image sharpness metric", *IEEE International Conference on Image Processing*, p. 2949-2952, 2006.

[FOL 94] FOLEY J.M., BOYNTON G.M., "A new model of human luminance pattern vision mechanisms: analysis of the effects of pattern orientation, spatial phase and temporal frequency", *SPIE*, *Computational Vision Based on Neurobiology*, vol. 2054, p. 32-42, 1994.

[FRE 38] FREUD S., *Abrégé de la psychanalyse*, PUF, Paris, 1938.

[FRE 98] FREDERICKSEN R., HESS R., "Estimating multiple temporal mechanisms in human vision", *Vision Research*, vol. 38, no. 7, p. 1023-1040, 1998.

[GAO 02] GAO W., MERMER C., KIM Y., "A de-blocking algorithm and blockiness metric for highly compressed images", *IEEE Transactions on Circuits and Systems for Video Technology*, vol. 12, no. 12, p. 1150-1159, 2002.

[GAS 07] GASTALDO P., PARODI G., REDI J., ZUNINO R., "No-reference quality assessment of JPEG images by using CBP neural networks", *ICANN 2007, Part II*, vol. LNCS 4669, p. 564-572, 2007.

[GHA 03] GHANBARI M., GUNAWAN I., "Reduced-reference picture quality estimation by using local harmonic amplitude information", *London Communications Symposium*, 2003.

[GUA 99] GUAN S.-S., LUO M.R., "Investigation of parametric effects using large colour differences", *Color Research and Application*, vol. 24, no. 5, p. 356-368, 1999.

[HAM 99] HAMADA T., MIYAJI S., MATSUMOTO S., "Picture quality assessment system by three-layered bottom-up noise weighting considering human visual perception", *SMPTE Journal*, vol. 108, no. 1, p. 20-26, 1999.

[HAN 94] HANGAI S., SUZUKI K., MIHAUCHI K., "Advanced WSNR for coded monochrome picture evaluation using fractal dimension", *Picture Coding Symposium*, p. 92-95, 1994.

[HEE 92] HEEGER D., "Normalization of cell responses in cat visual cortex", *Visual Neuroscience*, vol. 9, p. 181-197, 1992.

[HOR 96] HORITA Y., KATAYAMA M., MURAI T., MIYAHARA M., "Objective picture quality scale for video coding", *ICIP*, p. 319-322, 1996.

[ITU 02] ITU-R RECOMMENDATION BT.500-11, Méthodologie d'évaluation subjective de la qualité des images de télévision, Report, ITU, Geneva, Switzerland, 2002.

[ITU 05] ITU-R DOCUMENT 6Q/131-E, Comparison of DSCQS and ACR, Report, ITU, Geneva, Switzerland, 2005.

[ITU 07a] ITU-R DOCUMENT 6Q/208-E, Report on experiment of new subjective vidéo quality metrics SAMVIQ for mobile video, Report, ITU, Geneva, Switzerland, 2007.

[ITU 07b] ITU-R REC. BT.1788, Methodology for the subjective assessment of video quality in multimedia applications, Report, ITU, Geneva, Switzerland, 2007.

[ITU 08] ITU-T REC. P.910, Subjective video quality assessment methods for multimedia applications, Report, ITU, Geneva, Switzerland, 2008.

[KAR 93] KARUNASEKERA S.A., KINGSBURY N.G., "A distorsion measure for blocking artifacts in images based on human visual sensitivity", *SPIE, Visual Communication and Image Processing*, vol. 2094, p. 474-486, 1993.

[KAR 94] KARUNASEKERA S.A., KINGSBURY N.G., "A distorsion measure for artefacts in images based on human visual sensitivity", *ICASSP*, p. 117-120, 1994.

[KUS 03] KUSUMA T.M., ZEPERNICK H.-J., "On perceptual objective quality metrics for in-service pictre quality monitoring", *Third ATere Telecommunications and Networking Conference and Workshop*, Melbourne, Australia, 2003.

[LAR 02] LARABI M.-C., Codage et analyse d'images couleur: application à l'indexation de base d'images réparties, PhD thesis, University of Poitiers, December 2002.

[LEG 80] LEGGE G.E., FOLEY J.M., "Contrast masking in human vision", *Journal of the Optical Society of America*, vol. 70, no. 12, p. 1458-1471, 1980.

[LIU 02] LIU S., BOVIK A., "Efficient DCT-domain blind measurement and reduction of blocking artifacts", *IEEE Transactions on Circuits and Systems for Video Technology*, vol. 12, no. 12, p. 1139-1149, 2002.

[LUB 93] LUBIN J., "The use of psychophysical data and models in the analysis of display system performance", *Digital Images and Human Vision*, p. 163-178, MIT press, Cambridge, MA, 1993.

[LUB 95] LUBIN J., "A visual discrimination model for imaging system design and evaluation", *Vision Models for Target Detection and Recognition*, p. 245-283, World Scientific Publishing, Singapore, 1995.

[LUK 82] LUKAS J., BUDRIKIS Z., "Picture quality based on a visual model", *IEEE Transactions on Communications*, vol. 30, p. 1679-1692, 1982.

[LUO 00] LUO M., CUI G., RIGG B., "Derivation of a rotation function for the new CIE colour difference formula", *Proceedings of Colour and Visual Scales*, 2000.

[MAA 09] MAALOUF A., LARABI M.-C., FERNANDEZ C., "A grouplet-based reduced reference image quality assessment", *International Workshop on Quality of Multimedia Experience*, p. 59-63, 2009.

[MAA 10] MAALOUF A., LARABI M.-C., "A no-reference color video quality metric based on a 3D multispectral wavelet transform", *Qomex*, Trondheim, Norway, p. 11-16, 2010.

[MAN 74] MANNOS J.L., SAKRISON D.J., "The effects of visual fidelity criterion on the encoding of images", *IEEE Transactions on Information Theory*, vol. 20, no. 4, p. 525-536, 1974.

[MAR 96] MARTENS J., KAYARGADDE V., "Image quality prediction in a multi-dimensionnal Space", *ICIP*, p. 877-880, 1996.

[MAR 04] MARZILIANO P., DUFAUX F., WINKLER S., EBRAHIMI T., "Perceptual blur and ringing metrics: application to JPEG2000", *Signal Processing: Image Communication*, vol. 19, p. 163-172, 2004.

[MUI 05] MUIJS R., KIRENKO I., "A no-reference blocking artifact measure for adaptive video processing", *European Signal Processing Conference*, 2005.

[NAU 10] NAUGE M., LARABI M.-C., FERNANDEZ C., "A reduced-reference metric based on the interest points in color images", *PCS2010*, Nagoya, Japan, p. 610-613, 2010.

[ONG 03a] ONG E., LIN W., LU Z., YANG X., YAO S., PAN F., JIANG L., MOSCHETTI F., "A no-reference quality metric for measuring image blur", *Signal Processing and its Applications*, p. 469-472, 2003.

[ONG 03b] ONG E., LIN W., LU Z., YAO S., YANG X., JIANG L., "No-reference jpeg-2000 image quality metric", *International Conference on Multimedia and Expo*, p. 545-548, 2003.

[PAN 04a] PAN F., LIN X., RAHARDJA S., LIN W., ONG E., YAO S., LU Z., YANG X., "A locally adaptive algorithm for measuring blocking artifacts in images and videos", *Signal Processing Image Communication*, vol. 19, p. 499-506, 2004.

[PAN 04b] PAN F., LIN X., RAHARDJA S., ONG E., LIN W., "Measuring blocking artifacts using edge direction information", *International Conference on Multimedia and Expo*, 2004.

[PAP 00] PAPPAS T.N., SAFRANEK R.J., "Perceptual criteria for image quality evaluation", BOVIK A. (ed.), *Handbook of Image and Video Processing*, p. 669-684, Academic Press, 2000.

[PAR 05] PARRAGA C., TROSCIANKO T., TOLHURST D., "The effects of amplitude-spectrum statistics on foveal and peripheral discrimination of changes in natural images, and a multi-resolution model", *Vision Research*, vol. 45, p. 3145-3168, 2005.

[QUI 08] QUINTARD L., Evaluation de la qualité des dispositifs d'affichage couleur: des évaluations subjectives à la mesure objective, PhD thesis, University of Poitiers, 2008.

[RAM 09] RAMIN N., Vers une métrique sans référence de la qualité spatiale d'un signal vidéo dans un contexte multimédia, PhD thesis, University of Nantes, 2009.

[ROS 08] ROSSELLI V., LARABI M., FERNANDEZ-MALOIGNE C., "Perceptual color difference metric based on the perception threshold", *IS&T Image Quality and System Performance V*, 2008.

[SAA 10] SAAD M., BOVIK A.C., CHARRIER C., "A DCT statistics-based blind image quality index", *IEEE Signal Processing Letters*, vol. 17, no. 2, p. 583-586, 2010.

[SAH 00] SAHA S., VEMURI R., "An analysis on the effect of image activity on lossy coding performance", *Proceedings of IEEE International Symposium on Circuits and Systems*, vol. 3, Geneva, Switzerland, p. 295-298, 2000.

[SAZ 06] SAZZAD Z.M.P., HORITA Y., "Image quality assessment models for JPEG and JPEG2000 compressed color images", *IS&T Third European Conference on Color in Graphics, Imaging and Vision (CGIV)*, Leeds, England, 2006.

[SEN 01] SENANE H., SAADANE A., BARBA D., "Design and evaluation of an entirely psychovisual-based coding scheme", *Journal of Visual Communication and Image Representation*, vol. 12, p. 401- 421, 2001.

[SES 09] SESHADRINATHAN K., BOVIK A.C., "Motion-based perceptual quality assessment of video", *Human Vision and Electronic Imaging*, 2009.

[SHE 02] SHEIKH H., WANG Z., CORMACK L., BOVIK A., "Blind quality assessment for JPEG-2000 compressed images", *Asilomar Conference on Signals, Systems and Computers*, 2002.

[SIM 95] SIMONCELLI E., FREEMAN W., "The steerable pyramid: a flexible architecture for multi-scale derivative computation", *2nd Annual International Conference on Image Processing*, IEEE, p. 444-447, October 1995.

[SRI 03] SRIVASTAVA A., LEE A., SIMONCELLI E., ZHU S., "On advances in statistical modeling of natural images", *Journal of Mathematical Imaging and Vision*, vol. 18, no. 1, p. 17-33, 2003.

[STO 06] STOCKER A., SIMONCELLI E., "Noise characteristics and prior expectations in human visual speed perception", *Nature Neuroscience*, vol. 9, p. 578-585, 2006.

[TEO 94] TEO P.C., HEEGER D.J., "Perceptual image distortion", *International Conference on Image Processing*, p. 982-986, 1994.

[TOL 05] TOLHURST D., PARRAGA C., LOVELL P., RIPAMONTI C., TROSCIANKO T., "A multiresolution color model for visual difference prediction", *2nd Conference APGV*, p. 135-138, 2005.

[TON 99] TONG X., HEEGER D., DEN BRANDEN LAMBRECHT C.V., "Video quality evaluation using ST-CIELAB", *SPIE*, vol. 3644, San Jose, CA, p. 185-196, 1999.

[VLA 00] VLACHOS T., "Detection of blocking artifacts in compressed video", *Electronics Letters*, vol. 36, no. 13, p. 1106-1108, 2000.

[VOR 92] VORAN S.D., WOLF S., "The development and evaluation of an objective video quality assessment system that emulates human viewing panels", *International Broadcasting Convention*, Amsterdam, The Netherlands, 1992.

[WAN 00] WANG Z., BOVIK A.C., EVAN B.L., "Blind measurement of blocking artifacts in images", *International Conference on Image Processing*, vol. 3, p. 981-984, 2000.

[WAN 02] WANG Z., SHEIKH H., BOVIK A., "No reference perceptual quality assessment of JPEG compressed images", *IEEE International Conference on Image Processing (ICIP)*, p. 477-480, 2002.

[WAN 05] WANG Z., SIMONCELLI E.P., "Reduce-reference image quality assessment using a wavelet-domain natural image statistic model", *Human Vision and Electronic Imaging X*, vol. 5666, p. 17-20, 2005.

[WAN 07] WANG Z., LI Q., "Video quality assessment using a statistical model of human visual speed perception", *Journal of the Optical Society of America*, vol. 24, no. 12, p. 61-69, 2007.

[WAT 87] WATSON A., "The cortex transform: rapid computation of simulated neural images", *Computer Vision, Graphics an Image Processing*, vol. 39, no. 3, p. 311-327, 1987.

[WAT 93] WATSON A.B., "DCTune: A technique for visual optimization of DCT quantization matrices for individual images", *Society for Information Display Digest of Technical Papers*, vol. 1, p. 946-949, 1993.

[WEI 02] WEISS Y., SIMONCELLI E., ADELSON E., "Motion illusions as optimal percepts", *Nature Neuroscience*, vol. 5, p. 598-604, 2002.

[WIN 99] WINKLER S., "A perceptual distortion metric for digital color images", *Signal Processing*, vol. 78, no. 2, p. 231-252, 1999.

[WU 97] WU H., YUEN M., "A generalized block-edge impairment metric for video coding", *IEEE Signal Processing Letters*, vol. 4, no. 11, p. 317-320, 1997.

[XU 94] XU W., HAUSKE G., "Picture quality evaluation based on error segmentation", *SPIE 2308*, p. 1454-1465, 1994.

[YEN 98] YENDRIKHOVSKIJ S.N., Color reproduction and the naturalness constraint, PhD thesis, Technische Universiteit Eindhoven, The Netherlands, 1998.

[ZEP 03] ZEPERNICK H., KUSUMA T., "A reduced-reference perceptual quality metric for inservice image quality assessment", *Joint First Workshop on Mobile Future and IEEE Symposium on Trends in Communications*, vol. 10, p. 71-74, 2003.

[ZHA 97] ZHANG X.M., WANDELL B.A., "A spatial extension of CIELAB for digital color image reproduction", *SID Journal*, vol. 5, no. 1, p. 61-63, 1997.

List of Authors

Omar Aɪᴛ Aɪᴅᴇʀ
LASMEA UMR 6602
Blaise Pascal University
Aubière
France

François Bᴇʀʀʏ
LASMEA UMR 6602
Blaise Pascal University
Aubière
France

Pierre Bᴏɴᴛᴏɴ
LASMEA UMR 6602
Blaise Pascal University
Aubière
France

Jean-Christophe Bᴜʀɪᴇ
Laboratoire Informatique Image
Interaction (L3i)
La Rochelle University
France

Philippe Cᴀʀʀᴇ́
Laboratoire XLIM-SIC UMR CNRS 6172
Poitiers University
France

Majed CHAMBAH
CReSTIC
Reims – Champagne Ardenne University
France

Christophe CHARRIER
GREYC UMR CNRS 6072
University of Caen Lower Normandy
France

Samuel DELEPOULLE
Laboratoire d'Informatique Signal et Image de la Côte d'Opale
University of the Littoral Opal Coast
Calais
France

Eric DINET
Laboratoire Hubert Curien
Jean Monnet University
Saint-Étienne
France

Christine FERNANDEZ-MALOIGNE
Laboratoire Xlim-SIC
Poitiers University
Chasseneuil
France

Mohamed-Chaker LARABI
XLIM-SIC
Poitiers University
France

Jean LE ROHELLEC
Centre de recherche sur la conservation des collections
Muséum national d'histoire naturelle
Paris
France

Olivier LOSSON
LAGIS FRE
Lille 1 University
France

Ludovic MACAIRE
Laboratoire LAGIS
Lille 1 University
France

Bernard PÉROCHE
Laboratoire d'InfoRmatique en Image et Systèmes d'information (LIRIS)
Claude Bernard Lyon 1 University
France

William PUECH
LIRMM, UMR CNRS 5506
Montpellier 2 University
France

Christophe RENAUD
Laboratoire d'Informatique Signal et Image de la Côte d'Opale
University of the Littoral Opal Coast
Calais
France

Frédérique ROBERT-INACIO
IM2NP
ISEN
Toulon
France

Abdelhakim SAADANE
XLIM-SIC, UMR CNRS 6172
Polytech'Nantes
France

Alain TRÉMEAU
Laboratoire Hubert Curien
Jean Monnet University
Saint-Etienne
France

Sylvie TREUILLET
Laboratoire PRISME
Polytech'Orléans
France

Françoise VIÉNOT
Centre de recherche sur la conservation des collections
Muséum national d'histoire naturelle
Paris
France

Index